AF305265

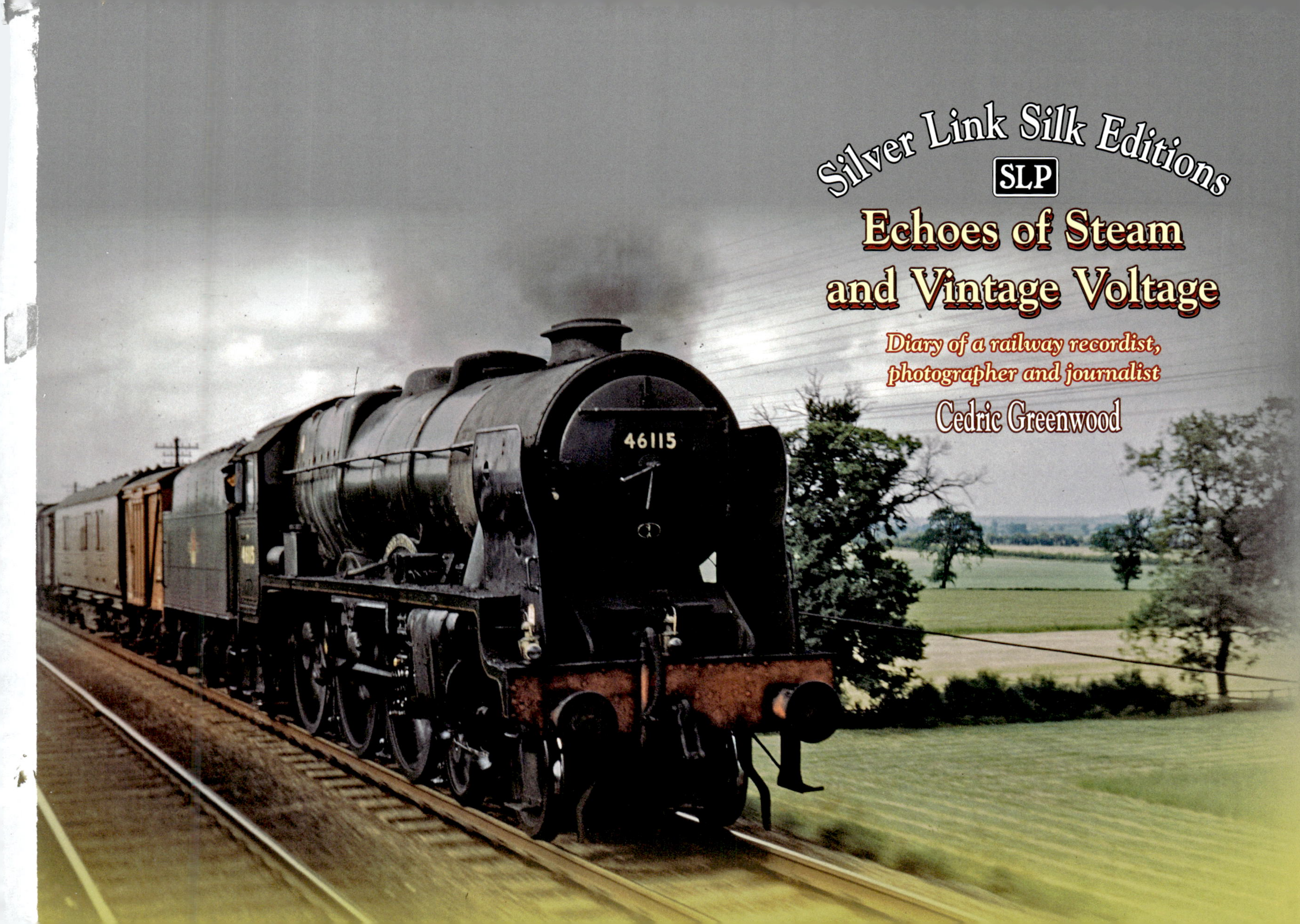

Silver Link Silk Editions
SLP
Echoes of Steam
and Vintage Voltage
Diary of a railway recordist,
photographer and journalist
Cedric Greenwood
46115

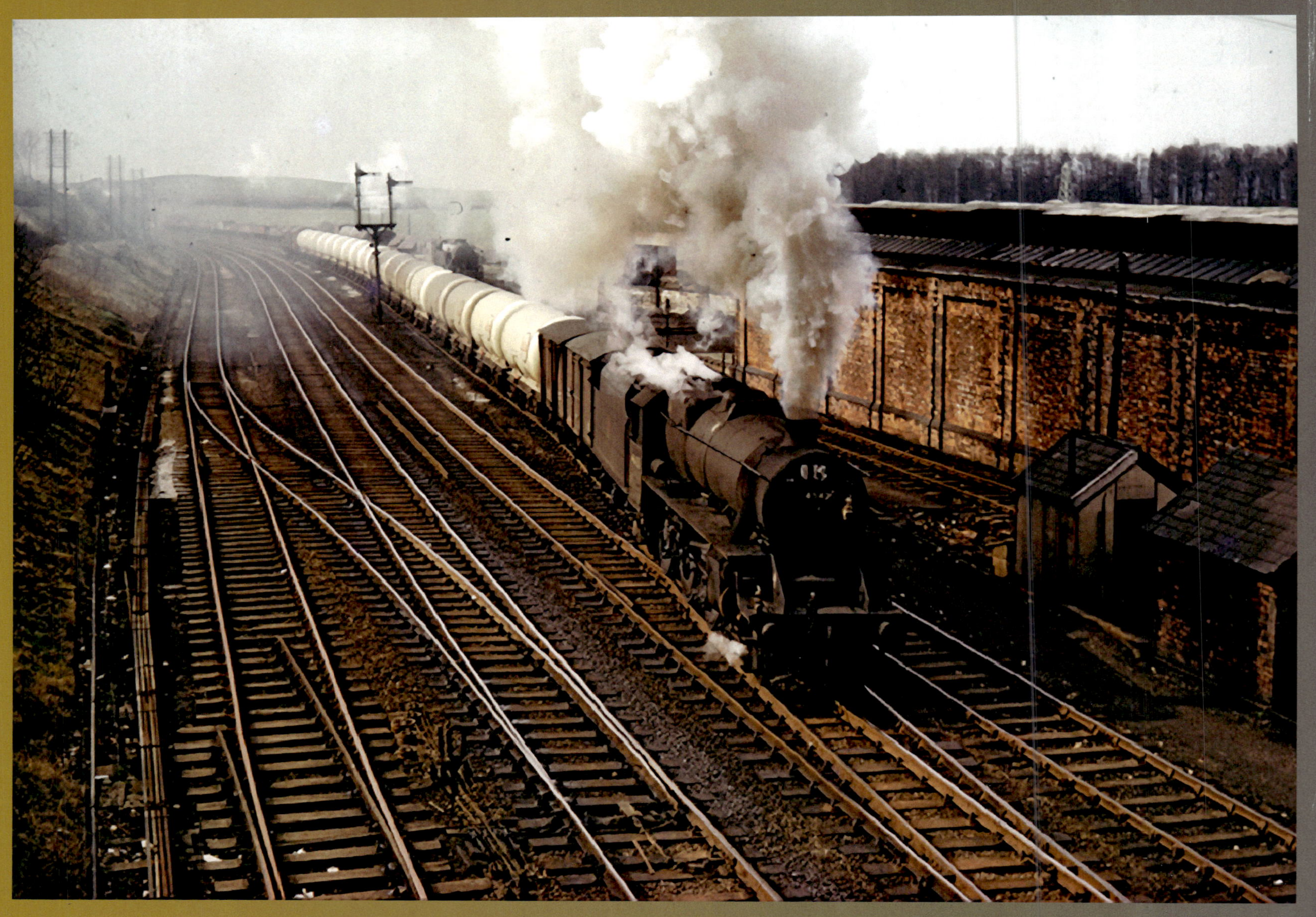

Silver Link Silk Editions

SLP

Echoes of Steam and Vintage Voltage

Diary of a railway recordist, photographer and journalist

Cedric Greenwood

Silver Link Publishing Ltd

First published in 2015

British Library Cataloguing in Publication
Data

A catalogue record for this book is available
from the British Library.

ISBN 978 1 85794 452 5

Silver Link Publishing Ltd
The Trundle
Ringstead Road
Great Addington
Kettering
Northants NN14 4BW

Tel/Fax: 01536 330588
email: sales@nostalgiacollection.com
Website: www.nostalgiacollection.com

Printed and bound in the Czech Republic

Bibliography

The following books were used for reference
in writing the text and captions of this
book:

Black Five, by Lancaster Railway Circle
British Electric Trains, by H. W. A. Linecar,
1949
Bygone Liverpool, by Ramsay Muir, 1913
The Directory of British Tramways, by Keith
Turner, 1996
The Face of London, by Harold Clunn, 1960
The Furness Railway, Volumes 1 and 2, by K.
J. Norman, 1994
The Groudle Glen Railway
*The Historical Guide to North American
Railroads*, by George Drury. 1985
The Isle of Man Railway, by James Boyd,
1967
LMS Branch Lines, by C. J. Gammell, 1988
London Midland in the Fells, by Derek
Huntriss, 1986
Manx Electric, by Mike Goodwyn, 1993
Rail Centres: Oxford, by Laurence Waters,
1986
Settle–Carlisle Railway By W.R. Mitchell and
David Joy 1966
South Shore, The Last Interurban, by William
Middleton, 1970

Front cover: Snow and steam over the fells. A
southbound freight train crests the summit of the
Settle and Carlisle railway at Ais Gill, 1,169 feet high
on the watershed and county boundary between
Yorkshire and Westmorland on 19 January 1966. The
sound of trains labouring up the 1 in 100 northern
ascent to Ais Gill echoed off the scar of Wild Boar
Fell (2,324 feet), Westmorland, in the background.

This train is 'Long Meg', a twice-daily load of
anhydrite from Long Meg quarry in Cumberland to
Widnes chemical works. 'Long Meg' was the heaviest
train on the 'Long Drag'. In these last years of steam
traction it was always hauled by a BR Standard Class
9F (freight) 2-10-0 locomotive, as seen here, snorting
a fine plume of smoke and steam in the cold air.

The gnome-like, stone bothy on the left is a
platelayers' hut for men working on the track. The
four-track layout here comprised two through lines
and a siding on each side for slow, loose-coupled
goods trains to pull in and let fast (continuous air-
brake fitted) freight and passenger trains overtake.

Ais Gill signal cabin, built in 1900 to a standard
Midland Railway design, has been removed to the
Midland Railway Centre at Butterley in Derbyshire.
Since the railway was reprieved from closure in 1989
it has seen an increasing number of long-distance
freight trains.

Back cover: The great hills ranging from Snaefell
(2,034 feet) to North Barrule (1,860 feet) form the
backdrop to the Manx Electric Railway between
Laxey and Ramsey, seen here with northbound
trolley car 7 of 1894 towing a trailer car at Ballaskeig
Beg on 17 August 1961.

Contents

Half title: When steam still worked the North Western main line: *Scots Guardsman*, an ex-LMS rebuilt 'Royal Scot' Class 4-6-0 heads an up parcels train at speed near Leighton Buzzard on 6 July 1962. The photograph was taken from an overtaking steam passenger train on the way to Euston. *Scots Guardsman* was stabled at Willesden (1A) but later moved north as steam was exiled south of Crewe. The engine is now preserved in working order.

Title page: Long freight trains waited in the down loop sidings at Oxenholme for banking engines to give them a push up Grayrigg bank. 'Black Five' No 45421 of 1937 passes Oxenholme loco shed (right) as it pulls a train of Esso oil tank wagons out of the sidings on 2 April 1964. The shed turntable can be seen through the arch of the smoke and more freight trains are queuing up in the sidings in the background. Oxenholme shed closed in 1962, after which Carnforth shed provided the bankers.

Introduction

The steam locomotive, one time king of the iron road, had been deposed by the diesel and electric invasion of British Railways and was making its last stand in north-west England in 1967 and '68. It seemed fitting that this area of grimy, heavy industry and rugged, majestic fell country between Crewe and Carlisle, the Pennines and the Irish Sea, should see the twilight of the steam age. I lived in the north-western fell country and steam trains, with their trails of steam and echoing rods and whistles, seemed to enhance the romance of the fells and dales but when the last steam train had gone the railway lost its romance. I had the good fortune to be living and working at Kendal in Westmorland during the 1960s. When I moved there from electrified Kent at the end of 1962 I was not to know that this would give me a grandstand seat in the final theatre of steam.

My first and lasting impression of Kendal was of the place where phantom steam trains rode through the night sky. I was hitch-hiking back home to Kent after a visit to Glasgow tramways with my friend Robin in December 1960. We arrived in Kendal after dark looking for bed and breakfast overnight. I perceived over the rooftops the images of trains apparently climbing through the sky with lines of dim lights from the carriage windows and the glow from the locomotive firebox lighting up the underside of their trails of smoke and steam as they climbed along the side of Hay Fell from Oxenholme to Grayrigg on the main line to Scotland.

Before and after my deferred National Service I was a reporter and feature writer for the *Kent Messenger* at Canterbury, and on 7 January 1963 I started work for the *Lancashire Evening Post* at its Kendal branch office. Kendal was on the Oxenholme-Windermere branch line, which was the first branch line into the Lake District, in 1846, the northern outpost of the last area of steam traction on British Railways, and the last steam branch line on the network. The branch saw its last steam passenger train on 29 July and the last steam freight on 3 August 1968, the very last day of regular steam traction on BR.

The area I covered for the newspaper also included much of the former London & North Western, or 'West Coast', main line between Lancaster and Carlisle, the former Midland main line between Settle and Carlisle, the former Midland branch line from Clapham to Low Gill (closed in 1964) and the former Furness Railway between Carnforth and Barrow with its branches to Hincaster (closed in 1963), Lake Side (closed in 1965) and Coniston (closed in 1962). There was also the former North Eastern Railway trans-Pennine line from Darlington to Tebay bringing Durham coal to Furness ironworks via Hincaster. This route closed in 1962 and my footplate 'chauffeur', Watson Sowerby, of Carnforth shed, was an exile from Kirkby Stephen East shed on that North Eastern route.

The Settle and Carlisle line was the Midland Railway's independent, impressive and scenic route to Scotland, the highest main line in England, forging a dramatic passage over the western flanks of the north Pennine Moors through the dales and moors of Yorkshire, Westmorland and Cumberland in a marathon of gargantuan earthworks, 17 viaducts and 14 tunnels in the 72 miles from Settle to Carlisle, to maintain a ruling gradient of 1 in 100. Railwaymen called it 'The Long Drag'; on this ruling gradient it's a 15-mile climb each side of the fells, north from Settle to Blea Moor and south from Appleby to Ais Gill summit at 1,169 feet.

I photographed these railways on my days off and wrote about them in the newspaper but that was not enough. I had long had a sensitive ear for the sounds of steam and vintage electric trains and tramcars, and my interests extended to old ferry and excursion steamers on estuaries and lakes. This is evidenced by my collection of 39 vinyl gramophone records of these subjects, mainly steam railways, both in Britain and North America. The sounds of steam and vintage electric trains and tramcars are like music to my ears. The Americans call it 'stack music', i.e. sounds from the smokestack. You can spend a whole evening looking at photographs or lantern slides of railways but the subject is still dead. As soon as you put on a gramophone record of railways the subject comes alive and you feel as if you have experienced it first hand. To me, sound brings steam trains and tramcars back to life in a way that picture books can never do, and I prefer to sit in the darkness with the sound and give free rein to my imagination than to see pictures of the subject.

Now I wanted to record railways that were familiar to me and sounds I liked that were not recorded on those commercial gramophone records. I acquired a portable tape recorder at the end of 1966 and recorded steam workings in Lancashire, Westmorland and Cumberland, from Manchester to Carlisle and on the Isle of Man. I recorded at the trackside, in the goods yard, in the shed yard, in the signal cabin, from the leading coach, from the brakevan, on the footplate, inside a tunnel and under the coaling stage. I also recorded interviews with a stationmaster and signalmen on the high and lonely reaches of the Settle and Carlisle railway.

Fortunately I also kept descriptive diaries from 1962 till 1968, which included my recording and photographic expeditions covering the end of the steam era, and most of the text that follows this Introduction is taken from those diaries, augmented by extracts from my tape scripts and from letters of the period, collected and recently returned to me by my old friend Robin Hogg. The diaries and letters, written straight after the events with the details fresh in my mind, conjure up a vivid word picture and atmosphere that would be impossible to recall and recreate from memory today. Without those contemporary records I would never have attempted to write this book.

When steam had finished we had to leave Kendal for our deaf son's education, life was less interesting but busier so the diaries ended but the letters continued. Life was not as eventful after the steam era but I did carry on tape-recording. The text of my contemporary extracts from the diaries and letters is enclosed in single quotation marks and the narrative that threads it together is completed in unquoted text.

After the steam era I went on to tape-record pre-war electric trains around London, Manchester, Liverpool and Glasgow, tramcars at Blackpool and ex-LNER paddle steamers on the Humber and the Firth of Clyde. During the steam era, in 1967, I recorded the late-Victorian tramcars on the Manx Electric Railway, described in Part 3. My interest in vintage electric traction extended to the 'interurban' electric railways of North America and I recorded the Chicago, South Shore & South Bend Railroad on the streets of Michigan City, Indiana, in 1972. In the end I resorted to recording the Guy buses of Chester City Transport in 1979 and Bristol buses of the Eastern Scottish Motor Traction Company out of Edinburgh in 1982. These Gardner-engined buses, with their deep-throated throb and conductors collecting the fares, were the last nostalgic sounds of a past era of public transport.

All these recordings are of a way of life that was a throwback to the old order and different from the alien new order that came in with the 1960s, the most decadent decade in modern history, socially, architecturally and for the railways.

I scripted each tape programme before recording, following a set, geographical or storyline sequence for each title, and left blank spaces between the sound tracks to insert the scripted narration afterwards, which had to be edited to fit the blank intervals between the sound tracks, thus announcing each subsequent sequence without talking over it. I narrated the programmes so that people could listen to them at home in the dark with the lights out and just the fire glow, so that one's domestic surroundings did not detract from one's imagination of the railway scenes, especially the nocturnes. A narration saves the listener switching on the light to read about the next sequence and that is one aspect of the commercial recordings I think is lacking.

Sometimes I was lucky to get the sounds I wanted first time but in many cases I returned to re-record the sequences until I got what I wanted. In some cases the recorded sounds were never sufficiently graphic to use on the final programmes when, many years later, I transcribed them to compact discs. I give a list of my ultimate CD programmes available below.

When I was in recording mode, I had to keep an eye on the volume needle so I thought little about photography, with the result that most of my illustrations were taken at other times, before or after the recordings, which is why in many cases the dates of the photographs are at variance with the diary dates of the recordings.

All the monochrome and colour

photographs in this book are mine, except where otherwise credited. The monochromes were taken with a 1925-vintage Kodak Brownie No 2 box camera, handed down by my Dad, using Ilford 120 film. The colour photographs are reproduced from transparencies taken with a Braun Paxette 35mm camera using Kodachrome (1) film; these slides have retained the colour well.

I have augmented the illustrations with a selection of my contemporary railway tickets, mostly those thick, card tickets, 2¼in by 3cm, that the booking clerk picked from a rack and stamped in a date punch, much quicker than today's computer-issued tickets. The fares seem amazingly cheap by today's standards but prices are related to wages and these fares are a salutary reminder of inflation and devaluation of the pound since then. Because of inflation I have not attempted to decimalise the £ s d fares. The oft-quoted 'D-day', 1971, exchange rate is as invalid for comparison with earlier decades as it is with today because it is tied to the pound, the value of which has changed radically over the last half century. £7 5s 10d in 1950 does not convert to £7.29 in today's money; in 2014 it equated to £611.90, because they were the average weekly wages for those years. Let's just say that before decimalisation there were 20s (shillings)

in £1 and 12d (pence) in 1 shilling (1s). In the 1960s few of us could afford to buy ciné projectors to show commercial railway films or ciné cameras to take our own films, let alone with sound track. With the birth of video the price of ciné cameras with sound came down and I bought one in 1982, but the price of film went up until by 1990 it cost us £15 for a three-minute film, much of which would end up in the waste paper basket on editing.

Videotape was very much cheaper and unwanted footage could be reused. I took my last ciné film in 1990 and in 1997 I started filming with VHS videotape, first editing on to tape, then from 2002 with d.v. mini-tape, edited on to d.v. disc. Since 1982 I have produced film programmes mainly featuring traditional tramways and interurbans in Europe.

Today we have the sights and sounds of railways readily available on DVD with hundreds of commercial railway programmes available, thus eclipsing the vinyl gramophone records and compact discs of railway sounds that were once sought after by railway enthusiasts, but for which there is little or no demand. As a throwback from the past, I still enjoy the sounds of steam trains marching through my house emanating from the gramophone or CD player while I'm working. When I

have the time I prefer just to sit and listen in the dark. The sounds help me to conjure up the total scene and atmosphere better than any still or motion picture. There were many sonic situations, such as night on the footplate or under the coaling tower, which would be very difficult to illustrate on film or video. Gramophone records had another advantage over DVDs in that British and North American records could be played on the same machine, but DVDs cannot because of regional differences in the discs and recorders. I can still enjoy the sound of live steam in my retirement as my back garden is within earshot of the North Norfolk Railway and trains climbing the 1 in 80 bank up Kelling Heath.

Finally, as this is an introduction, let me introduce you to the people and things whose names recur through the text, notably Ruth, my wife, Karl, my elder son, and Raven Scar, our grey stone house on Windermere Road in Kendal. Vintora was my name for my Lambretta motor scooter, which I rode over the hills beyond Kendal on business and on most of these railway adventures. Robin Hogg, of north London and later St Alban's, is my best friend, from National Service days, a kindred spirit, one of what John Betjeman called 'us of the steam and the gaslight'.

My confederates in steam at Kendal

included Percy Duff, the Borough Treasurer, Richard Holloway, one of the town's leading solicitors and clerk to Windermere Magistrates, and Jack Dawson, Chairman of Sedbergh Rural District Council. Other friends in steam at Kendal, to whom I was indebted for 'bush telegraph' information about the railways, were Stan Berry, Alan Birtwistle, Mrs Kathleen Preston, John Proctor and Jim Slater.

My thanks also go to Douglas Frior, of Melton Constable, Norfolk, for transcribing and editing my tape recordings on to the ultimate compact disc programmes for me. The CDs we produced from these recordings are listed below. Copies are available from him through his Internet website www. bygone-transport.co.uk.

'Smoke Over Kendal': Steam passenger and freight workings on the Windermere branch and at Oxenholme, recorded from March to September 1967: 67 minutes.

'The Long Drag': Steam freight and signalmen on the Midland line over the roof of England, recorded from May to October 1967: 50 minutes.

'Isle of Man Journey': By steamship, horse tram, electric tram, petrol tram and steam train, recorded in August 1967: 70 minutes.

'Riding the Iron Horse': On the footplate of a 'Britannia' with a night freight from Carnforth to Carlisle, recorded on 14 December 1967: 46 minutes.

'Steam Journey Through Lancashire': The 'Belfast Boat Express', recorded from the leading coach and on the footplate on 20 January 1968: 56 minutes.

'Steam's Last Duty': Stanier steam shunting and shifting freight at Ulverston, Kendal and Carlisle, recorded February to August 1968: 48 minutes.

'Whitehaven Coal Railway': NCB railways at Haig colliery and Whitehaven harbour and the cable incline link, recorded in May 1969: 30 minutes.

'Vintage Voltage': Electric multiple unit trains of 1927-39 around London, Manchester, Liverpool and Glasgow, recorded from 1968 to 1977: 74 minutes.

'South Shore Line': North America's last 'interurban' electric railway on street in Michigan City, Indiana, and on board to South Bend, recorded in August 1972: 33 minutes.

'LNER Paddle Steamers': The Humber ferries *Wingfield Castle* and *Lincoln Castle*, recorded in 1974-75, and the Clyde excursion steamer *Waverley*, recorded in 1981: 47 minutes.

'Blackpool and Glasgow trams': Tramcars in service at Blackpool, recorded in 1976, and Glasgow cars at Crich museum, recorded in 1987: 40 minutes.

'Chester Guy Buses': Buses of 1953 to 1969 recorded in the garage, in the lower saloon and in the cab in 1979 and 1982.

Overleaf: Snorting a fine plume of smoke and steam, an ex-LMS 8F 2-8-0 toils up the 1 in 100 gradient through Ribblesdale past Selside signal cabin with a northbound freight on 12 October 1967.

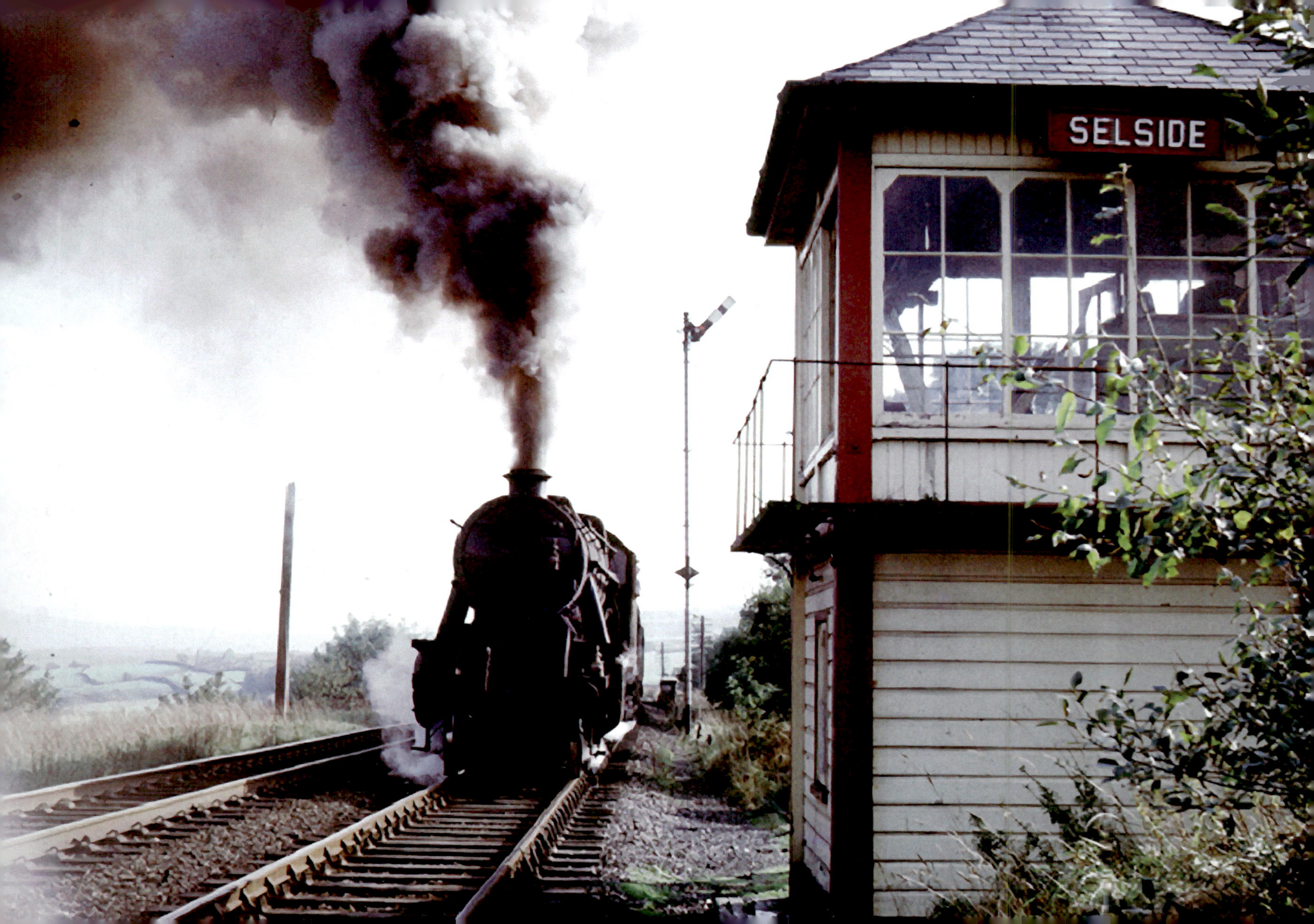
SELSIDE

Part I Oxford to Oxenholme, 1946 – 1966

My interest in railways was purely aesthetic, photographic, architectural and aural. I never collected engine numbers nor did I have much knowledge of the technical or engineering aspects, but I could admire the orderliness and disciplines of railway operations and I was fascinated by the historic ramifications of the railway network, the interlocking of manual signalling – and the sounds in the signal cabin. I liked the general railway scene and photographed the railway in the landscape and townscape, its stations, old carriages, goods brakevans and signal cabins as well as the locomotives. The listed stations and the old signal cabins are the last vestiges of the golden age of railways, and the last of the manual signal cabins are now fast disappearing.

My induction to railways started at Oxford about 1946, when I was eight, and my interest culminated at Oxenholme and ended with the demise of steam traction on British Railways in 1968. We lived at Oxford from 1944 to 1949 and Oxford General station was the gateway to discovery. It was the springboard for our post-war family holidays by the Great Western Railway

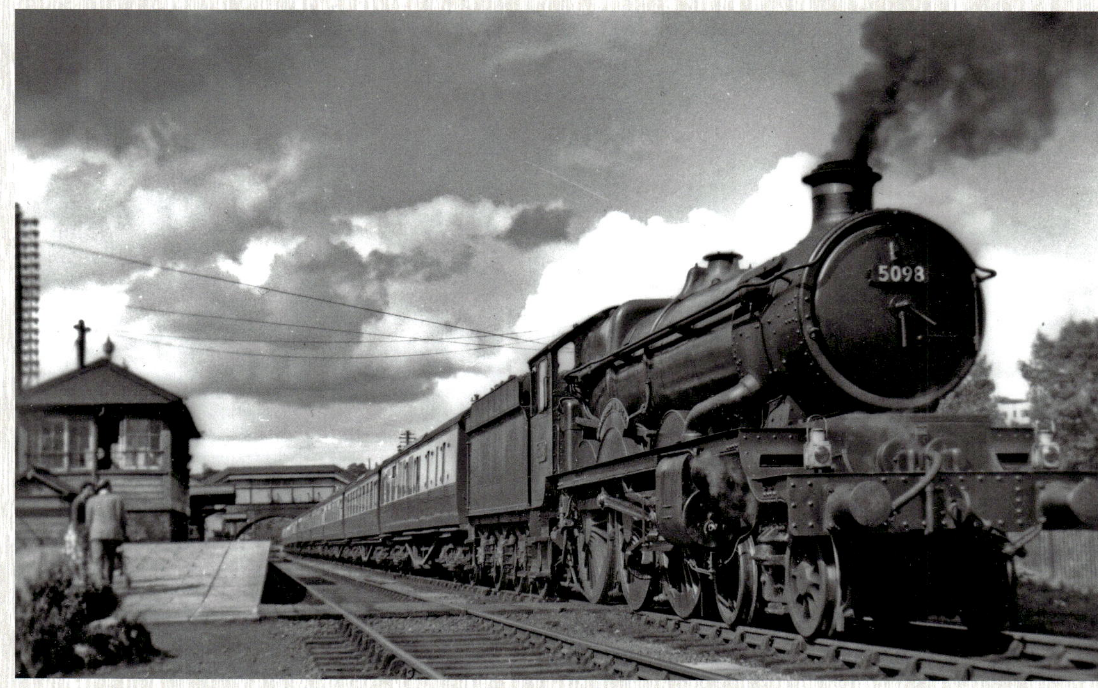

This was my first railway photograph, at age 11. The down 'Cornish Riviera Express' stops at Par, junction for Newquay, one afternoon in 1949. The train left Paddington at 10.30am, first stop Plymouth, next stop Par at 4.02pm, then Truro, Gwinear Road and St Erth, arriving in Penzance at 5.25. It is headed by Great Western 4-6-0 locomotive No 5098 *Clifford Castle*, in this classic composition reminiscent of wooden jigsaw puzzles of the period. Par signal cabin (left), on the south end of the up platform, was built about 1879, extended in 1893 and still operates the points and semaphore signals regulating the diesel trains of today. The covered footbridge has been replaced by a modern one without a roof and the tall telegraph pole has gone.

and Southern Railway in Somerset, Devon and Cornwall in 1946-49 and our move to Merseyside in 1949. Dad worked in the Post Office Telephones and moved home every time he had promotion so I stayed on as a boarder at Magdalen School, Oxford, where I had started as a dayboy from age 10, while he moved around the country. When he transferred from Oxford to Liverpool we moved home to Wallasey and I had the pleasure of going home by the GWR from Oxford to Birkenhead for the school holidays at half-term and the end of term from 1949 to 1952.

As a boarder in Oxford I spent my spare time browsing in second-hand bookshops and record shops and venturing beyond the town centre to Gloucester Green bus station, the two railway stations, LMS and GWR, and exploring Oxfordshire, Berkshire and Buckinghamshire by bus and branch line. Wednesday afternoons were 'sports afternoons' at school but sports were not compulsory and my 'sport' was running and jumping on moving goods brakevans during the afternoon shunting in the LMS goods yard, having first released the handbrakes on all the vans in the sidings, and riding to the bufferstops. Obviously we had no notion of 'health and safety' in those days.

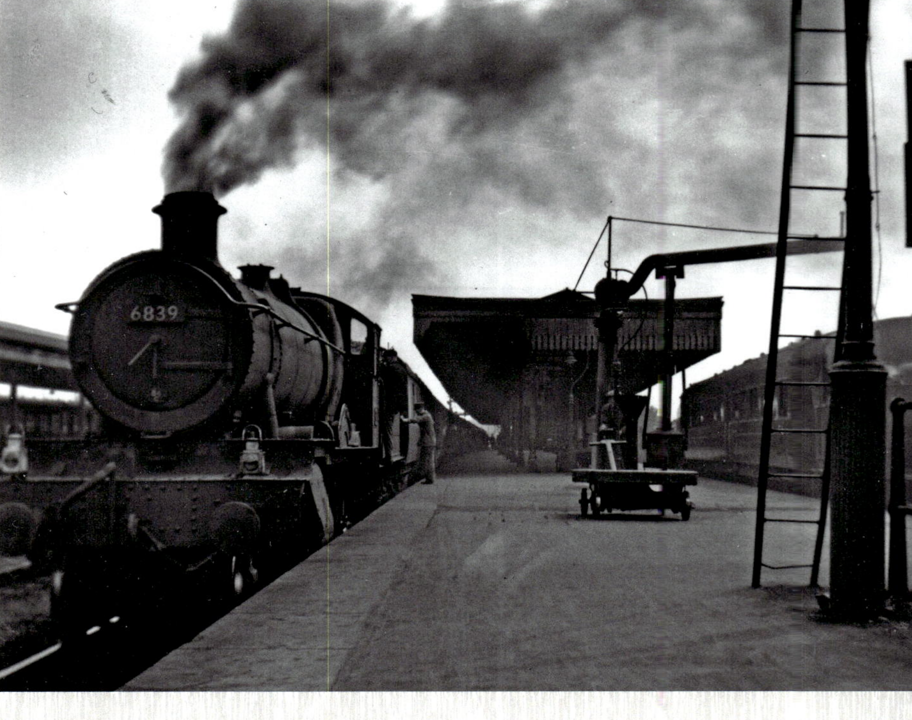

Smoke filters the afternoon sunshine at Oxford General station on the former Great Western main line. This busy station lay alongside the sleepy LMS terminus, divided only by its road approach to the up platform. This was the scene at the north end of the down platform in 1953 with Great Western 4-6-0 locomotive No 6839 *Hewell Grange* (left) at the head of a train from Paddington to Wolverhampton. In the bay platform on the right is a '1400' Class tank engine with an auto-trailer for the Woodstock branch.

The four tracks between the main up and down platforms were busy with freight on the centre tracks and with passenger trains calling at the platforms on journeys from Paddington to Hereford and to Wolverhampton, from Weymouth to Wolverhampton, from the Kent coast and Bournemouth to Birkenhead, and from Bournemouth, Swindon and Swansea to York. Thus Oxford General saw an interesting mixture of GWR, Southern and LNER locomotives and carriages. Local branch line trains ran to Princes Risborough, Fairford and, from 1951, to Bletchley.

The up and down platforms were over 900 feet long, each accommodating two trains via scissors crossovers halfway along, linking the centre tracks with the platform tracks. The station buildings, dating from 1852, were weatherboarded like stations in the Wild West, and the canopies dated from 1893, when they replaced an overall roof. The old, wooden, gas-lit station lasted till 1970-72, when it was rebuilt in the austere modern idiom – and it has since been rebuilt again.

Looking north from the down platform at Oxford General, where trains left for Hereford, Wolverhampton, Birkenhead and York. This 1953 picture was taken to feature the platform furniture: the water column, brazier, gas lamps and the signals with their ball-and-spike finials, notably the large bay platform signal in the off position with the screen on the post showing when the line was clear from the down main platform. All the signal posts and semaphores in this picture are the original Great Western wooden ones, which were replaced by steel signals in 1959 and electric signals in 1973. Also in the picture we can see the Great Western's soot-black, weatherboarded, engine shed on the left, the LMS engine shed in the background to the right, Oxford Station North signal cabin and the tower of St Barnabas church on the extreme right. The church tower is the only structure in this photograph to survive today.

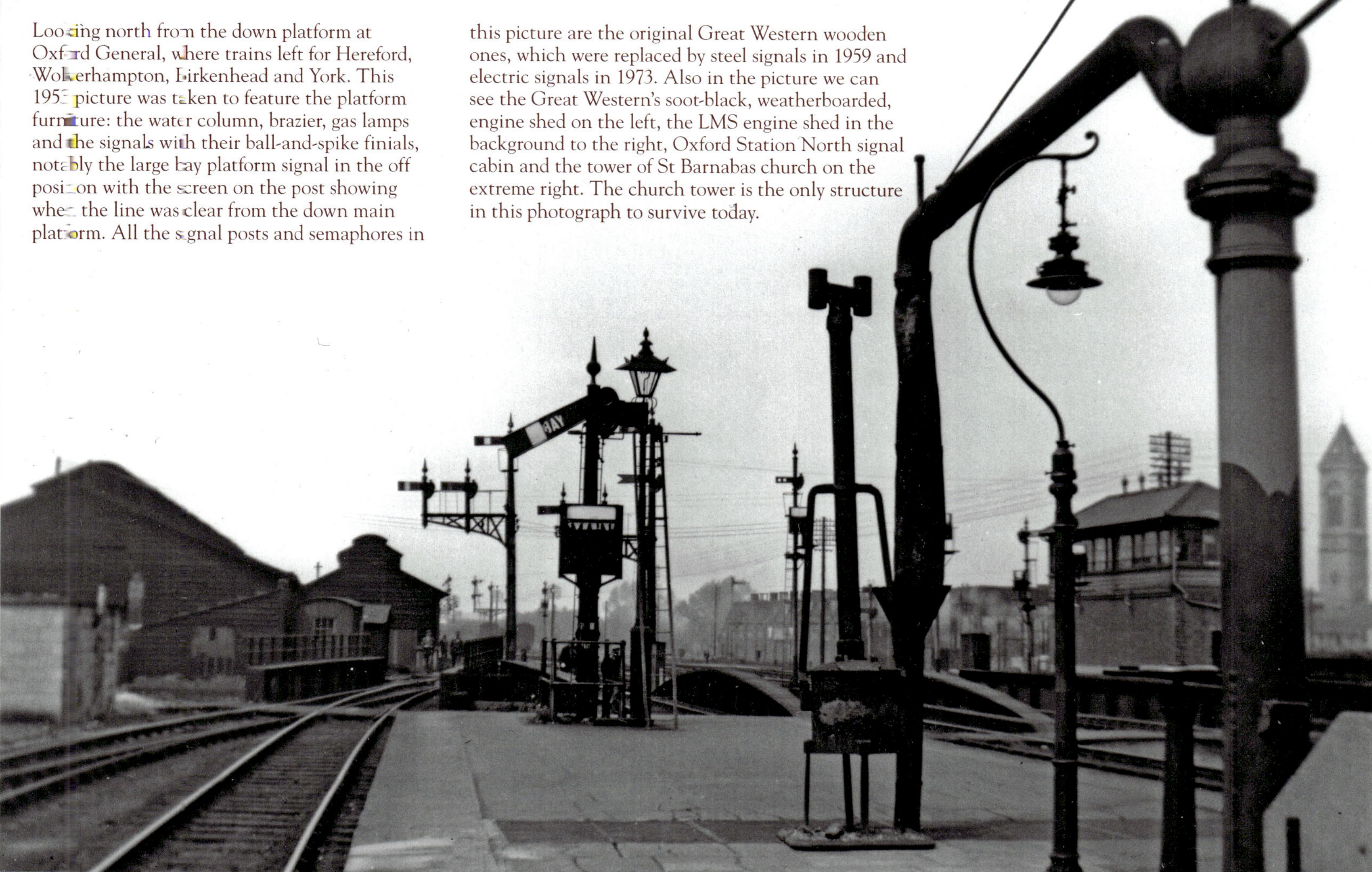

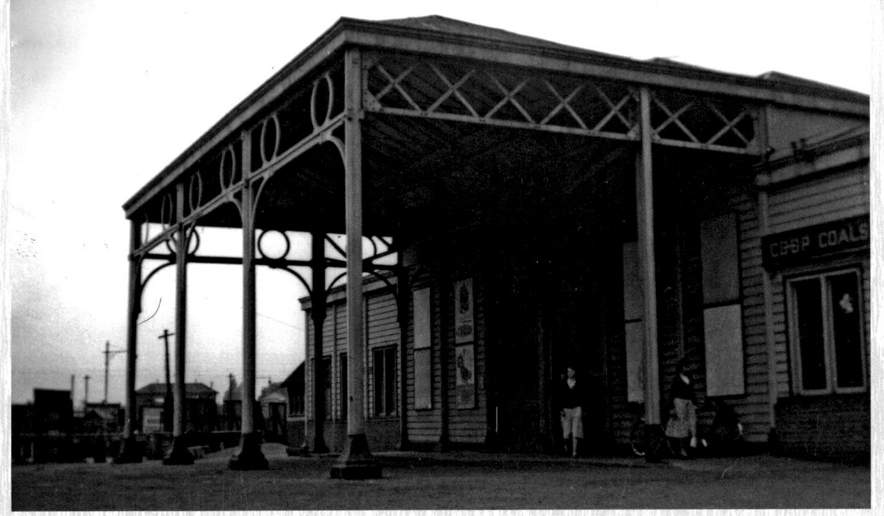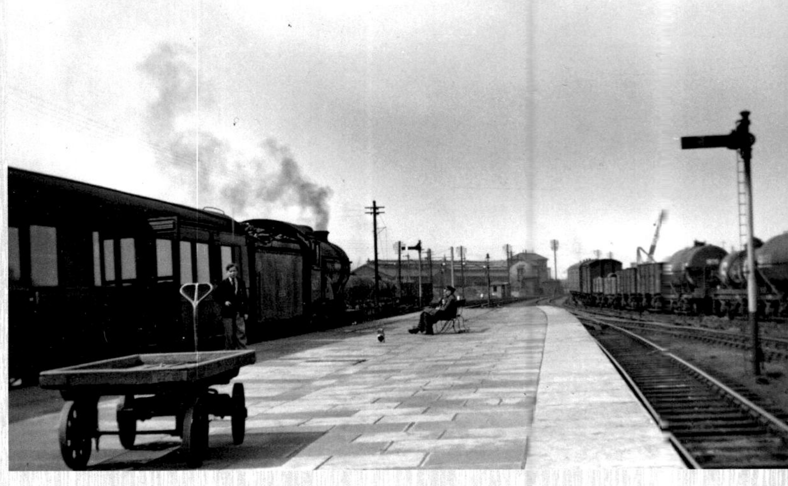

Above left: The university city banished its railways to a point half a mile from the city centre on the road west. While the GWR station was on a through main line, the LMS station next door was the terminus of a 31-mile branch line from Bletchley on the former LNW main line. This grand portico fronted a weatherboarded, gas-lit building and one island platform with only eight passenger trains a day when this photograph was taken in 1950, but was surrounded by a large goods yard. The portico and the frame of the trainshed were constructed of prefabricated cast-iron sections by Fox, Henderson Ltd, who built Crystal Palace in 1851, the same year as this station opened on the corner of Park End Street and Rewley Road.

A hundred years later the station closed to passenger trains, which were switched to Oxford General, but the goods yard remained open till 1984. The site has been redeveloped with a plain, modern business school and there is no sign that there was ever a railway station here; however, the portico and trainshed have been saved and resurrected around a new island platform at the Buckinghamshire Railway Centre at Quainton near Aylesbury.

Above right: Oxford LMS station, Rewley Road, with its island platform, was the terminus of the former LNWR branch line from Bletchley. The station saw only eight passenger trains a day when this picture was taken in 1950: seven to Bletchley and one to Verney Junction only. Three Bletchley trains ran on to Bedford and one of those ran through to Cambridge. The line was generally worked by ex-LMS engines from Bletchley, but this ex-LNER 'D16' Class 4-4-0 locomotive is on the one round trip of the day from Cambridge, the only direct railway service between the two great university cities. The engine crew sits in the afternoon sunshine awaiting the 2.42 departure for Bletchley, Bedford and Cambridge. A school friend, Roger Lowman, stands by the leading coach.

In between passenger trains the locomotive shunted the goods sidings on both sides of the passenger station. Tracks from this terminus funnelled past the LMS and GW signal cabins in the background, where a double-track swing-bridge over a branch of the River Isis was the sole access to the LMS terminus.

This station closed to passengers in 1951, when Bletchley trains were diverted through Oxford North Junction into the adjacent Oxford General station on the Great Western main line. The service was augmented to ten trains a day and steam gave way to diesel multiple units in the 1960s but the service ended in 1967. The former Bletchley Line later reopened for passenger trains for 12 miles from Oxford to Bicester with 11 trains each way on weekdays and nine on Sundays but this service has been suspended till 2015 while the line is being relaid and upgraded to Bletchley with the longer-term plan to reopen the through route between Oxford and Cambridge.

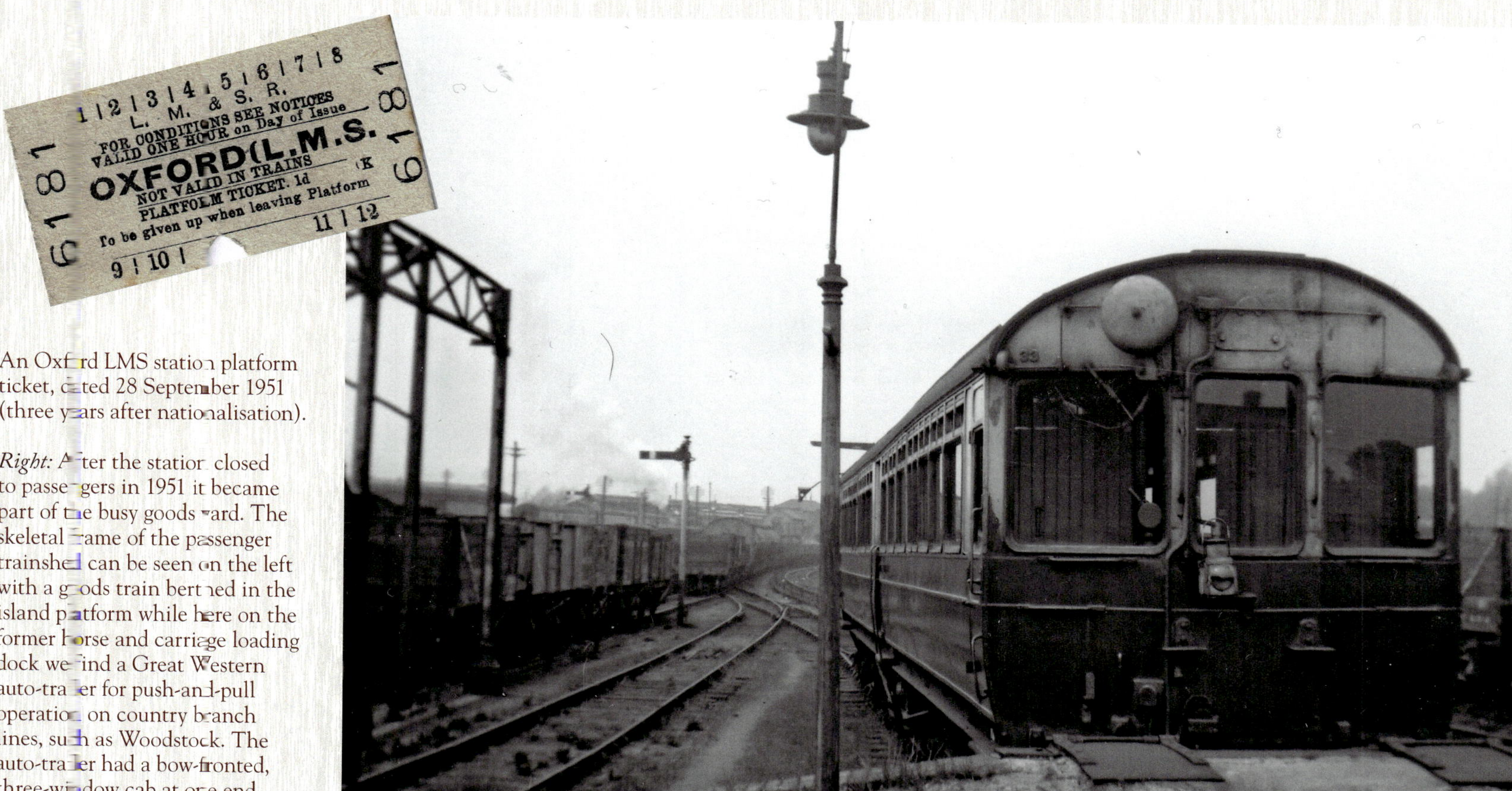

An Oxford LMS station platform ticket, dated 28 September 1951 (three years after nationalisation).

Right: After the station closed to passengers in 1951 it became part of the busy goods yard. The skeletal frame of the passenger trainshed can be seen on the left with a goods train berthed in the island platform while here on the former horse and carriage loading dock we find a Great Western auto-trailer for push-and-pull operation on country branch lines, such as Woodstock. The auto-trailer had a bow-fronted, three-window cab at one end for the driver, who remotely controlled the locomotive when running in reverse. It also had a large warning gong above the cab windows and centre doors to a large saloon with longitudinal seats like the lower saloon of an old tramcar. The older auto-trailers originated as steam rail motors with a self-contained, small steam locomotive and footplate at one end of the vehicle and the remote driving cab at the other. This coach was built in 1908 as a steam rail motor and was converted to an auto-trailer coach in 1928. Later auto-trailers were built new as driver trailer coaches identical to this.

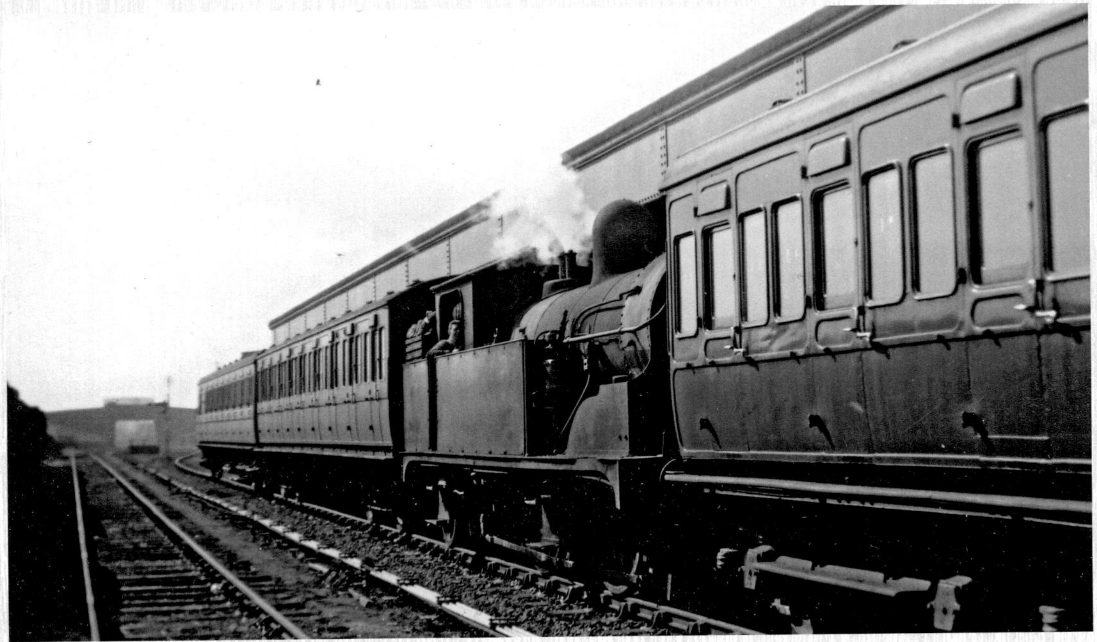

Herne Bay is on the north Kent main line from London to Ramsgate, but found itself on the end of a branch line with trains of pre-Grouping stock after the east coast tidal surge on 1 February 1953 washed out 4 miles of the main line across Chislet Marshes between Herne Bay and Birchington. This is one of the emergency push-and-pull trains that connected Herne Bay and Whitstable with the Dover main line at Faversham. It is pictured at Herne Bay station with a reboilered ex-London & South Western 2-4-0T 'M7' sandwiched in the middle of four elderly carriages with a remote driving cab at each end. This service operated from 2 March to 20 May 1953, while the railway reinstated the roadbed across the marshes and heaped a protective earth bank alongside. The main line to Thanet reopened on 21 May pending completion of a concrete sea wall from Birchington to Reculver.

From 1 February to 1 March Herne Bay and Whitstable were cut off by rail as the sea had also flooded the line across Seasalter Level between Whitstable and Faversham. The Canterbury & Whitstable Railway, which had closed on 1 December 1952, was reopened between 6 and 28 February to deliver coal for Whitstable and Herne Bay. The C&WR originally opened in 1830 to carry Tyneside coal from Whitstable harbour to Canterbury.

We had to get permission from the headmaster to go 'up town'. To us this included the railway stations, which were half a mile on the other side of the town centre. My friends and I were exposed by a photographer on the front page of the *Oxford Mail* waving off the last passenger train from Oxford LMS station in 1951. The headmaster, Bob Stanier, made no comment but I don't suppose he disapproved; his uncle was Sir William Stanier, the Great Western Works Manager at Swindon from 1912 and Chief Mechanical Engineer of the LMS from 1932 to 1944, and there was a facial likeness. Oxford's two stations were among my places of regular pilgrimage until I left boarding school at age 17.

Dad was promoted again from Liverpool to Canterbury in 1952 so for my last three years at boarding school we were living at Herne Bay and I still travelled home by steam train, via Paddington and Victoria. The main line to Ramsgate passed within view of our house on the semi-rural outskirts of Herne Bay and I liked to watch the trains in the night from the top of a signal post at nearby Blacksole Bridge.

During the school holidays I spent odd days in London, rising at 3.40am and walking 2 miles down dark country lanes to Herne Bay station to catch the early morning workmen's train, the 5am from Margate and 5.19 from Herne Bay. The workmen's return ticket to London and back, returning by any train, 120 miles in all, cost only 4s 8d. It was a train of ex-South Eastern & Chatham, wooden, compartment stock with a 'birdcage' lookout above roof-level in the guard's van. Some compartments had seats on one side only. We had to change at Chatham on to an electric multiple unit of converted ex-SECR steam-hauled, non-corridor, compartment stock to London Bridge or Cannon Street. Thus London Bridge station became my regular railway Mecca, continuously busy with its electric multiple units, many of them pre-war, and occasional steam trains, and this experience would lead me back to record the Southern Electric and other vintage electric traction when steam had finished.

My first contemporary description of a railway journey was a travelogue of the Great Western route from Oxford General to Birkenhead Woodside during my travels home from boarding school in 1949-52, when I was aged 11 to 14. This was purely a travelogue of the lineside scene, such as I found many years later in a second-hand copy of the Great Western's 95-page guide book *Paddington to Birkenhead* published in 1925 as Number Two in the series 'Through the Window' (Number One being *Paddington to Penzance*).

The Birkenhead route was scenic and interesting, passing through the Chiltern Hills, Warwickshire and the Black Country, dipping into the Welsh hills between Shrewsbury and Chester and taking in five grand, architectural stations on the way: Paddington, Birmingham Snow Hill, Shrewsbury, Chester General and Birkenhead Woodside.

When I was living in Kent I also travelled this route on the through train between Margate and Birkenhead via Guildford in August 1954, at age 16, to spend two weeks' holiday photographing the streets, docks and ferries of Merseyside. I also travelled the route from Paddington to Woodside in May 1960 with *King George V* at the head as far as Wolverhampton; this was the start of a hitch-hiking and youth-hostelling tour of Wales and Cornwall with Ruth. Based largely on my notes in 1951, I wrote a travelogue of the journey from Paddington to Woodside as the opening narrative to my book *Merseyside: The Indian Summer* (Silver Link, 2007), a detailed description of Merseyside in the 1950s, illustrated mainly with the photographs I took on that trip in 1954.

My first description of a train journey, with the focus on the railway rather than the lineside scene, is taken from a diary of my travels in 1955-56. In those days

the main lines into Kent were electrified only as far as Gillingham, Maidstone and Sevenoaks. Through steam trains ran from Victoria to Tunbridge Wells, Dover and Ramsgate but to get to east Kent from Charing Cross, Cannon Street or London Bridge we had to ride an electric train to Chatham or Gillingham and change there to a steam train from Victoria.

**London Bridge to Herne Bay
4 April 1955**

'London Bridge railway station is the war-torn survivor of the 1851 Italianate brick and timber buildings with provisional post-war restitution. There are two stations in one: the high-level through station on the former South Eastern Railway to Charing Cross, all on viaduct, and the ground-level terminus of the former London, Brighton & South Coast Railway under a cavernous iron and glass trainshed. The high-level station is a complex warren of underground passages and offices, long ramps in tunnels up to the platforms, long footbridges spanning the platforms and dungeon-like steps down to Tooley Street.

'In the dark of the evening I stood on the west end of platform 1 watching the ghost-like electric trains appear round the bend along the viaduct from Charing Cross and Cannon Street. I could hear the roar and purr of the AEC RT buses in the street below. The streetlights illuminated the taller buildings that overlook the railway viaduct but gloom prevailed on the north side of the platform, the Tooley Street, Bermondsey, prospect. The former South Eastern Railway offices and large warehouses abut on to the viaduct, and through the narrow gaps between them can be seen dim gas wall lanterns lighting the sett-paved approaches to the great warehouse gates on the opposite side of the street. A steam train, a rare thing in this station, came in for a long rest in platform 2.

'I was soon sitting in the compartment of an electric train rattling along south Thames-side via Woolwich and Gravesend to Gillingham. Most of the passengers had alighted before we reached Chatham. The train headed through the tunnels and cuttings of the Medway towns on its last lap to Gillingham. I got out on to a long, cold, uninviting platform and the empty train slid out of service away into the night towards the sheds. The platform was empty but for a small group of Chatham sailors seeing their girlfriends off, four "Teddy boys" and two ill-looking young men in railway uniform who lounged on a trolley and talked in low tones. The silence was sometimes interrupted by lewd and loud laughter from

each end of the platform and by brilliantly lit, empty, electric trains that came dashing in to the end of their last run. As each train arrived the young railwaymen collected the tickets, raided the train for newspapers and magazines and slammed the doors.

'I waited here for an hour and I was standing in the hearth of the drab waiting room when the approach of the 9.37 was heralded by a long, low, eerie whistle. The station shook as, out of the tunnel the train, headed by a rebuilt Merchant Navy Pacific, came thundering and clanking alongside the platform. As the train slid to a stop the compartment lights went out and the carriages were plunged into darkness. I groped my way around in one of those saloon carriages that resemble dining cars without tables. Two recumbent figures lay asleep in the otherwise empty carriage. The train started off. It was beginning to spit with rain outside. We chuffed through the murky sidings, past rows of goods waggons, off into the night. As we gathered speed the saloon lights flashed on, much to my annoyance; I preferred to be in darkness because it enabled me to see out of the window; now all I could see was my own reflection. Disappointed and bored, I went to sleep.

'Ten to 15 minutes later the brakes were jammed on for the stop at Sittingbourne

and as we drew into the platform the lights went off again and we made the rest of the journey in darkness. As we left Sittingbourne, shadows and streaks of light moved across the saloon ceiling from the lights in the streets below. Glad now that the dynamo – or whatever system of lighting was on this train – had failed, I settled into a reclining position along the seat with a good view out of the large window. We were soon rocketing and swaying down deep cuttings. The thick, black smoke with a red tint of firebox glow on the underside dispersed in the woods on each side of the cutting.

'Then the dark, empty train was clattering over the joints and points, sending loud echoes down the sleeping back streets of Faversham. After a grim reception there, the train stumbled through the yards and sidings, left the London-Dover line and headed north-east across the desolation of Graveney Marshes and Seasalter Level. We stopped at Whitstable and at Swalecliffe Halt.

'As we neared Herne Bay I raised myself from my comfortable position, sorry that this journey was nearly at an end – but then those passengers who were going on to Thanet probably got no such inspiration or "kick" out of it as I did; they merely had further to go and did not appreciate their longer journey. I stood by the door at the end of the saloon and surveyed the length of the carriage with the two sleeping figures, the silhouettes of the large seats (with headrests) against the night sky through the windows and the shadows moving across the ceiling. The engine began to get desperate and showered sparks in the telephone wires over the hedgerows. Then the brakes were thrust on and we stopped in a series of jerks as if the driver had suddenly realised we had arrived at Herne Bay.

'It was raining fairly heavily by now and, too poor to take a taxicab, I donned a sou'wester and trudged off along the footpath to Eddington Lane. The train chugged off slowly up the hill towards Blacksole Bridge, Bogshole Bridge, the marshes and the Isle of Thanet. With amazing intuition and foresight, Dad, guessing that I would arrive on the 10.30 at Herne Bay, came down and met me halfway and hauled me off up home to Mill Lane on the back of his motorised tandem [with a petrol Power Pak on the back wheel].'

My favourite perch for watching trains at Herne Bay was the little platform, used by the lamp man, on top of the signal post in the cutting west of Blacksole Bridge. It was a lower-quadrant, semaphore, distant signal and access was by an iron ladder up the side of the post ('Post' rhyming with 'cost'). I only used this observation post at night so as not to be seen. At this location the 'up' trains go downhill and the 'down' trains go uphill. This line to Ramsgate was not electrified till 1959.

Watching the trains from a signal post at Herne Bay
14 September 1955

'At Blacksole Bridge I climbed over the low, wooden fence from the deserted road and scrambled down the side of the cutting in the dark shadows of the bridge down on to the railway tracks. The black night had descended by now and Bogshole Bridge, at the summit of the gradient, stood dramatically silhouetted against the haze of Margate lights, 10 miles distant. I walked in silence on the stout, wooden sleepers down the gradient to my signal post. I made the strange ascent up the near vertical ladder, stood on the little iron platform at the top and leaned on the waist-high railing on each side. The signal downhill towards Herne Bay station turned green. An East Kent double-deck bus grunted quietly over Blacksole Bridge; it looked giant and top-heavy over the cutting. Then, with a soft wheeze, my signal went slowly down. Now my light would show green in the other direction and a train was signalled each way. Crickets twittered in the long grass on the sides of the wide, deep cutting.

'Suddenly a dim, orange light appeared under Bogshole Bridge as if held poised for its descent. It was the train from Ramsgate. The light came flickering down the gradient towards Blacksole Bridge, under which burst a hefty, hissing Schools class locomotive, which came roaring past, followed by its train of carriages, pattering and echoing in the cutting down the hill, casting lights on the ground around it, the sound diminishing around the bend until I could hear it no longer and I presumed it was at rest in Herne Bay station.

'After a while I heard a whistle from the direction of the station and what I thought was the sound of the train going west out of Herne Bay station – but no, the chugging continued slowly and laboriously and its sound became increasingly distinct. Soon a flickering, reddish light appeared, moving slowly and smoothly through the dark night. On it came, steadily, around the bend. Sparks were thrust vertically out of the locomotive chimney into the night sky. Nearer and nearer came the monster, followed by dozens of small, rectangular, dim lights. With its thick, grey smoke billowing skyward and taken by the north-east wind, the fuming monster passed beneath, shaking my signal-top perch. Sparks shot skyward and were lost in the darkness. I was suddenly dazzled by the glaring light from the locomotive firebox, which was open as the fireman fuelled it up the hill. All was darkness again as it chugged on its way and the dark carriages slid beneath me, the lights from their windows cast on the grass banks of the cutting.

'I descended the ladder down the signal post and trudged back up the track on which that last, Thanet-bound train had just passed. As I left my signal post, a soft wheeze put the signal up again. It was all over. Deadly silence surrounded me once more in the dark cutting with the exception of my feet disturbing the stones between the sleepers. I clambered up the side of the cutting and hit the road for home.'

I left school at Christmas 1955 and started work as a newspaper reporter and feature writer for the *Kent Messenger* based at Canterbury branch office on 1 January (which was not a public holiday then). I was conscripted to deferred National Service in the RAF in 1960-62, when I met Robin. Back in 'civvy street', I married Ruth Amos at Margate in 1962, and by 1963 we were living at Kendal in Westmorland and I was reporting for the *Lancashire Evening Post*. In those days the 'Lanky Post' covered

Westmorland and Cumberland too, as far north as Workington. I worked from the Kendal branch office at 94 Stricklandgate and later at 48 Stramongate with the northern editor, Harry Griffin, and the *Farmers' Guardian* reporter Alan Birtwistle. I covered a wide area from Kirkby Stephen in the east to Ravenglass in the west and from Morecambe Bay in the south to Ullswater in the north. Passing through this area were all the ex-LNW, Midland, Furness and North Eastern Railway main lines and branches I described in my Introduction.

Ruth and I moved to Kendal to be on hand for the fell walks we had enjoyed on holiday during our three-year courtship. Little did I realise then that North West England would be steam's last stronghold on British Railways, but it soon became apparent that this area was an island of the old order surrounded by a rising tide of the new diesel and electric railway scene. By 1965 the wires were being strung along the North Western main line south of Crewe. One had to travel by diesel train from Euston to Rugby, by electric train from Rugby to Crewe, and by steam to the north. My trail had led me from Oxford to Oxenholme, a country junction on the 'West Coast' main line for the Windermere branch, and this station would be the last temple of my worship of the

steam locomotive on British Railways. In pursuance of the steam locomotive I would see much more of the fell country I had come for.

**Euston to Preston
3 January 1965**

On returning home from a Christmas visit to our parents in Kent, I recorded the following in my diary. 'The terminus at Euston, with its massive Doric propylæum and its lofty Great Hall waiting room, had been nearly all demolished and a rectangular concrete structure was being built in its place. It was a very bleak and scruffy looking station and had a small, mean, drab waiting room in contrast to the comfort and grandeur of the Great Hall. I followed our journey down the main line in an LMS route book I bought in 1948. *Track of the Royal Scot (vol. 1, Euston to Carlisle)*. Our train was hauled by a diesel locomotive, stopping at Watford and Bletchley, to Rugby Midland, and an overhead-electric locomotive from Rugby, stopping at Nuneaton Trent Valley, Tamworth, Lichfield Trent Valley and Stafford to Crewe.

'The train waited in Crewe station for about 30 minutes for a change of locomotive so I walked to the north end of the platform to see what form of locomotion we were going to have. I was surprised and delighted to see a steam locomotive backing on to our train. It was Britannia class 70043, *Lord Kitchener*. As we journeyed north it was good to see the steam drifting past the carriage window and to hear the locomotive's clanking rods and chime whistle as it hauled us across Cheshire's neat, pleasant countryside, over the Manchester Ship Canal and the river Mersey, stopping at Warrington Bank Quay and Wigan North Western to Preston. Between Warrington and Wigan the industrial plain, with large, black factories, canals, wastelands, derelict coal mines, slag heaps, railway sidings, gas lamps, locomotive water tanks etc, was bathed and silhouetted in the red afterglow of sunset in the western sky. Ruth pointed to a silhouetted slagheap and two chimney stacks and said: "Isn't that beautiful?'"

Photographing the Windermere branch 17 February 1965

Warned that half the steam passenger trains on the Windermere branch were to be replaced by diesel multiple units from 1 March 1965, I set out to take photographs of steam scenes along the line, travelling by bicycle, motor scooter, bus and on foot.

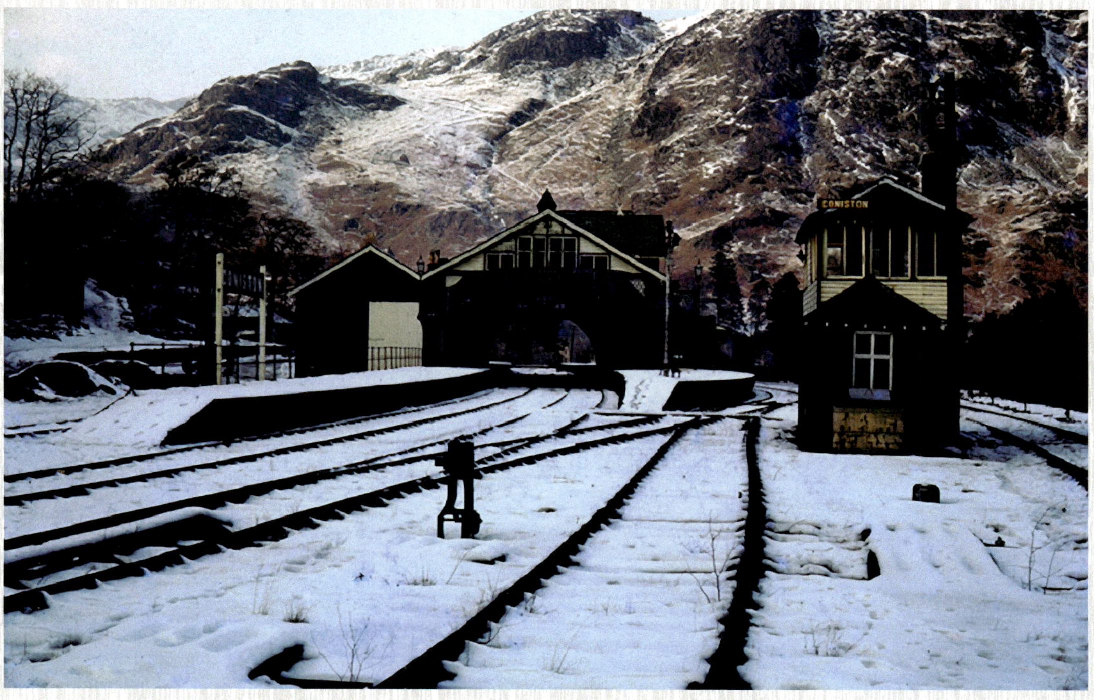

Coniston station, terminus of the former Furness Railway branch line from Foxfield, is seen against its theatrical mountain backdrop on 13 February 1963. Here it is complete with its overall roof, footbridge, signal cabin, signal posts, nameboards and the yard crane behind the running-in board – everything except its signal arms – more than four years after closure to passengers on 6 October 1958, and ten months after closure to goods on 30 April 1962.

The branch opened in 1859, this station building dates from 1862, and the terminus was enlarged in 1896. The single line behind the signal cabin led to a small engine shed where the branch engine stayed overnight. The Coniston branch was built to carry copper ores mined in these mountains.

The footbridge survives today at Ravenglass terminus of the 15-inch-gauge railway into Eskdale, a ground frame cabin from the north end of the station is now on a garden railway in Coniston, and the Furness Railway's elegant and luxurious 42-ton steam yacht *Gondola* of 1859 still plies from Coniston pier on Coniston Water after rotting under water for three years and being restored for the National Trust.

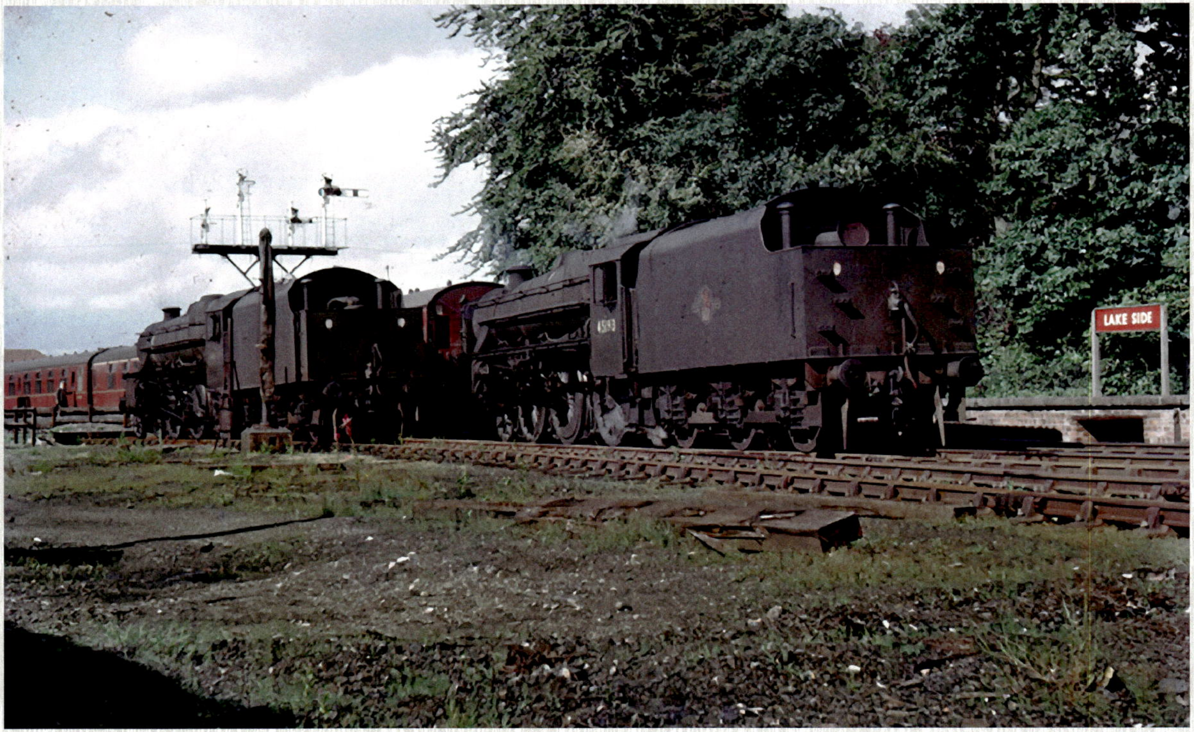

Clanking coupling rods and squealing flanges were the sounds I most liked to capture on my steam railway recordings and here they are in close-up, covered with oil and grime, on 'Black Five' No 44870 at Lake Side on 1 August 1965.

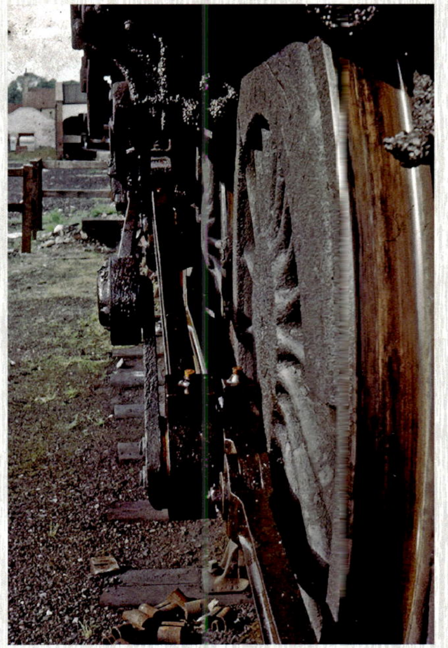

Two 'Black Fives' stand at the Lake Side terminus of the former Furness Railway branch line from Ulverston on 1 August 1965. Engine No 45193 on the right was built by Armstrong Whitworth at Newcastle in 1935, while No 44870 on the left was built by the LMS at Crewe in 1945. Here at Lake Side the trains met the railway-owned steamers on Windermere plying to Bowness and Ambleside. No 45193 was about to leave, tender first, with the passenger train seen alongside the station platform.

The summer-only passenger train service closed on 6 September 1965. Freight services continued between Plumpton Junction and Haverthwaite till 1967, but that section was lifted to make way for an upgraded A590 Barrow trunk road and the remaining section of line from Haverthwaite to Lake Side was restored to steam in 1973 as the Lakeside & Haverthwaite Railway.

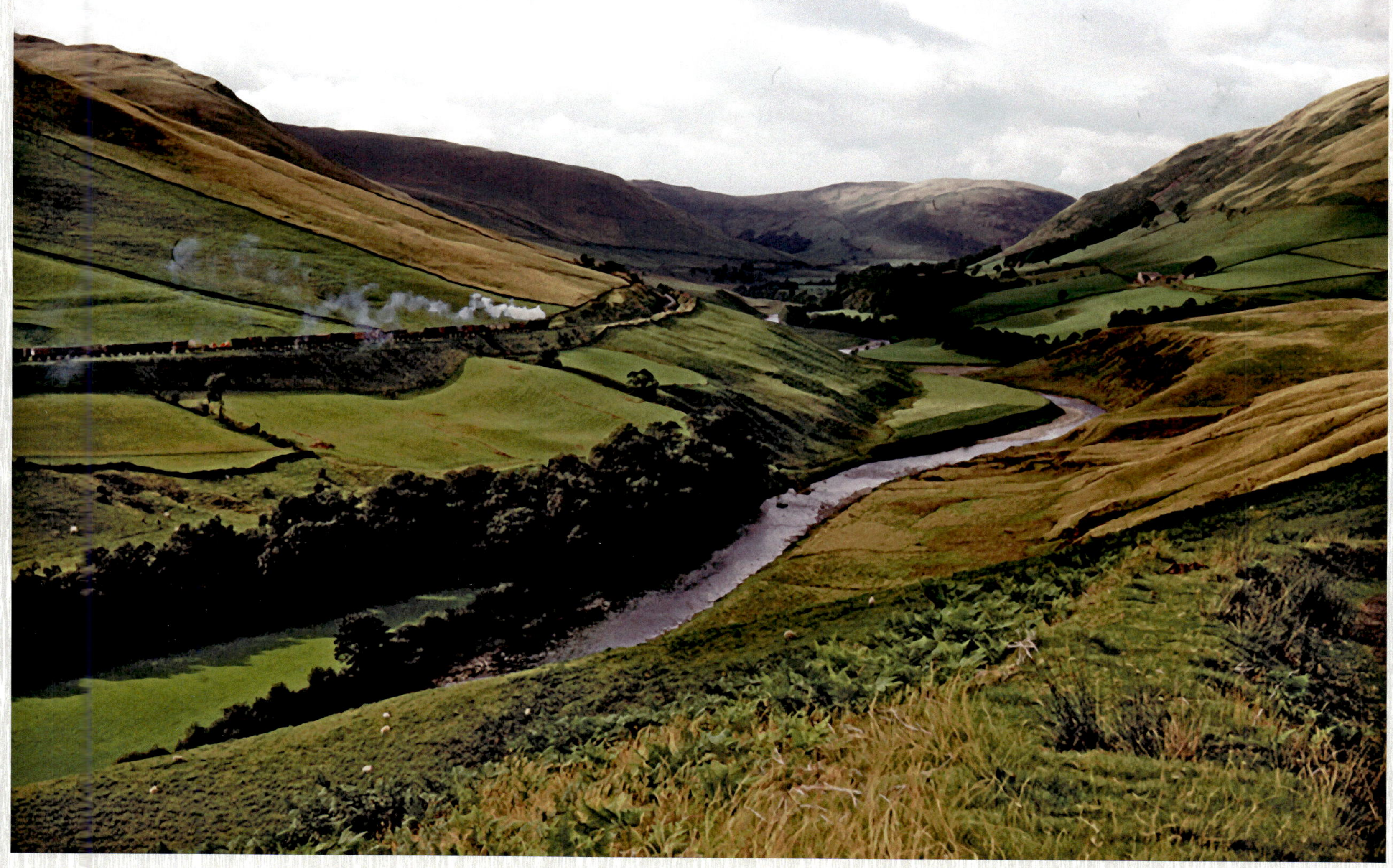

Steam in the landscape. A northbound freight on the 'West Coast' main line between Grayrigg and Tebay on 15 August 1963 is diminutive against the fells over 1,500 feet high on each side as it runs around the shoulder of Grayrigg Forest into Lunesdale. The railway uses the gap cut by the river through the fell barrier that links the North Pennine Moors with the Cumbrian Mountains. The River Lune rises in Ravenstonedale and flows south by Kirkby Lonsdale and Lancaster into Morecambe Bay.

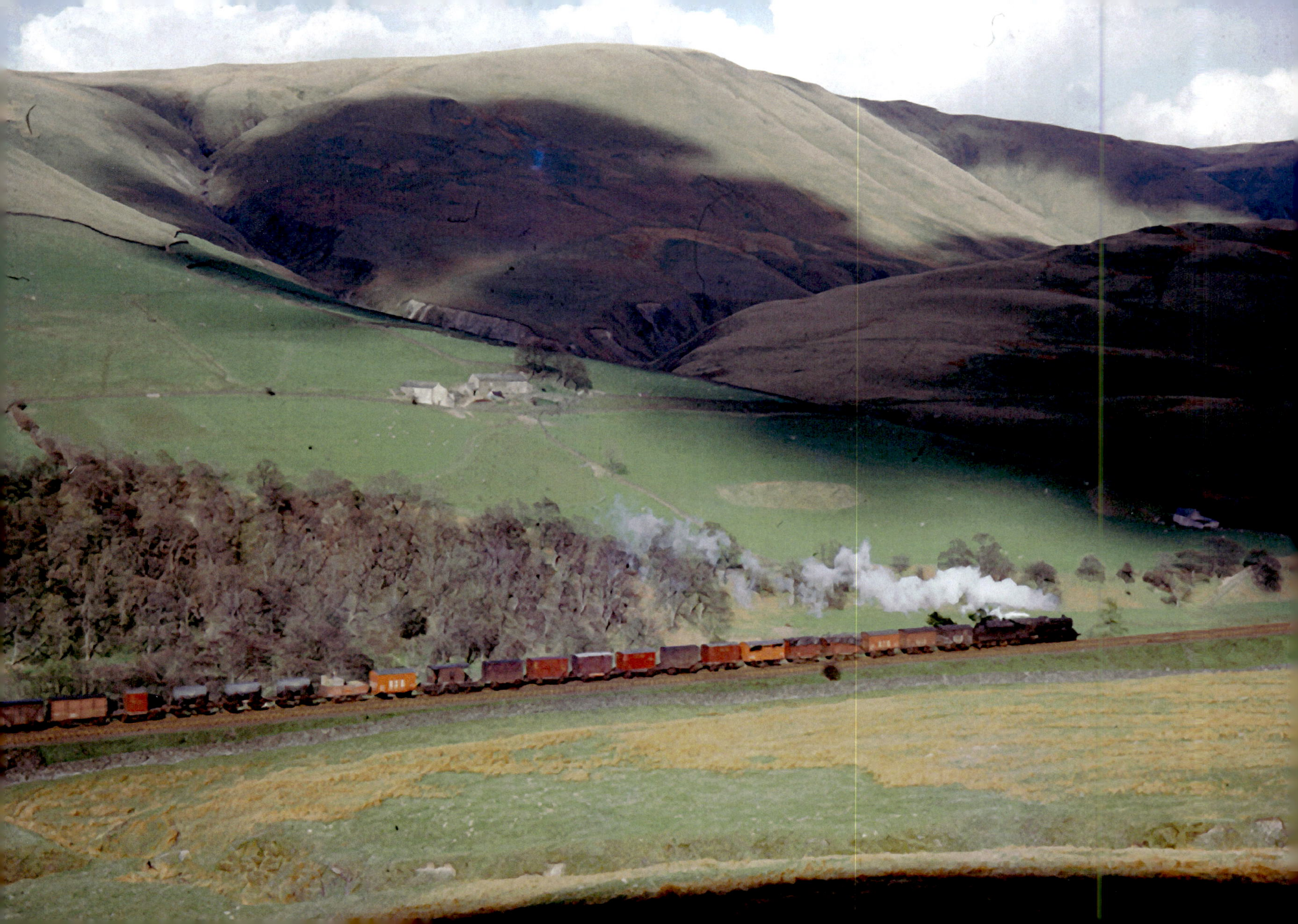

Left: A southbound freight on the LNWR main line, headed by a 'Black Five', runs through Lunesdale at Carlin Gill, the ravine, on the boundary of Westmorland and Yorkshire, on 1 May 1963. In the background is Uldale Head (1,553 feet) and High Carlingill Farm on the route of the Roman road from Lancaster to Carlisle. The railway has since been electrified with overhead catenary and the M6 motorway now runs along the slopes in the foreground.

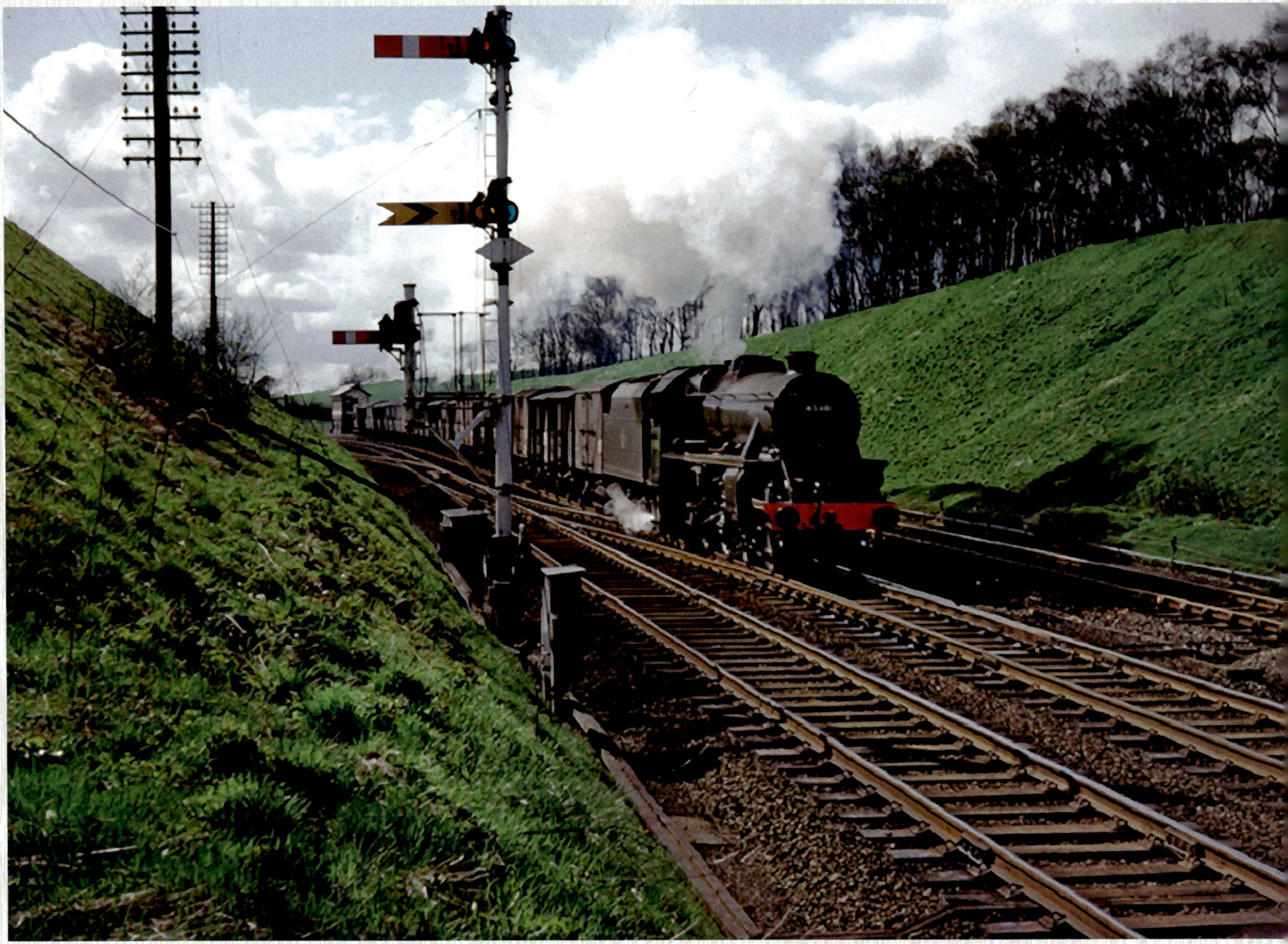

Right: Cresting the top of Grayrigg bank, 'Black Five' No 45481 heads a northbound freight through the site of the former Grayrigg station on the LNWR main line between Lancaster and Carlisle on 1 May 1963.

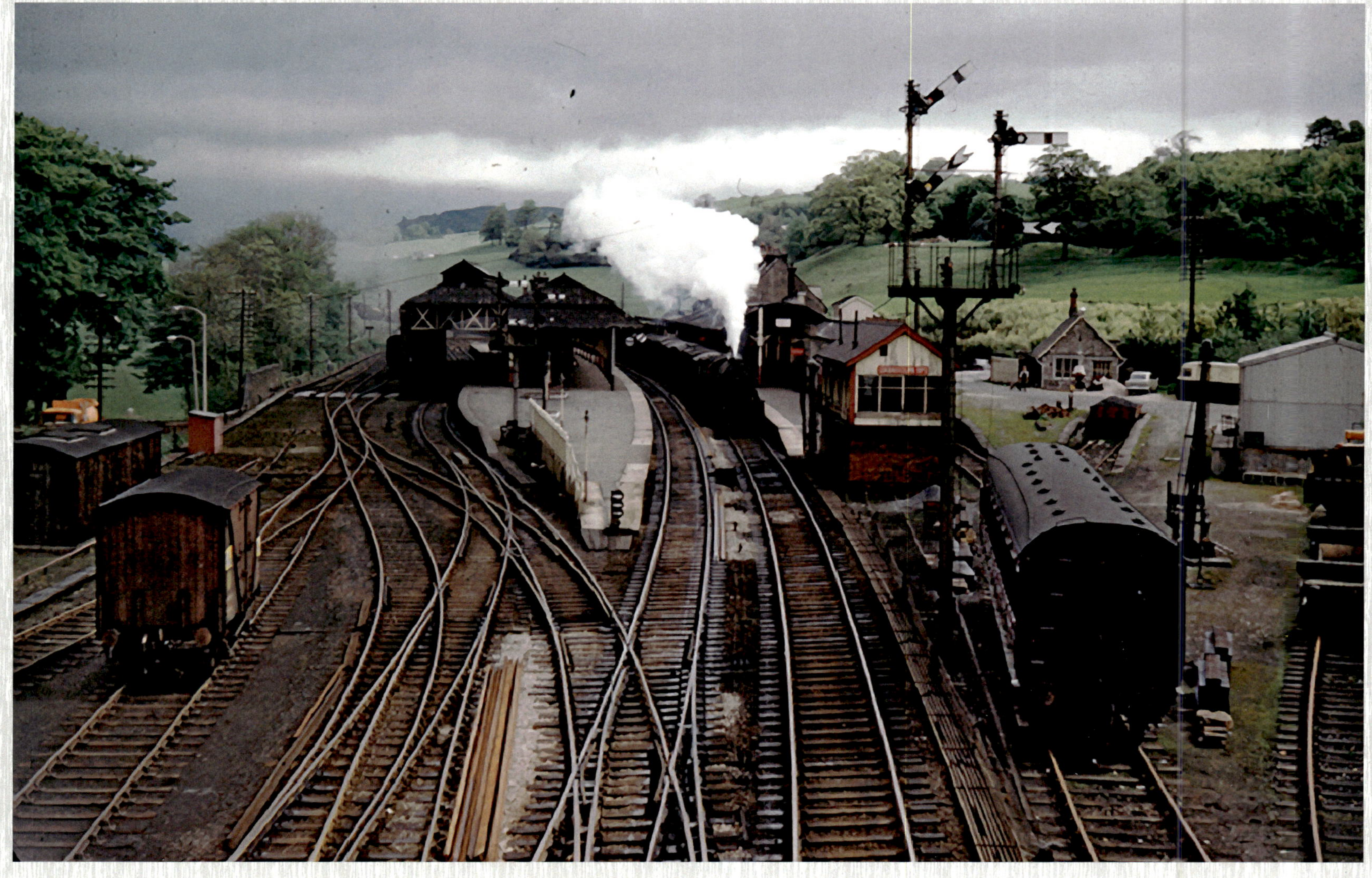

Oxenholme, a country junction in Westmorland, on 29 May 1962. Here the Lancaster and Carlisle railway begins the ascent of Grayrigg bank on the first leg of the assault on the fell barrier on the 'West Coast' main line to Scotland. The Windermere branch forks off to the left. Kendal is the first stop on the branch, just 2 miles down the line. At this time Oxenholme was the point where heavy freight trains and long passenger trains stopped to pick up a banking engine to help push them up Grayrigg bank and the branch line was busy with passenger trains, goods trains, cattle trains and parcels trains. Oxenholme, with its refreshment rooms, signal cabins, freight yard and engine sheds, was a railwaymen's village but it was in decline at this time along with the railways.

The engine shed closed in 1962 and the goods sidings were lifted in 1969. In 1973 the main line was electrified as part of the 'West Coast' route to Scotland, the double-track branch line was singled and all excursion, freight and parcels traffic ceased. At the same time the signal cabins closed and the semaphore signals were replaced with coloured lights. Diesel and electric traction ended the banking ritual of steam days.

The station appears much the same today, including the roofs over the down main platform and the Windermere bay. The limestone buildings on the island platform have gone but those on the up platform remain, now cleaned up, with hanging baskets of flowers. The sidings on the right survive today but those on the left have been replaced by a car park. The station has been renamed 'Oxenholme (the Lake District)' although it is not in the Lake District; the national park boundary is 6 miles down the Windermere branch.

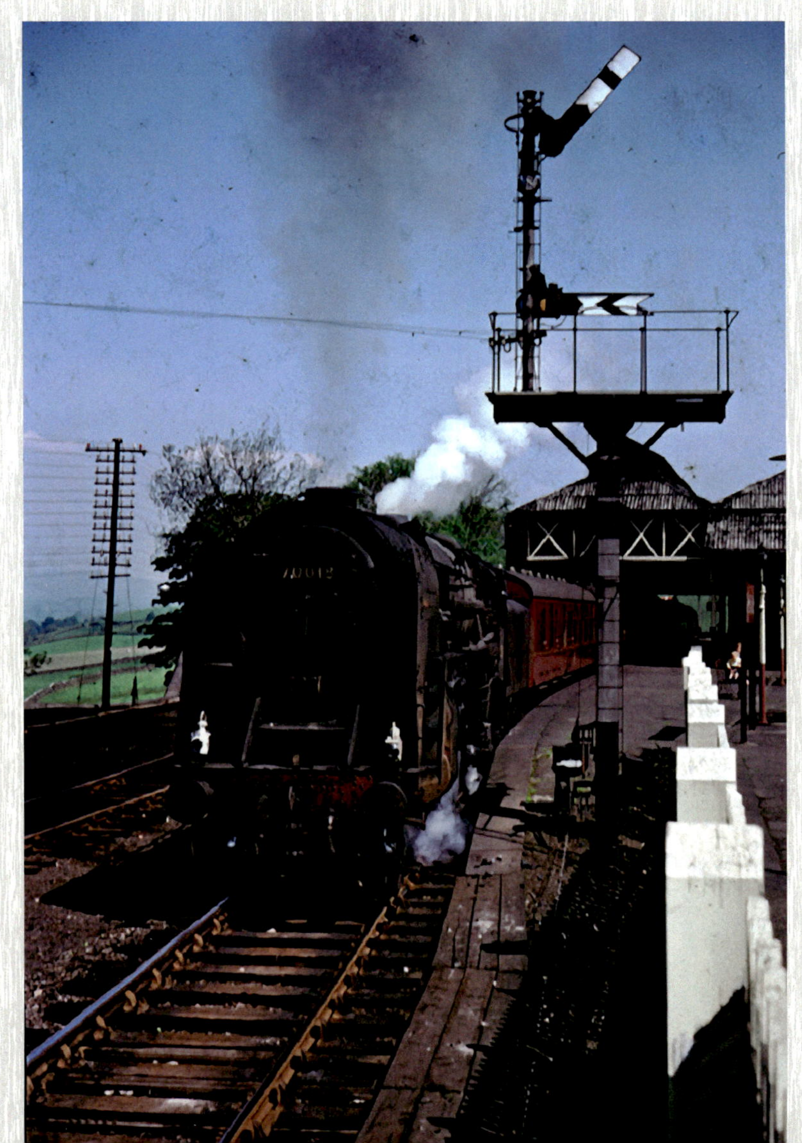

'Britannia' No 70018 *Flying Dutchman* leaves Oxenholme's bay platform with the up 'Lakes Express' on 3 June 1965. The engine will head the train to Crewe, handing over to an electric locomotive to take it on to Euston. The picture shows the overall roof and retaining wall of the Windermere branch bay platform that provided a good sounding board for recording the echoing bark and clank of steam locomotives entering the station as they crested the top of the 1 in 80 gradient from Kendal.

I visited several scenic locations on three days during February, finishing on the 25th at Windermere '…where in the sunlit quiet a steam locomotive waited, wreathed in steam at the head of a passenger train, with seagulls wheeling about and a panoramic backdrop of snow-capped mountains. I returned home via Burneside station, with its staggered platforms and a rugged stone station house, in which I waited in the warm office with a coal fire to photograph the last train before dusk.'

Steam holds its own on the Windermere branch
7 March 1965

'All the trains on the Windermere branch are still steam hauled but for one passenger train hauled by a diesel locomotive, which returns light from Windermere. Most of the local passenger trains were due to be replaced by diesel multiple units from March 1st, leaving only the through trains to and from Preston, Manchester Victoria and Crewe to be operated by steamers, but the service is still steam and no diesel multiple units have shown up.

'A railwayman told me that there was not enough diesel stock available yet. There is such a big turnover in diesel locomotives and multiple units breaking down and catching fire so frequently that we still see a lot of steam on the LNW lines north of Crewe.

'We have a lot of Britannias with chime whistles up here now that they have been banned south of Crewe owing to the low clearances of the overhead electric wires. The morning train from Windermere to Manchester Victoria, which had been diesel-hauled for about six months, is back to steam with one of these Britannias. Many of the locomotives up here now have diagonal yellow bands on their cab sides meaning they are banned south of Crewe. As the overhead catenary advances north towards Carlisle, steam engines will become more and more concentrated in the north-west corner of the country.'

BR Standard Class 5MT locomotive No 73141 brings the up 'Lakes Express' into Kendal station on its way from Windermere to Euston on 12 August 1964. The steamer would hand over the train to an electric locomotive at Crewe. Through coaches of the 'Lakes Express' went from Euston to Blackpool, Keswick and Whitehaven and vice versa.

The Windermere branch has since been singled and Kendal station has lost its canopies and been reduced to an unstaffed halt with a small, slate-stone shelter on the down platform (left). The up platform and the parcels sidings beyond have been replaced by a car park. The station offices behind the down platform have been built up to a four-storey building, in matching slate, housing the town's doctors' surgery and pharmacy with offices above, and the freight yard, on the down side, has been redeveloped as an industrial estate, incorporating the former large. stone-built goods warehouse. The train service has improved, with 17 trains a day each way between Oxenholme and Windermere, Monday to Saturday, and 12 on Sunday. Some trains go to Manchester Airport but there are no more through trains to Euston.

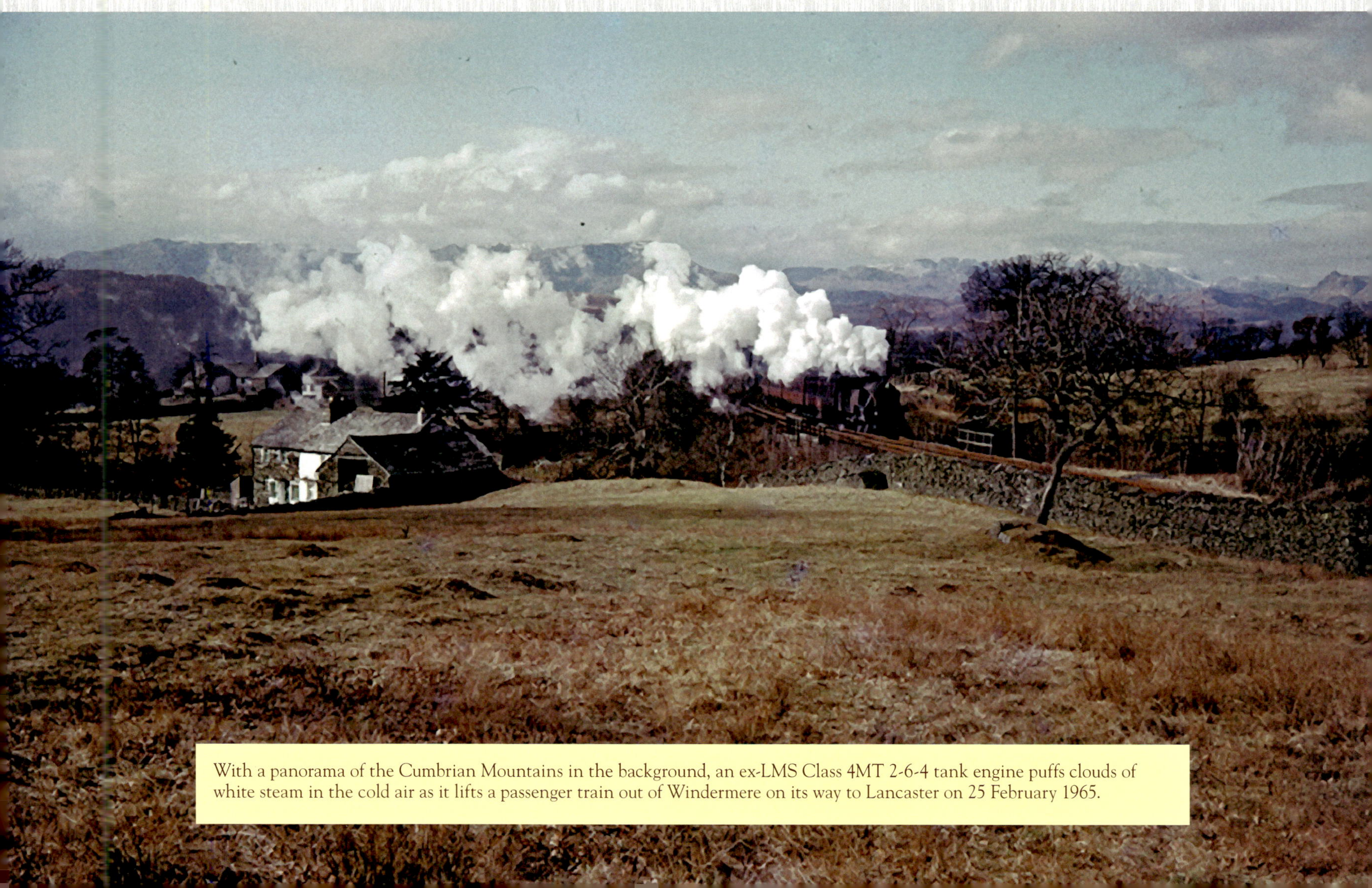

With a panorama of the Cumbrian Mountains in the background, an ex-LMS Class 4MT 2-6-4 tank engine puffs clouds of white steam in the cold air as it lifts a passenger train out of Windermere on its way to Lancaster on 25 February 1965.

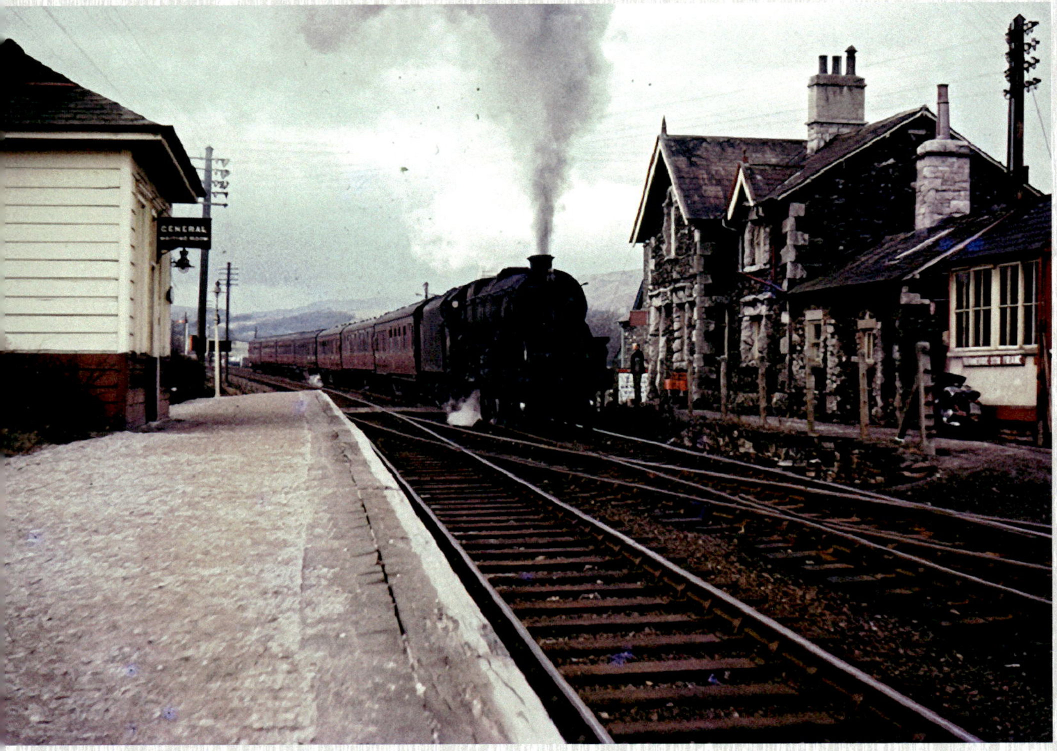

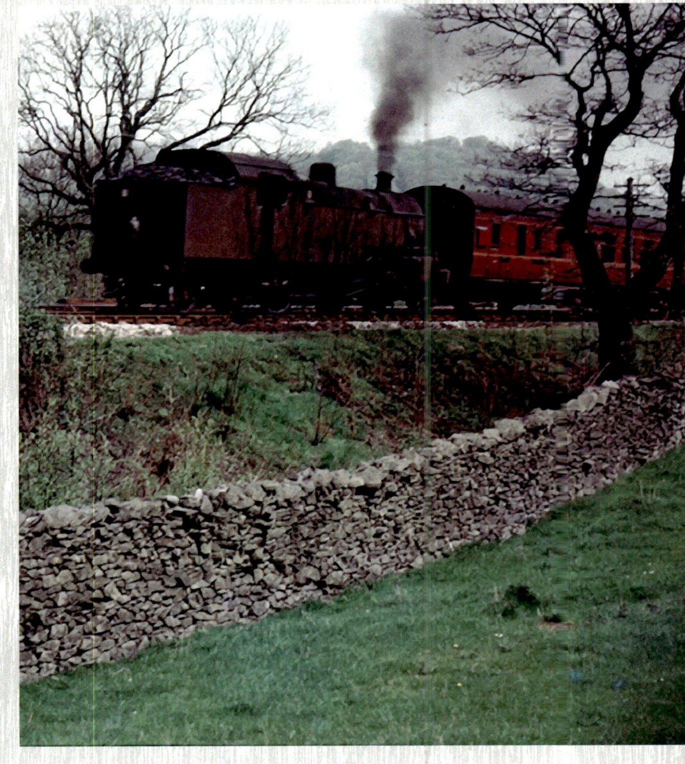

A seven-coach train, headed by a BR Standard Class 5, calls at Burneside on its way from Windermere to Lancaster on 25 February 1965. The two platforms were staggered, end to end. The locomotive is alongside the rugged stone station house, where on this cold day I waited for this train by the coal fire in the waiting room. The down waiting shelter is on the left, the ground signal cabin is on the right and the crossover was for goods trains serving Burneside paper mill.

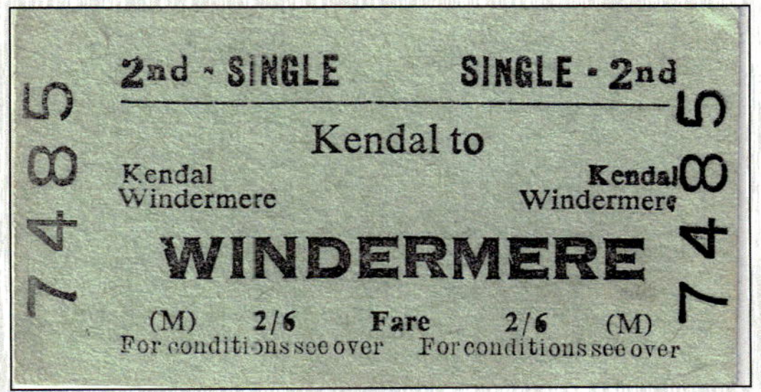

An ex-LMS Fowler Class 4 2-6-4 tank engine with the Windermere branch train heads bunker-first west of Staveley on 12 May 1965. Grime covers the engine number on the side of the bunker.

A Kendal to Windermere ticket dated 15 September 1966, fare 2s 6d.

Local diesel service
3 June 1965

'In the event, the diesel multiple unit local train service on the Windermere branch, which was due to start on March 1st, was postponed till June 2nd. Today I took Ruth and Karl by train from Kendal, headed by a Britannia, to Oxenholme to take some photographs of this characteristic LNW stern, stone, railway station before it might be modernised. I was surprised to see a diesel multiple unit train roll slowly in, destined for Windermere. I found that the service had started the day before.

'One two-carriage unit from the closed Carlisle-Silloth line, now stabled at Carnforth, is sufficient to work all the local services between Windermere and Oxenholme, Carnforth or Lancaster but all the through trains from Crewe, Manchester Victoria and Preston are still hauled by steam locomotives, mainly 5MTs and Britannias, and, of course, all the goods trains are still steam-hauled too.

'There are five steam, three diesel multiple unit and one diesel locomotive-hauled passenger trains down the branch to Windermere each day and four steam and three diesel multiple unit passenger trains back. One of the steam engines works back light and the diesel locomotive is a stray, which takes an early afternoon train to Windermere, runs light back to Kendal and takes the evening parcels train south.'

Ribblehead to Dent on foot
19 June 1965

'A friend of mine from Wallasey, Allan Clayton, who was staying with us for two days, drove me in his car via Kirkby Lonsdale and Ingleton and up the roller-coaster road along the foot of Raven Scar [a limestone cliff] to Ribblehead railway station, 1,050 feet high in the Yorkshire moors. There we left the car and walked north alongside the old Midland Railway main line, taking scenic views with steam trains. Our progress was slow because my right leg was in plaster with a large boot on my foot after dropping down an unguarded 4-foot water board excavation outside my front gate.

'We waited in Blea Moor signal cabin, with the wind whistling around it, while a few diesel trains passed, to photograph the next steam train. Then we walked over the moor, under which the railway tunnels for 1 mile 629 yards. At first we strayed over mosses and bogs but then hit the trail made by the tunnel builders in the early 1870s, passing the soot-black tops of the three ventilation shafts and the great heaps of stone dug out of the tunnel, hauled up the shafts and dumped on top of the moor. From the summit, 1,650 feet high and 500 feet above the tunnel, we had a wonderful view down upper Dentdale, verdant and beautiful, and while we were descending steeply to the railway we saw two steam passenger trains passing and then a steam goods train. Smoke poured from the tunnel mouth for at least 15 minutes after the last train had gone through.

'We still had a mile to walk to Dent station when the last stopping passenger train of the day, which we intended to get back to Ribblehead, came steaming up the line towards us and we took a picture of it crossing Arten Gill viaduct. While Allan walked by road over Gayle Moor back to Ribblehead to get his car, I walked on to Dent station, at 1,145 feet the highest railway station in England, where I sheltered in a goods brakevan on a siding during a rain shower and then waited in the warm signal cabin until Allan arrived. The signalman showed us some photographs he had taken of The Waverley (Edinburgh to St Pancras) express train snowed up at Dent in February, 1963. Allan drove us through Dent and Sedbergh back to Kendal.'

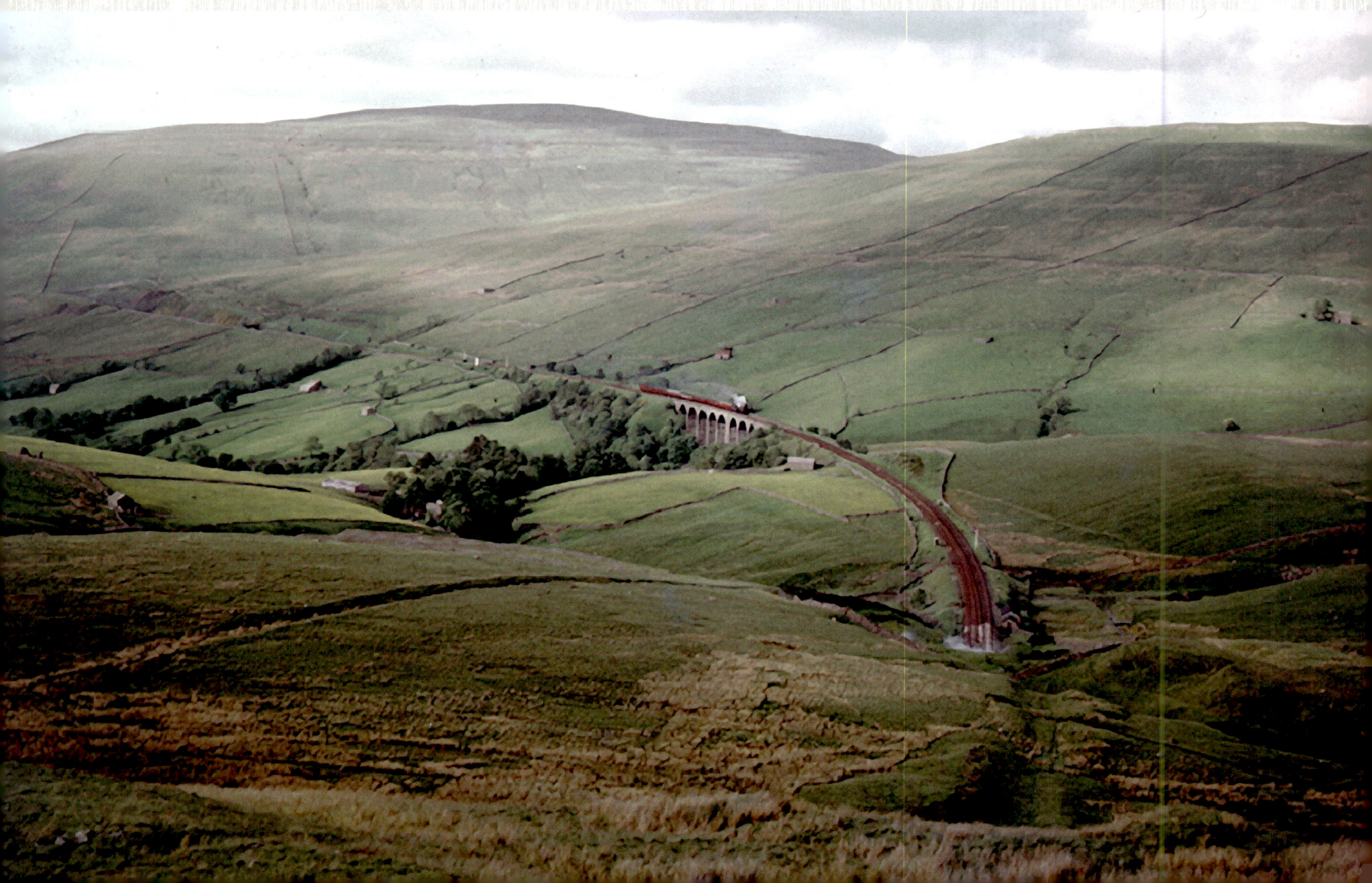

The Midland Railway over the roof of England: the Settle to Carlisle line is viewed from Blea Moor with a southbound steam passenger train crossing Dent Head viaduct on 19 June 1965.

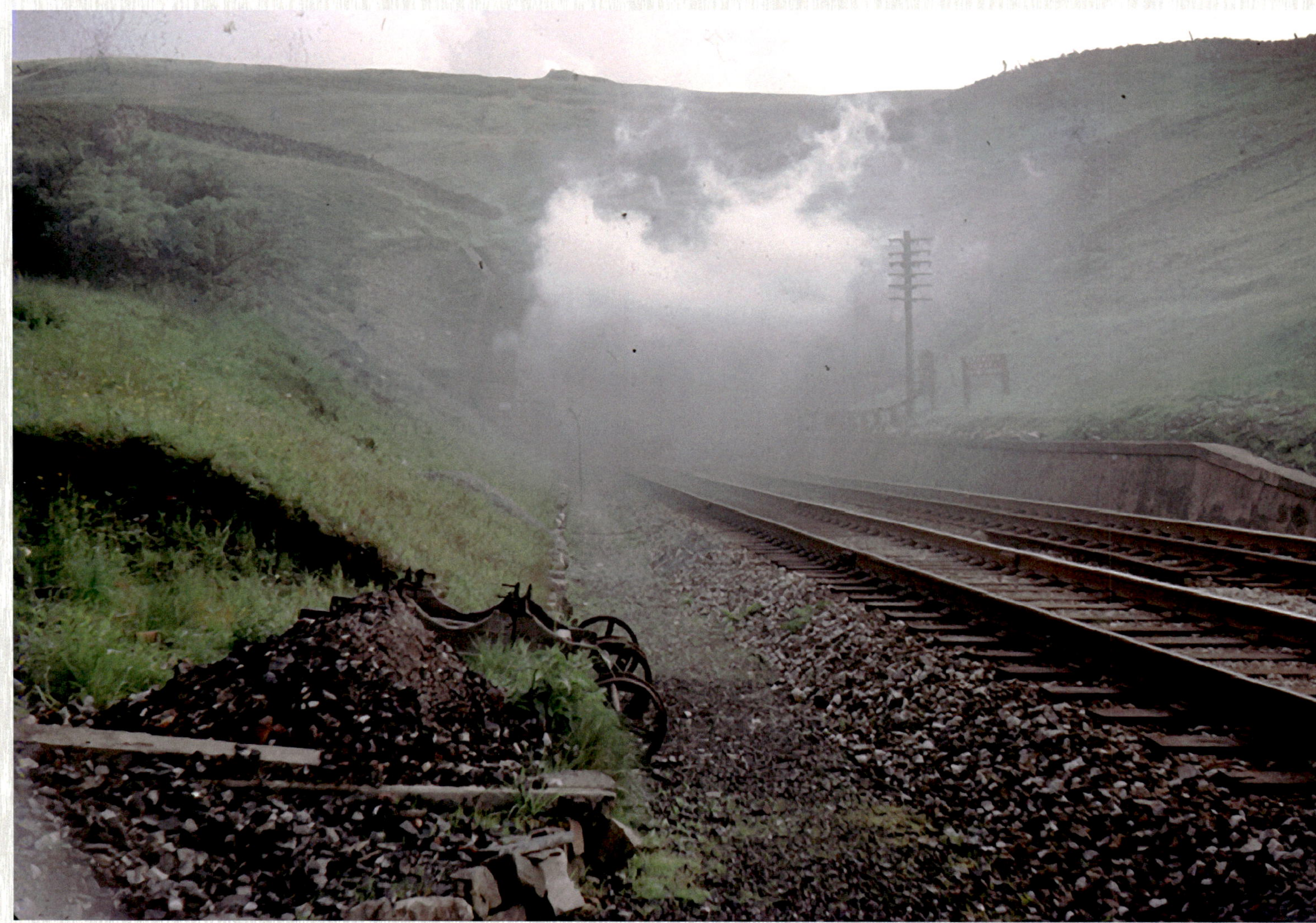

Smoke still pours from the north portal of Blea Moor tunnel 10 minutes after the last of three steam trains had passed through it within a 10-minute period on 19 June 1965.

The last 'Jubilee' on the Windermere branch
29 June 1965

'I watched Jubilee class locomotive 45697 *Achilles*, built by the LMS in 1934, clean and green with a red buffer beam, heading the up Lakes Express (Windermere to Euston) alongside Castle Road, Kendal. I believe this was the last Jubilee on the Windermere branch.'

Manchester before Metrolink
28 August 1965

'Ruth, Karl and I travelled by train, headed by a Black Five, from Kendal, stopping at Oxenholme, Lancaster, Garstang & Catterall and Preston, to Manchester Exchange [ex-LNWR, closed 1969]. For much of this journey I looked out the windows at the locomotive pounding along the shiny wet rails. I wore Ruth's sunglasses as soot spectacles; they must have looked incongruous in the rain and the gloom. It was fascinating entering Manchester through the dark, old, industrial districts with Emetty, derelict stations.

'Motor traffic was heavy, as was the traditional Manchester rain, as we walked across the city centre via Victoria Street, Market Street, Piccadilly and London Road to the other railway terminus for the next stage of our journey. On the south-east side of Piccadilly and on London Road it was good to see the trolleybus wires and a few trolleybuses of Manchester and Ashton-under-Lyne Corporations on the joint service between the two towns [dewired at the end of 1966].'

The former LNWR and Great Central joint station, London Road, was remodelled by British Rail in 1960-65 with a new frontage on the old trainshed and renamed Piccadilly. The station is half a mile from Piccadilly, which has been renamed Piccadilly Gardens, although the gardens are now very much smaller than they were when it was called Piccadilly – a combined case of misleading nomenclature. Of the new station I wrote:

'The modern fabric, bare and bleak to start with, wore badly and already looked drab and shabby before the station rebuilding was complete. The station smelt of fumes from the diesel trains. The new image British Rail was trying so hard to cultivate was a depressing one.

'From Manchester Piccadilly we travelled in a train drawn by an overhead-electric locomotive to Crewe, thence by diesel locomotives to Bristol Temple Meads and Exeter St David's. On this journey I never saw a diesel locomotive from Kendal to Manchester; it was all steam. From Shrewsbury to Exeter I never saw a steam locomotive; it was all diesel. Nearly all those handsome, brassy, Great Western locomotives had gone for scrap.'

Cab ride on the last day of the Lancaster-Heysham electric railway
1 January 1966

'I went to take some pictures of the Lancaster, Morecambe and Heysham electric railway on this its last day of operation. I rode my motor scooter, Vintora, down the A6 to Skerton, thence to every point where a road crosses the railway, across the bleak marshes and around the pleasant residential back of Morecambe to Heysham's desolate, scruffy harbour.

'It was a dark day with rain showers and a cold wind. I took seven photographs of the electric trains at five locations. Wreaths hung on the ends of the of some of the trains, which bore on their dark green panels the words "Last Day", "Au Revoir" and "Adios Amigo" and I saw a railwayman at Lancaster Green Ayre station chalk up "A victim of public apathy" on a train.

'When the daylight became too dark for further photography I went to Lancaster Castle station to ride a train. At Morecambe Promenade terminus the motorman, changing ends, asked me if I would like to ride in the cab. I said I would. He said he was not supposed to take public in the cab but, as it was dark, no one would see.

'We glided smoothly and silently in the 1914-vintage ex-London & North Western Railway rolling stock from north London along the glinting steel rails through the darkness, passing an oncoming steam locomotive as we approached Lancaster. The acceleration was terrific, with no jerks, despite the weight of these old cars, with their solid construction, switchgear and transformers, which gave them such a smooth, steady ride. With their silent traction motors these trains would not have been a suitable subject for sound recording. [In his book *British Electric Trains* (1949), Howard Linecar said the riding qualities of these trains were considered to be without equal in the country.] It seemed to me a retrograde step to close the line and replace it with noisy, vibrating, fumy, two-car diesel multiple units on a longer, roundabout route via Bare Lane at a time when overhead-electric traction was replacing diesel in other parts of the London Midland Region.

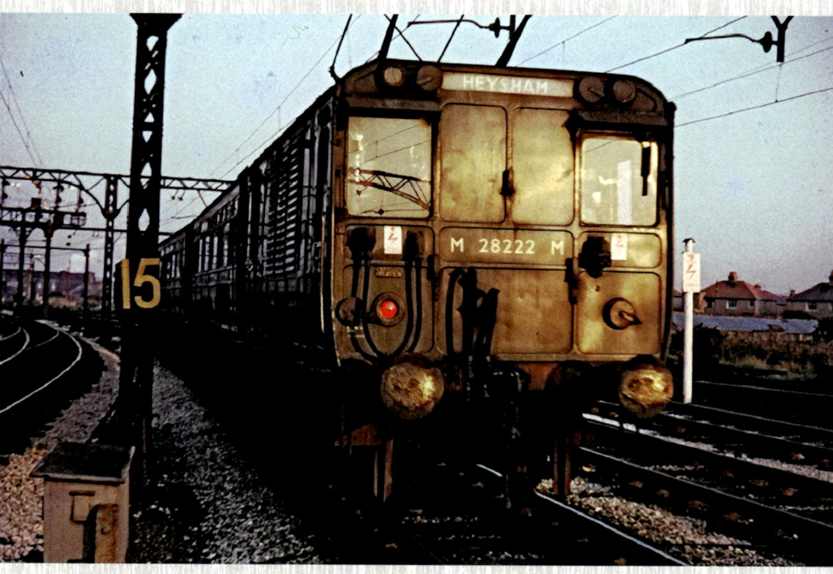

The cab end of a 1914-vintage, ex-LNW three-car electric multiple unit train on the Lancaster, Morecambe and Heysham line of the former Midland Railway, leaving Morecambe Promenade terminus on 15 October 1964. These trains were built for the Euston-Watford 630-volt d.c. four-rail electrification. They were retired in 1940 but kept in store and transferred to the Lancaster-Heysham line when it was re-electrified in 1953.

This 8½-mile route was, in 1908, the first railway to be electrified on the single-phase a.c. overhead system, operating 6,600-volt multiple unit trains with bow collectors. The 1908 Midland stock remained in service till 1951, when steam traction took over while BR converted the line to 50 hertz. The traction cars of the ex-LNW stock were fitted with pantographs and mercury-arc rectifier-transformers to convert the current to 750 volts d.c.. This experiment led to BR's 50 hertz, 25,000-volt a.c. system that became standard for main-line electrification.

The direct electric line between Lancaster and Morecambe closed on 1 January 1966, replaced by diesel multiple units on the indirect route via Bare Lane, and trains now only continue to Heysham to meet the Belfast ferries.

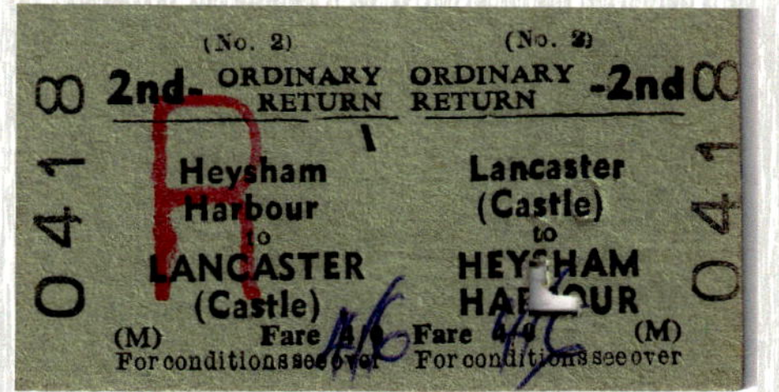

A last day return ticket on the electric railway between Lancaster Castle and Heysham Harbour, 1 January 1966, fare 4s 6d.

'At Castle station I did not want to surrender my ticket, which was a return covering the whole length of the electric railway to be closed, between Lancaster Castle and Heysham Harbour, and stamped with the date of the last day of operation. When no-one was looking I slipped off the platform at one end of the train, crossed two tracks and a deserted platform and, hidden by the train from the platforms where all the activity was going on, scrambled up a grass bank and climbed over a 5ft 6in tall fence to the station forecourt, where Vintora was parked.'

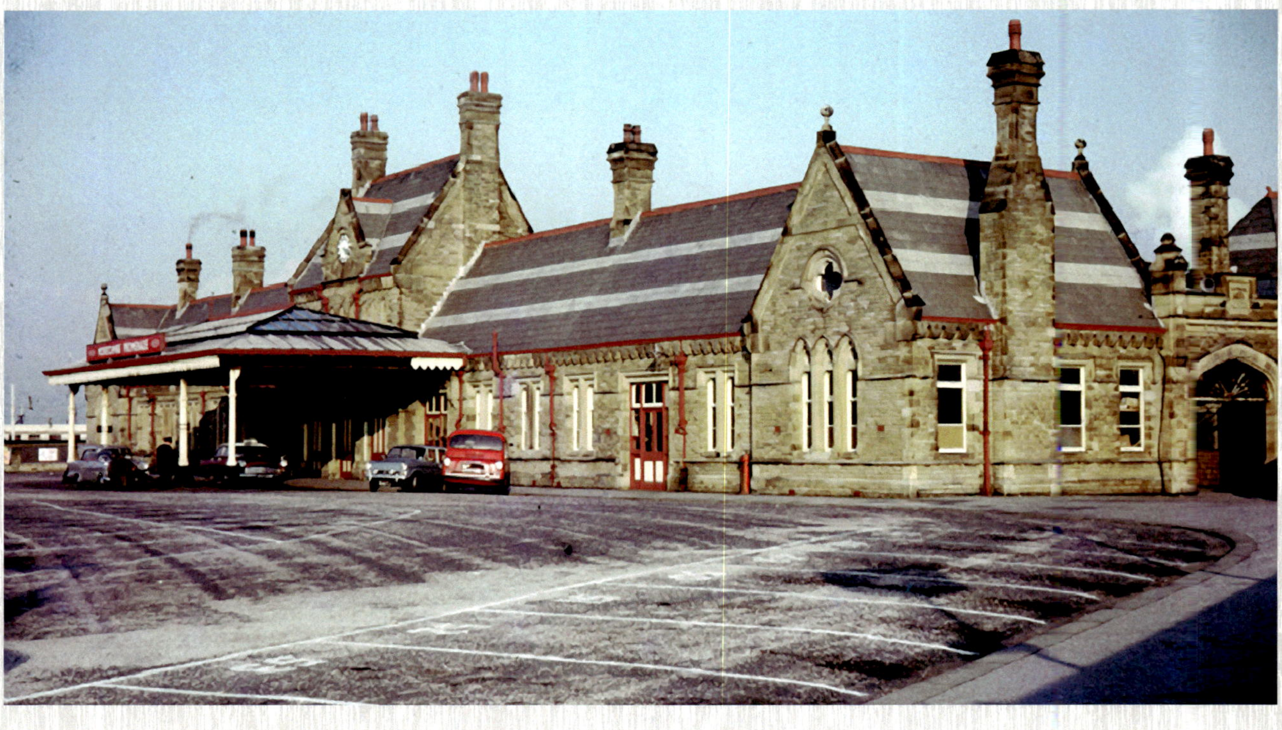

People came from Leeds, Bradford and Skipton by the Midland Railway to Morecambe Promenade station for their holidays on the Lancashire coast. It was the opening of this railway that created Morecambe as a seaside resort. The line was extended in 1907 from the original terminus in Northumberland Street to this handsome four-platform terminal building on the sea front, designed by Thomas Wheatley and built in honey-coloured stone with a large, iron, coach portico, tall chimneys, a dormer clock and quatrefoil windows in the gables.

Behind the facade was a spacious concourse hung with flower baskets and festooned with ivy, leading to the four platforms, with occasional steam trains to Bradford, Leeds, Manchester and Crewe, and infrequent 1914-vintage electric multiple unit trains that reversed here on their 8½-mile trip between Lancaster and Heysham. The station was photographed on 15 October 1964.

The experimental high-voltage a.c. overhead-electric railway closed in 1966, replaced by diesels on the indirect route via Bare Lane, and trains now continue to Heysham only to meet the Belfast ferries. In 1994 the remaining line into Morecambe was cut back a quarter of a mile from the Promenade terminus to a new platform on the site of the original terminus, and the Promenade station closed. It is now a listed building, restored and used as an arts centre, tourist information office and restaurant, while the concourse and platforms have been replaced by a cinema and market hall. The station forecourt is now mainly lawn.

Oxenholme and Kendal
13 January 1966

'Ruth and Karl returned home from Westgate-on-Sea after attending her dad's funeral I caught a diesel multiple unit train from Kendal up to Oxenholme junction to meet Ruth and help her with Karl and the luggage in changing on to the branch train. As I waited on this dark, stone station, a succession of steam-headed goods and parcels trains and lone steam locomotives passed through every few minutes with steam swirling around the gas lamps. The Stanier and Fairburn Class 4 2-6-4 tank engines, which pushed the heavy goods trains up Grayrigg bank, came clanking down the fell and echoing through the station to take up the next one.

'The London-Perth train came in, headed by a diesel locomotive. Ruth's head appeared out of a window and when I opened the door there was little Karl standing in front of her. I lifted Karl out and took Ruth's case and the three of us waited in the waiting room with a roaring coal fire and Midland Railway seats with the initials MR carved in the backrests in old English or Gothic lettering; they must have come from another station.

'The Manchester to Windermere evening train came into the station, headed by a Britannia class locomotive, and we travelled in the compartment nearest the locomotive down the branch to Kendal. Karl and I watched the train leaving Kendal from the north end of the platform with a fierce display of sparks from the slipping driving wheels as it started and orange-tinted smoke piled into the cold night sky as the train disappeared down the line into the darkness.'

Steam in the snow on the roof of England
19 January 1966

'The day was intensely cold with blue sky and sunshine so I went up to the Midland Railway main line through the Pennine Moors to take some pictures

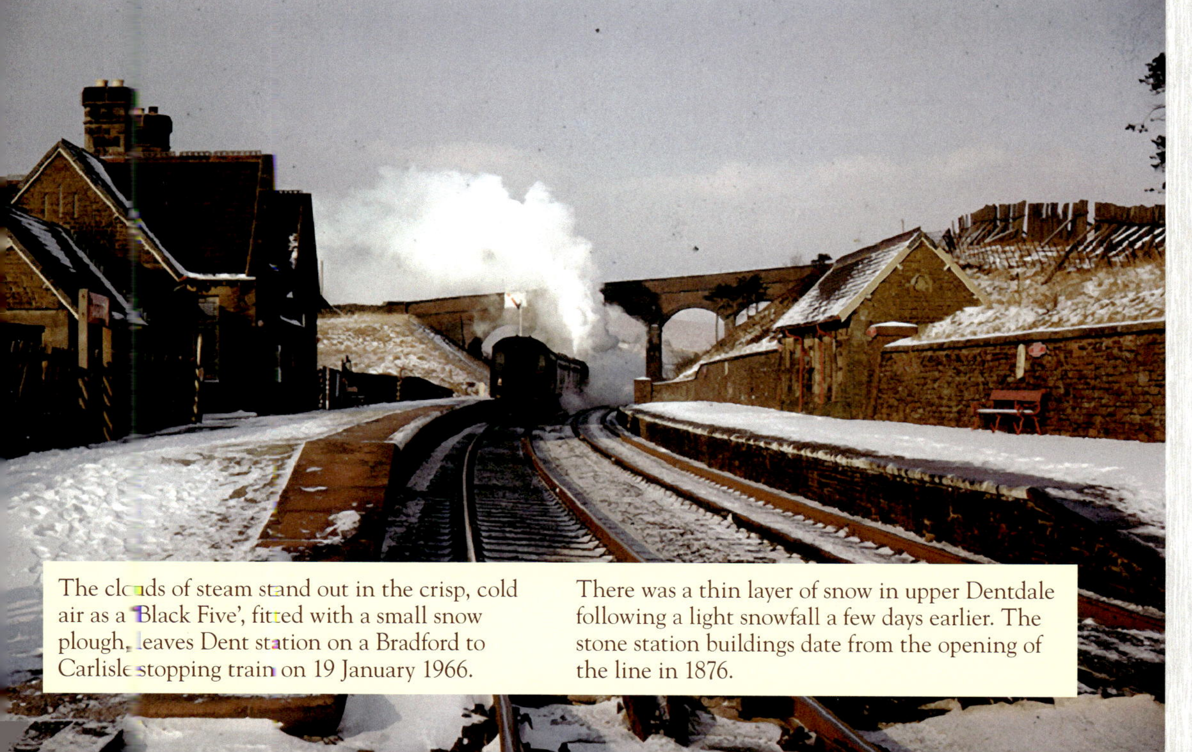

The clouds of steam stand out in the crisp, cold air as a 'Black Five', fitted with a small snow plough, leaves Dent station on a Bradford to Carlisle stopping train on 19 January 1966.

There was a thin layer of snow in upper Dentdale following a light snowfall a few days earlier. The stone station buildings date from the opening of the line in 1876.

of steam trains with the smoke and steam showing up boldly in the cold air. It was the coldest day we had had since 1947; the maximum temperature was 28 degrees F (minus 4 degrees C). I rode Vintora against an ice-fanged, east wind via Sedbergh to Dent railway station at 1,145 feet. There was a thin layer of snow in upper Dentdale, snow covered the station platforms and the steam locomotive at the head of the stopping passenger train I photographed was a Black Five fitted with a small snow plough.

'I rode back down Dentdale to Sedbergh, where I supped a large bowl of hot vegetable soup, then rode up Garsdale, back into the snowy moors – bleak wastelands that looked as cold, dead and desolate as the surface of the moon – to Ais Gill, the summit of the Midland main line, 1,169 feet high on the watershed boundary of Yorkshire and Westmorland. There I took several pictures of steam-hauled goods trains surmounting the summit from the south and north, snorting piles of smoke and steam straight up in monarchial plumes. Between trains I waited in the warmth of Ais Gill signal box and by the roaring fire in the adjacent, stone-built platelayers' hut, which looked like a house for gnomes. When the light began to fade I rode Vintora back via Sedbergh to Kendal. I don't think I had ever felt so cold as I did on this day but I was

rewarded with just the pictures I wanted and I thought the expedition very enjoyable and worthwhile.'

**Oxenholme station at night
1 February 1966**

'Late at night I rode my bicycle, Anderstroam, up to Oxenholme railway station to see the night trains go through. I arrived at the station about 11pm. The station was locked up and in darkness. I walked through the stationmaster's garden and climbed over the wall on to the north end of the up platform, crossed the lines to the down platform and stood there in the pool of light cast by the one gas lamp left alight near the water column for any steam locomotive to fill up with water. The station was just the setting for a ghost train, with the stern, stone buildings, the dark cavern formed by the overall roof and the slate-stone wall of the branch line bay platform, the flickering pilot flames in the extinguished gas lamps and the streetlight outside the station illuminating the tall trees silver-grey against the black night sky.

'I took a flashlight photograph of a steam locomotive chugging slowly north past the water column and the signal post with its red and green aspects lit by an oil lamp. I watched several goods trains and a mail

train, down from the fells, tearing through on their way south. One of them was a diesel-hauled Freightliner train going at a terrific speed. A lone banking engine came clanking down the fells as I left the station at midnight, waiting for the engine to echo through the station to drown my footsteps past the stationmaster's house.'

**Carnforth engine shed
16 March 1966**

'Yesterday Vintora had a puncture in the rear tyre in Carnforth on my way to the Morecambe PSV Society to give an epidiascope show of my pictures of British buses. Luckily, today was my day off, so I took Ruth and Karl with me by train to Carnforth to take Vintora to a garage for a new tyre. We went by train, sitting in the compartment next to the Britannia class locomotive, stopping at Oxenholme and reaching 75mph between Oxenholme and Carnforth.

'After taking Vintora to a garage, shopping and having dinner, we visited Carnforth loco-shed. It was like a live museum with the great, black, grimy, oily locomotives wreathed in steam and smoke – a study in black and white: black iron, black shed and white steam. The locomotives, mostly ex-LMS Black Fives, looked sadly neglected, dirty and decrepit, as British Rail, dedicated to diesel, is allowing the steamers to run down. It is a wonder they can carry on working so long but they are still more reliable and less troublesome than the new diesels.

'Back on Carnforth station we saw two steamers on passenger trains, one on the Furness line, the other on the LNW line, both going south. We also saw one diesel locomotive, grimy and ugly like a war machine, its cab windscreens covered with a film of blue diesel oil smuts from its own exhaust – in fact it was the first diesel locomotive we had seen that day. A Britannia brought in a passenger train, which we boarded and rode in the compartment nearest the engine to Oxenholme, where we changed to the Windermere branch train, headed by a depressing, growling diesel locomotive, and rode down the branch back to Kendal.'

**Round-up of steam on BR
9 April 1966**

'At this stage it was clear that north-west England would see the twilight of the steam age on British Railways and that it would become the Mecca for steam railfans. No longer do steam locomotives shine black, green or crimson at the head of crack passenger expresses. They still haul some passenger trains but are now mainly relegated to freight duties and look sadly neglected, grimy and drab.

'The only steam lines out of London are on the old London & South Western from Waterloo and the Great Central from Marylebone. As one travels north-west from London through the Midlands one sees more and more steam locomotives. Steam still works passenger and freight in West Yorkshire, the Wrexham area, along the main line from Crewe to Holyhead and in southern, eastern and central Scotland and freight only in the Tees-Tyne area. The north-western counties from Cheshire to Cumberland are the centre of steam's domain in Britain.

'Steam loco-sheds in Cheshire are at Crewe North, Stockport Edgeley, Northwich, Chester Midland and Birkenhead. Lancashire has more steam sheds than any other county; there are 18 of them including five around Manchester (Heaton Mersey, Didsbury, Newton Heath, Agecroft and Patricroft) and four around Liverpool (Speke Junction, Edge Hill, Bank Hall and Aintree); the others in Lancashire are at Bolton, Warrington (Dallam), St Helen's (Sutton Oak), Wigan (Springs Branch), Burnley (Rose Grove), Preston (Lostock Hall), Blackpool, Carnforth and Barrow. Westmorland has a shed at Tebay and Cumberland has two sheds at Carlisle (Upperby and Kingmoor) and one at Workington. There are also sheds at Buxton in Derbyshire and at Croes Newydd in Denbighshire working freight in this area.'

**My first ride on the footplate
16 April 1966**

'This was officially forecast to be the last day of rostered steam haulage on local passenger trains calling at all stations between Lancaster and Carlisle and on the Windermere branch. They were to be replaced by diesel multiple units. In the morning and afternoon I took photographs at Staveley, Kendal, in Lunesdale and at Tebay. The station at Tebay was a strange place: a deserted, unroofed, grim, Victorian Gothic station in begrimed red sandstone; the water column stood in the middle of the down platform with puddles and a scattered heap of coal for the brazier.

'In the evening I rode the last rostered steam passenger train on the Windermere branch from Kendal to Windermere. It was headed by Black Five 45195, which made a grand finale of passenger steam in the Lake District. There were no wreaths or fireworks – no fireworks, that is, except for the showers of red hot cinders as this 31-year-old locomotive regained the 10 minutes it had lost on the way from Crewe on the scheduled 21-minute, 8-mile run, stopping at Burneside and Staveley, and arrived at Windermere dead on time at 10.13pm.

'To keep my ticket I got out on the wrong side of the train, dropped on to the tracks and left the station through the carriage sidings and over a fence. I couldn't face the anti-climax of doddering home on a slow, metallic, neon-lit Ribble bus after that experience so I re-entered the station through the front passenger entrance and got a lift on the locomotive footplate back to Kendal on its run light back to Carnforth loco-shed. This was my first ride on a steam locomotive – apart from a Birkenhead dockside saddle-tank engine about 1950 – and I was thrilled.

'The station gas lamps were extinguished and the locomotive backed the carriages out of the station to the points, uncoupled and ran forward to the turntable, leaving the carriages to roll by gravity into the carriage sidings with the guard on board braking them. The Windermere signalman, a former driver on the now closed Coniston branch, came on the locomotive to get some coal from the tender for the stove in his cabin. We went round on the turntable, the guard doused the last gas light in the station yard and came on board to ride the engine back to Carnforth. The engine slid slowly through the dark station yard to the signal cabin, where the signalman shovelled several hundredweight of coal from the tender out of the cab doorway into the air. The shovelfuls of coal disappeared through a cloud of steam into the darkness and landed with crashing sounds on the railway bank next to the cabin. The roaring fire in the locomotive firebox lit up the rugged, merry faces of the driver, fireman, guard and signalman as they yarned in their strong north Lancashire accents. I was in my element in this environment of iron, coal and steam.

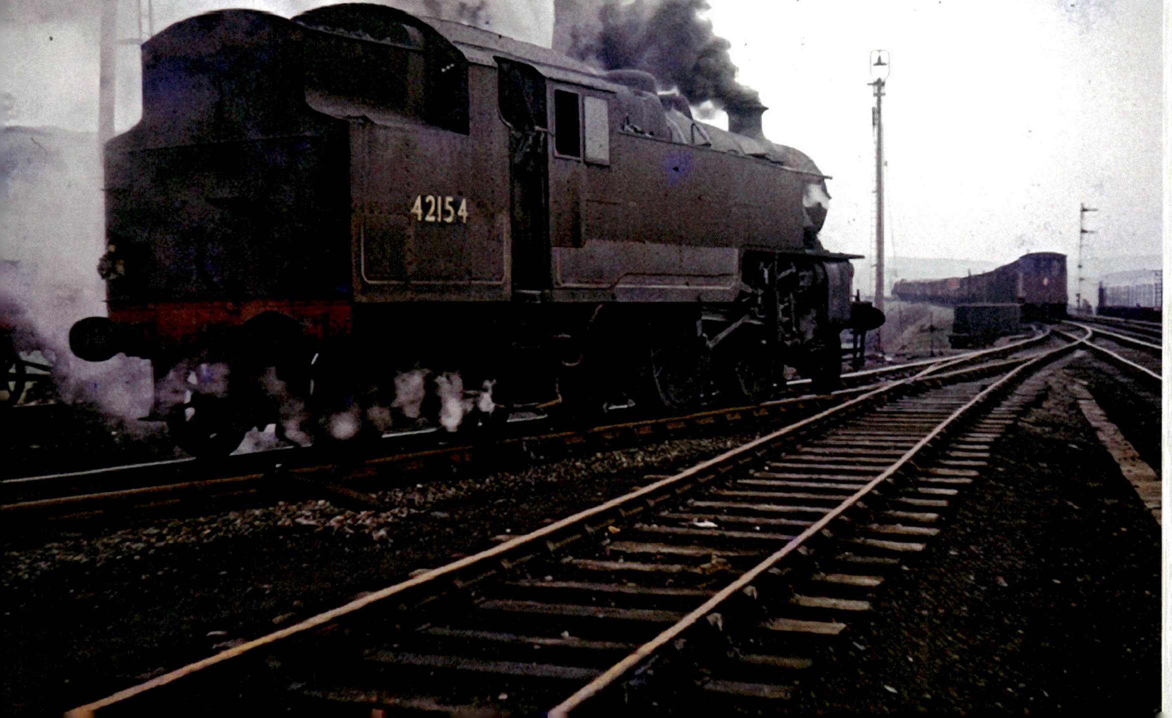

Ex-LMS Fairburn Class 4MT tank engine No 42154 on Tebay shed sidings is about to bank a steam-headed goods train up Shap Fells on 16 April 1966.

'Then the signalman climbed off and the locomotive started on its journey. Its motion was rather vehement, the alternating movement of the connecting and coupling rods on each side made it nose from side to side while, for some unaccountable reason, it jogged up and down as if it were running along the sleepers! Then I realised why steam locomotives were called iron horses – because of their galloping motion. How the locomotive held together on one run, let alone 31 years of running, I don't know but it must have been very strongly built. Unlike North American locomotives, British locomotives do not carry a headlamp to throw a beam along the track ahead, probably because our permanent way is fenced. This shaking monster went plunging blindly headlong through the pitch-blackness up to 55 miles an hour.

'After passing through Burneside the driver closed the throttle to slow down and drop me at Kendal. We echoed through Kendal station, which was in darkness and locked up, and chuffed on to where the railway runs alongside Castle Road. The locomotive stopped, I jumped down, crossed the down track, climbed over a stone wall to the road and watched the locomotive chuff off into the darkness on its way home to Carnforth. Then I became an ordinary, civilised pedestrian and walked home, feeling elated and ho-ish after that tremendous and memorable experience.'

Dieselisation of the Windermere passenger trains
18 April 1966

'Diesel multi unit trains replaced steam-hauled passenger trains on the Windermere branch today, although steam engines still worked the freight. The new service, starting with a new timetable, operated between Windermere and Carnforth, where passengers had to change, replacing the former through steam train services to and from Preston, Manchester Victoria and Crewe. The first of the diesel multiple unit trains ran along the branch this morning – 20 minutes late.

Steam is back
22 April 1966

'Six days after the official last steam passenger train on the Kendal and Windermere branch and on the fifth day of the new diesel service, a steam locomotive hauled the London express along the branch today after the diesel locomotive had broken down. The steamer, a Black Five, headed the 1.45pm arrival at Windermere from London and took the 4.15pm out of Windermere for London. Both the up and down trains south of Crewe were hauled by overhead-electric locomotives.'

Steaming on
2 August 1966

'When the official last steam passenger train on the Oxenholme-Windermere branch ran on April 16th to give way to an all-diesel service, local railfans said steam would be back. They said that the diesels would break down and that there was not enough diesel multiple unit rolling stock available for the high summer service but the railways' divisional commercial manager at Preston, Mr G. G. Fell, said: "Wait and see."

'So the railfans waited … and since then we have seen progressively more steam passenger trains as diesel motors have failed and serviceable stock has become depleted. The holiday season, too, has created a shortage of diesel multiple units and now, at the height of the season, there are three or four steam passenger trains down the branch every day – about the same number as under last winter's timetable. There must have been at least 100 steam passenger trains on the Windermere branch since the official last one ran on April 16th. It seems that steam will die a slower, more gradual death.'

An appreciation of the DMUs
19 August 1966

On a day visit with Ruth and Karl to Grange-over-Sands: 'The diesel multiple unit trains we rode both ways between Kendal and Carnforth were the oldest kind, built at Derby in 1954-55 and rather like classic North American interurban electric cars in appearance, standing high off the ground, with upright, polygonal ends, three tall cab windows across the front and high-domed roofs with headlamps. They swept smoothly and quietly [maybe we were riding the trailer car] along continuous, welded rails and swayed with a somewhat tramcar-like motion along 60ft-section track. The ride from Carnforth back to Kendal with a view through the motorman's cab of the track ahead was fascinating and exciting. The foothills of the Cumbrian Mountains gradually closed in and the countryside on the southern approaches to Kendal looked rich-green and idyllic in the evening sunshine.'

The last standard tramcars in Blackpool and Fleetwood
29 October 1966

'I rode Vintora via Milnthorpe, Lancaster, Cockerham and Shard Bridge to Fleetwood to photograph Blackpool Corporation standard tramcar 147 of 1924, said to be the last traditional British standard tramcar in public service, on a final tour of the system to Fleetwood and Starr Gate organised by Blackpool Tramways Association. My main interest was in photographing the tramcar in the streets of Fleetwood – the last street tramway in Britain – to capture for the last possible time the once commonplace but now passing scene of a double-deck, standard tramcar in a street. Up to this time Fleetwood was served only by single-deckers, now all streamliners of the 1930s.

'At about 2.40pm two strange yet familiar and unmistakeable, tall, rectangular shapes, silhouetted in the low afternoon sunlight, appeared at the far end of the street. The shapes materialised into two Blackpool standard trams. So many tramfans booked a ride on No 147 that the Blackpool Tramways Association had to hire a second tram, No 159, of 1927, an illuminated standard car, outlined and decorated with coloured lights. Both trams were about to be withdrawn and sent to museums. In contrast to the streamlined tramcars on the Blackpool-Fleetwood service today, these two were like apparitions from a past age, droning, rocking and clanking along the street, loaded with ecstatic tramfans leaning out of the windows, crowding the platforms and hanging on to cameras, ciné cameras and tape recorders.

'I clicked my pictures, leapt on to Vintora, tore after the trams, overtook them and took another picture of them in North Albert Street. Then I followed them to the terminus at the ferry. It was only the second time standard trams had ever been to Fleetwood, the previous visit being a similar fantrip the previous October. Reversing at Ash Street, the trams made two return trips through Fleetwood's streets for photographers to capture this historic scene.

'I followed the trams from Fleetwood through Cleveleys and Blackpool to Starr Gate, riding Vintora abreast of No 147 and stopping to photograph it at selected locations. These two antiquated, wooden, spoke-wheeled tramcars cut a strange anachronistic profile as they rocked across the flat countryside between Broadwater and Rossall and along the deserted promenade from Little Bispham to Starr Gate, now the domain of their streamlined successors. [The heritage tram era lay in the future.]

'I had booked a ticket for this tour so I parked Vintora at Starr Gate and rode No 147 back along the promenade to the Tower and Rigby Road depot. I sat in the front, upper vestibule, looking ahead along the track, down the stairs to the motorman operating the controller and behind me through the austere, dark brown, varnished,

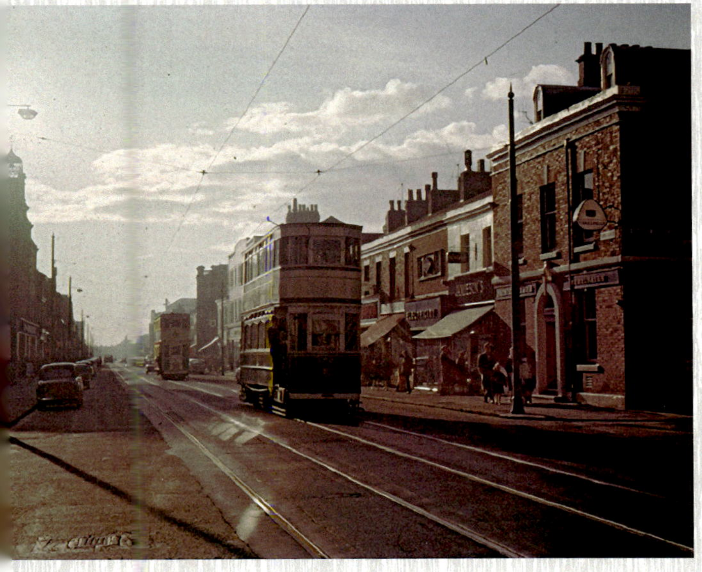

Half in silhouette against the low autumnal afternoon sunlight, like apparitions from a past age, two Blackpool standard tramcars appear along Lord Street, Fleetwood, on 29 October 1966. Significantly these were the last traditional British standard tramcars in public service and were traversing what was the last street tramway in Britain at that time on a special tour of the system before being withdrawn and sent to museums. The leading car, No 147 of 1924, went to Ohio in America but is now back in Blackpool's heritage fleet. The second car, No 159 of 1927, is now at the East Anglia Transport Museum near Lowestoft. At the time of this photograph No 159 was outlined with coloured light bulbs for the Blackpool Illuminations.

in London, Sheffield and Edinburgh, the Gosforth Park Light Railway at Newcastle, the Swansea & Mumbles Railway centenary, the life of a streetcar motorman in Montreal, trolleybuses and the London to Brighton vintage commercial vehicle rally. It was a fascinating film show to round off a memorable day.

'I rode Vintora via Shard Bridge, Cockerham, Lancaster and Burton back to Kendal.'

wooden saloon with is passengers sitting close together and upright on the narrow, wooden seats, nonchalantly being rocked about as in a small steamship on a rough sea. From Manchester Square to the Tower I rode on the longitudinal seats in the lower saloon, which was filled with the droning of the motors and the grinding and clanking of the wheels under the floor. From the Tower to Rigby Road depot I rode on the front platform next to the motorman. It was a fine, winter's day, the daylight had held out well and darkness came down as No 147 turned off the promenade, entered Lytham

Road and moved very slowly along the last 100 yards of track into the depot, flattening hundreds of souvenir pennies.

'I rode a modern service car from Manchester Square to Starr Gate to collect Vintora and drove alongside the tramway north to Cleveleys West Drive Methodist Church Hall to see the longest film programme of tramways ever screened in this country. We saw Blackpool tramways in 1954, the streets of Norwich from an open-top tramcar in 1902, the last days of trams

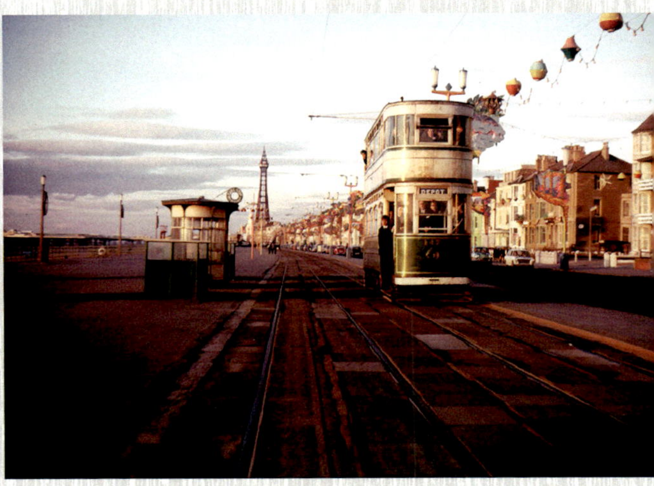

Blackpool standard tramcar No 147 is seen again on the same tour on an almost deserted Promenade at the end of the holiday season with the 520-foot Blackpool Tower in the background. On the left is one of the then standard tramway passenger shelters in cast iron with semi-circular ends, glazing all round and a circular stop sign on the roof.

On 29 November 1966 I wrote: 'As a result of a mail order I received a Philips portable tape recorder worth £27 6s, payable in weekly instalments of 14s 4d. I wanted it to record the early utterances of Karl, who was just starting to talk, and of the child Ruth was expecting, and for outdoor recordings of tramways, steam and electric railways, steamships, the sounds of Merseyside, seabirds etc.' In the event I recorded only the railways, tramways and steamships.

This was a 9-volt, battery-powered, all-transistor machine that recorded at one and seven-eighths inches a second – not the most sophisticated equipment for recording but it was all I could afford and gave good results, as clear as those on my many proprietary gramophone records of railways; like a camera it depended on how it was used. I carried it in a light-tan leather case, made to fit, with a strong woven nylon shoulder strap and it was quite heavy to carry about, even as a portable machine, weighing 10½lb, or 4.75kg, including the six XL 1.5-volt batteries.

In all my recording quests I rarely got the sounds I wanted first time because they weren't graphic enough. I was a perfectionist and I nearly always had to go back to retake them until I got just what I wanted, though those trips were not always recorded in the diaries and many of the recordings I made, including Paddington to Birkenhead, most of the electric railways of London, and the Eastern SMT in Midlothian, were never transcribed to compact discs; they only remain on tape that can no longer be heard because the machinery for playing them is obsolete.

A Wagnerian 'Britannia'
17 December 1966

'Ruth and I left Kendal in a diesel multiple unit train to Carnforth, where we changed to a Barrow-Euston train hauled by a Britannia class steam locomotive to Crewe, thence by an overhead-electric locomotive to Euston. The Britannia was Wagnerian with its wailing Wild West chime whistle and great clouds of steam and smoke spiralling in the wind through the tall, skeletal trees. There were several signal checks and, as we clanked and trundled slowly across the dismal, wet, south Lancashire plain in the gloom between 3 and 3.30pm, it seemed that we could not reach London by the scheduled time of 7pm. However, from Crewe we sped along behind the electric locomotive at 100 miles an hour through the darkness of evening and the lights of London's suburbs appeared before we had time to adjust ourselves to the transition from north to south. The train continued racing unchecked into London with the houses flashing past at an alarming rate, such as we had never experienced before, and we slowed down only a mile or two before Euston terminus.'

Four steam engines at Kendal
26 January 1967

'I took Karl down to our usual railway observation post, the footbridge spanning the marshalling yard, running tracks and parcel van sidings north of Kendal station, from which we saw up to four steam locomotives simultaneously. An Ivatt Mogul was shunting the yard when we arrived, a Black Five came in from Windermere with a goods train and started moving stock around, another Black Five came in from the south with a parcels train and, in the background, a steam passenger train puffed north from Oxenholme on the main line along the side of Hay Fell.'

LNER coaches at Kendal
6 February 1967

'The parcels trains in the sidings north of Kendal station are always mainly ex-LNER Gresley coaches with beaded panels and tapered roof ends. I covet one of these coaches every time I see them and I take the numbers of coaches in particularly good condition in the hope of buying one. [I wasn't sure what I would do with it but I envisaged adapting it to look like an American interurban car and driving it on the road with flexible caterpillar rails… if I could get it licensed!] These classic old coaches were originally finished in varnished teak livery with white roofs and they still look extremely elegant against the standard LMS and BR stock.

Steam to Barrow and a diesel cab ride back
11 February 1967

'In the evening I rode Vintora via Burton to Carnforth and tape-recorded the 8.19 steam passenger train to Barrow from the leading coach. The locomotive, Britannia 70051 *Firth of Forth*, looked like a moving volcano charging through the night with a bright, fiery glow on its clouds of smoke. I returned from Barrow in the driver's cab of a two-car diesel multiple unit train. The driver seemed glad to have somebody to talk to; most days he drove a steam locomotive in the company of a fireman. He said he preferred driving steam locomotives to diesels and told me of runs on steam locomotives that were, he said, 'a beauty to handle', notably Midland Compounds, Princess Royals and Princess Coronations. I rode Vintora back via Burton to Kendal.'

'The Zulu' from Paddington to
Birkenhead
4 March 1967

I rode a railway enthusiasts' special train, "The Zulu", from Paddington to Birkenhead, commemorating the end, the following day, of this through service, which the Great Western Railway started as long ago as 1861. With the new timetables from March 6th passengers will have to go electric from Euston to Liverpool instead. "The Zulu" was an old GW nickname for the Birkenhead express. I know this line north of Banbury better than any other trunk line in Britain from my journeys between boarding school at Oxford and my home in Wallasey from 1949 to 1952 and I can still recite, in order, the names of all the 83 stations and halts – many of them now derelict or closed – in the 165½ miles from Oxford General to Birkenhead Woodside, an average of one station every two miles. Nearly every night at boarding school I used to get under the bed sheets and imitate the sounds of a train – the engine and carriages – on certain sections of the journey from Oxford to Birkenhead. Now I wanted to make a tape recording of the real thing.

'Oxford was on the original route from Paddington to Birkenhead via the Thames valley, eclipsed by the "cut-off" through the Chilterns from 1910, which shortened the route by 18¼ miles. I could change at Banbury or ride through trains from the Kent coast and Bournemouth via Oxford to Birkenhead in the summer. I had previously travelled on "The Zulu" from Paddington to Woodside on May 8th, 1960, behind *King George V* as far as Wolverhampton.

'Steam was now banned between Paddington and Banbury so a diesel locomotive hauled the train from Paddington through High Wycombe to Banbury General, where Great Western steam locomotive 7029 *Clun Castle*, beautifully restored in the company's Brunswick green livery with "GREAT WESTERN" along the side of the tender and its polished brasswork gleaming in the sunlight, was waiting in the bay platform to take over. There were crowds of people on Banbury station and at Birmingham Snow Hill, Wolverhampton Low Level,

Shrewsbury and Chester General just to watch it stop there. Many people gathered in fields between Banbury and Solihull to photograph it and wave it by. All the bridges over the line from Solihull into

Birmingham were lined with spectators, the engine whistling to them at each bridge. Railwaymen photographed it from the trackside and men digging fields stopped and turned to watch it go by and doffed their hats in salute. The sight of a Great Western Castle class locomotive steaming through the countryside inspired affection and admiration, recalled grander days on the railways and represented a passing age of social history, of philosophy, of life.

'However, it is impossible to relive regular steam journeys of the past on a railway enthusiasts' special with the train crowded with fans armed with cameras, ciné-cameras and tape recorders and, being an extra train, caution and stop signals checking its progress, so that these journeys are not typical. I was only recording my favourite sections of the route but, owing to slow progress past signals between Acocks Green and Birmingham, I only just made it into Wolverhampton Low Level before the first side of the tape ran out although there should have been eight minutes to spare according to the schedule. At Chester the train reversed and a BR standard class

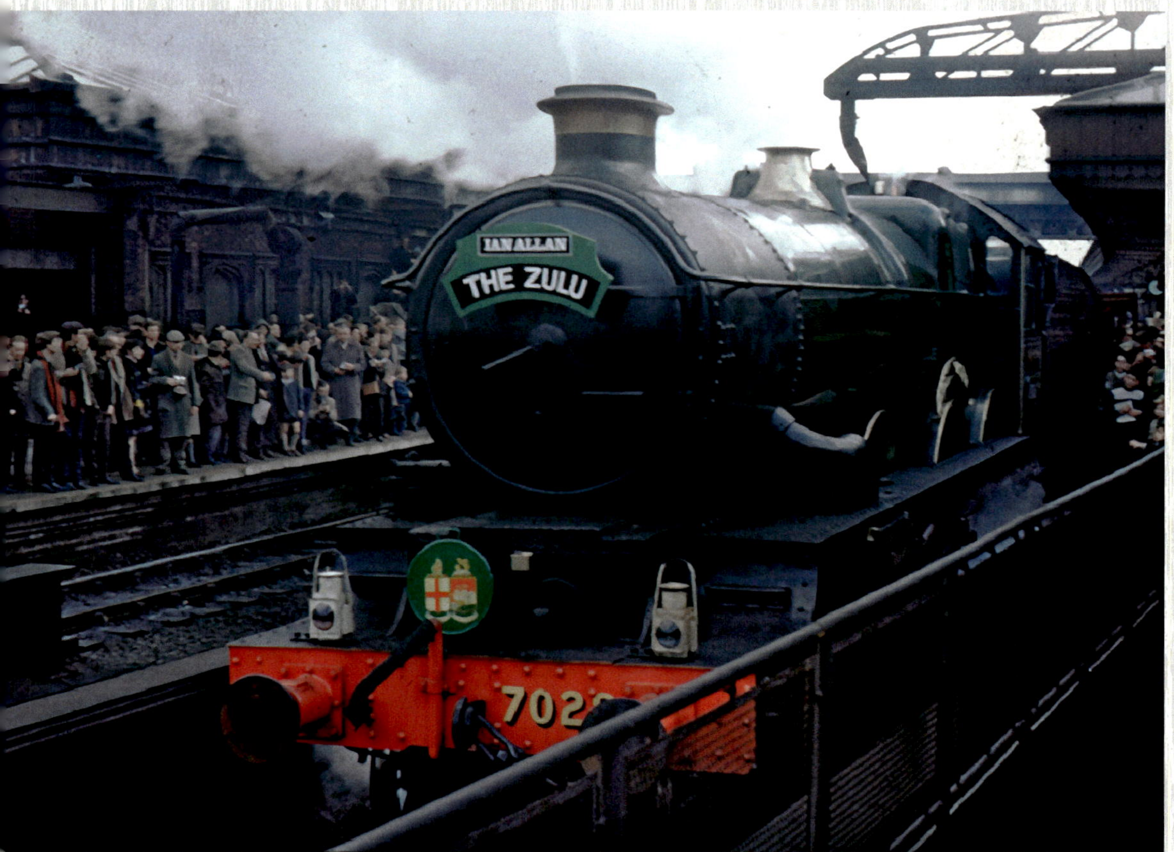

Crowds throng the platforms to watch Great Western 4-6-0 No 7029 *Clun Castle* stop at Shrewsbury with 'The Zulu' special train to mark the end of through services between Paddington and Birkenhead on 4 March 1967.

5 took over from *Clun Castle* for the final stage of the run to Birkenhead.

'I had missed my cue for recording the section from Chirk to Ruabon, so when the train arrived at Birkenhead I caught the next train, steam hauled, back to Gobowen and recorded a service train behind a standard class 5 to Chester and a Stanier class 4 tank engine to Birkenhead, and got much better recordings than on the special. The journey from Chester to Birkenhead was particularly memorable with the locomotive vigorously packing plenty of punch into its beat, sparks flying straight up into the (by then) night sky and soot covering my goggled face as I leaned out of the window.

'The last half mile of the journey to Birkenhead was a fitting finale with a sense of drama. From the viaduct over South Tranmere and Lower Tranmere we had a panoramic view over the Mersey and Liverpool, lit by a myriad glittering lights of the city and ships reflected in the river. The view was then eclipsed by the serrated range of high, black sheds and the towering cranes of Cammell Laird's shipyards. The train clattered and echoed through junctions with lines fanning out on both sides to the carriage sidings, shipyards, gas works, engine sheds and the docks. We slid through the disused Birkenhead Town station, closed since 1945, on a curve at the mouth of the tunnel under the headland on which Birkenhead stands. With brakes on, the train descended the 1 in 95 gradient of the curving tunnel through 565 yards of Stygian gloom. At the end of the tunnel an electric gong passed the window and flanges squealed as the train curved into the grand,

A Paddington train is drawn up in platform 1 at Birkenhead Woodside station, the northern terminus of the legendary Great Western Railway empire on the Mersey bank. The twin-arched trainshed spanned five platforms with a motor road for luggage vans between platforms 1 and 2 and framed the Queen's Arms Hotel and the clock tower of Birkenhead Town Hall in this photograph taken on 17 May 1959.

The GWR ran six trains a day each way between here and Paddington via Wrexham, Birmingham and Banbury, other trunk services to Pwllheli, Bournemouth and Margate, and through coaches to numerous destinations from Cardiff to Sandwich. The GWR also ran local joint services with the LNWR/LMS to Chester, Helsby and West Kirby via Hooton. The great train shed echoed to a total of 90 arrivals and departures a day.

The station was closed and the listed building demolished in 1967 and it is now the site of office blocks, including the Land Registry, and a car and bus park.

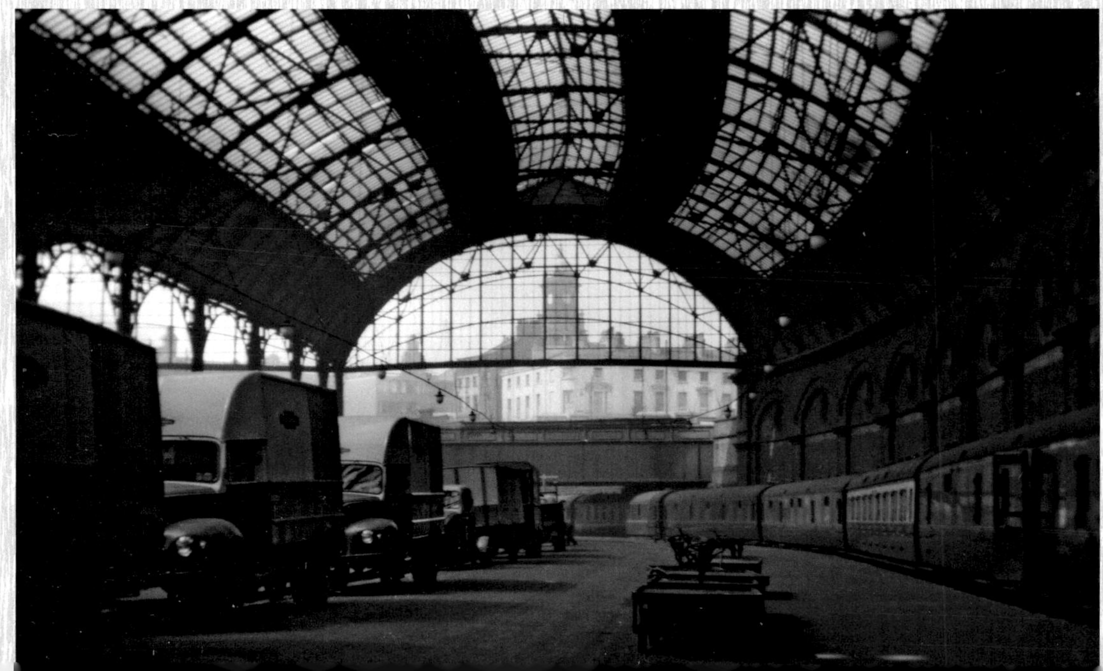

cavernous, dimly lit trainshed on the river bank with the superstructure of a ship in dry dock peering over the station wall at the outer end of the platforms. I can still hear the echoes of slammed carriage doors and the thump-thud of porters unloading mailbags and parcels beneath that cavernous roof in the gas-lit gloom.'

'It was wonderful to be able to catch any train between Chester and Birkenhead, knowing that it would be steam-hauled. It must have been the most intensive steam passenger service on BR before the end of the current timetables. On the three days of my holiday, March 2nd, 3rd and 4th, which I called "Operation Birkenhead", I rode three steam trains into Woodside and two out, and the great terminus, with its twin-arched roof and dramatic entry through the tunnel, became a kind of second home. Indeed it had been the Ultima Thule of my aspirations over the last 18 years. With only diesel multiple units disgracing it from now on, I shan't really be sorry that it will soon be closed.'

It would be difficult to make a pilgrimage along the route from Paddington to Woodside today. Such is the fragmentation of railway operations, one would have to start at Marylebone, change at Birmingham, Wolverhampton and Chester and finish at Birkenhead Hamilton Square.

My television debut
6 March 1967

'At night, just before going to bed, I overheard through the wall of the house, the voice of the news reader on our adjoining neighbours' television saying "…locomotive 7029, Clun Castle…" I knocked on their front door and they let me watch a newsreel of the Paddington to Birkenhead special. I got in just in time to see a shot of myself leaning out of a carriage window with my motor scooter goggles on as soot shields as I was tape-recording the train.'

We had no television at that time and it was our adjoining neighbour, Mrs Ruth Hartley, who, as a mail order catalogue agent, had ordered my tape recorder that led to me to making that railway journey and many more to follow.

Karl's first footplate ride
22 March 1967

I was returning with Karl from Preston '…by diesel locomotive-hauled train to Carnforth, thence by a smooth-running, quiet, diesel multiple unit [in the trailer car again?] through the sunlit south Westmorland countryside of green hills and grey stone farmsteads to Oxenholme and Kendal. At Kendal station I took Karl for a short ride on the footplate of a steam locomotive, a 1947 LMS Ivatt Mogul 4MT, on a parcels train from the up platform down to the crossover and back into the down platform. Karl (aged three) was rather fearful and cringed a bit when the locomotive started moving – rumbling and shaking – but he got used to it by the time we reversed and seemed to appreciate the run back into the station – or maybe he was looking forward to alighting from this hissing monster.'

Recording on the footplate
30 March 1967

'I recorded the oral introduction to the freight side of my tape programme "Smoke Over Kendal" against the background sound of a Black Five standing hissing in Kendal freight yard. Then I started the freight sequences with the Black Five, No 45193, making up a train in the yard, which I recorded from the guard's van coupled to the chimney end of the locomotive, followed by a ride on the locomotive steaming hard as it took the train up the 1 in 80 gradient to Oxenholme on its way to Carnforth. As we approached Oxenholme, above the clanking, hissing and steaming sounds on the footplate, the tape recorder picked out the high-pitched "crows" of a banking engine and a train engine on the main line signalling to each other that they were ready to move with a freight train up Grayrigg bank. The driver, who invited me for the footplate trip, got me a lift on a Stanier 8F, No 48211, on another freight back down the line to Kendal.'

New friends in steam
31 March 1967

'The borough treasurer of Kendal, Mr Percy Duff [successor to the famous Alfred Wainwright], is interested in steam railways and, when I took him three *Evening Posts* he wanted with railway articles I had written, I told him about the good recordings I had made the previous day. As I had my tape recorder with me he said: "Well come on, let's hear it." So there I was … playing steam locomotive noises to the borough treasurer in his office in the Town Hall.

'I had my recorder with me because I was on my way to Kendal freight yard to re-record my oral introduction to "Smoke Over Kendal". This was again with the hiss of a Black Five standing in the background and just when I mentioned the Britannia among the surviving classes of working steam locomotives, there came a whistle from a Britannia, whose presence I had not known of, in Kendal station. As I finished my introductory narration the Britannia came past with a parcels train and I was able to

follow my introduction with a recording of it. I couldn't have timed it better if I'd tried.

'The driver of the Black Five was Watson Sowerby, the one who drove me up to Oxenholme the previous day, and he got me to play him my recording of that in a lineside hut. He said he was fascinated by steam locomotives and offered me a ride on the footplate with him any time I liked, anywhere he was going.'

Breaking Karl in to the footplate experience
3 April 1967

'Late in the afternoon I took Karl to Kendal railway goods yard and on the footplate, with driver Watson Sowerby, of a BR standard class 5 shunting for about half an hour. Karl was still rather fearful and sat grimly on the fireman's seat on the right hand side of the cab, holding on tight and watching the fireman driving and the driver firing.'

Driving the engine
7 April 1967

'I rode with Watson Sowerby on the footplate of Stanier 8F locomotive 48438 with the late afternoon freight from Kendal to Burneside and back. What a

wonderful way to travel: on a great, black, iron contraption with coal and steam and the floors of the locomotive and tender moving different ways and much rumbling and grinding and squealing of flanges and clanking of rods. The train to Burneside was one empty truck and, of course, a guard's van. After shunting them into the sidings at Burneside the locomotive went back to Burneside lower crossing, where the driver opened the door to the tender, letting an avalanche of several hundredweight of coal crash on to the floor, then shovelled and booted it out of the cab doorway into a heap between the tracks – a regular, unauthorised, private delivery from Mr Sowerby to the crossing keeper for his cottage fire.

'Meanwhile the guard was rolling six trucks and his van by gravity out of the sidings down to the locomotive. They gained some speed as they rolled towards us and crashed into the tender with a terrific noise but we did not feel the slightest tremor on the locomotive. Then off we set back to Kendal. As we approached the town the driver gave me brief instructions on the operation of the vacuum and steam brakes, the regulator and the forward and reverse gear. I thought he was telling me out of interest but he left me to stop the train on the up line opposite Kendal freight yard, where he got down from the footplate with his flask of tea and disappeared into the shunter's hut.

'I then had to run the engine around the train, using two crossovers, take it over on to the down line, shunt it in sections into the sidings, make up a new train from the sidings and back it down gently on to vans being loaded in the goods warehouse for Watson to take the train away to Carnforth. This I did on my own under the supervision of the fireman and the directions of the shunter, who did most of the work, running about, switching the points, waving his arms and uncoupling and coupling-up the trucks. I was driving the locomotive for about 15 or 20 minutes. It was a great feeling controlling this steam giant and moving the trucks through the yard with a brass-handled, hissing, vacuum brake, rather like on an electric train or tramcar. I recall an engineman saying: "Anyone can drive an engine but it's stopping it in the right place that counts!"

'Not all footplate trips are as rough as I had on Black Five 45195 from Windermere to Kendal last April (16th). I'm told that every locomotive has a different character, a different temperament and a different motion, and so it seems from my short experience of this pleasure.'

End of the line from Clapham to Low Gill
4 April 1967

'Work starts this week on lifting the track of yet another of the few railway lines through the fell country, that from Clapham to Low Gill. Track gangers working seven days a week will take four months to lift the line. In its 23 miles, the line traverses five portions of the three counties of Yorkshire, Lancashire and Westmorland and once served, in order, stations at Clapham, Ingleton (Yorkshire), Kirkby Lonsdale (Lancashire), Barbon, Middleton-on-Lune (Westmorland), Sedbergh (Yorkshire) and Low Gill (Westmorland). Although Kirkby Lonsdale is in Westmorland, the station was over the boundary in Lancashire.

'The line was opened from Clapham to Ingleton in 1849 and from Low Gill to Ingleton in 1861. The passenger train service was withdrawn in 1954 and the freight service in 1964. The double-track permanent way has since been maintained in good condition for the diversion of trains from the Midland and North Western main lines when these lines were blocked by derailments or snow but it was thought locally that the line was being kept to divert Leeds-Carlisle trains from Hellifield to Low Gill if and when the Settle-Carlisle section of the Midland line was closed, as it

was to be under the Beeching plan. In fact the Clapham-Low Gill line was originally built as a main line for Midland trains between Leeds and Carlisle but, because of the uncooperative attitude of the North Western towards the running of Midland trains over their metals, the Midland built a direct line over the Pennines from Settle to Carlisle and the Clapham-Low Gill line was never anything more than a local branch line. The future of the Settle-Carlisle line is still in doubt under the Minister of Transport's latest railway plan and, if it is closed, trains between Leeds and Carlisle would have to go via Carnforth and reverse there instead of going via Ingleton.'

An evening with Percy Duff
11 April 1967

'Percy Duff, the borough treasurer, invited me to his home in Burneside Road to show me his lantern slides and play his tape recordings of steam trains, most of which were on the LNW main line over Shap Fells at Grayrigg and Scout Green. His recordings of trains at Grayrigg were made from the signal cabin with the sounds of bells and levers.'

**The banker ritual at Oxenholme
27 April 1967**

'On Tuesday and Wednesday the previous
week I had made recordings at Oxenholme
of a banking engine clanking down the
fell and echoing through the station and
a heavy freight plodding through the
station and stopping for a banker, but the
south-west wind blew away the sound of
the banked freight going up the fell. After
days spent waiting for the right weather
conditions – a still day or a slight north
wind – and hours spent waiting for a banker
to join on a freight after it had gone through
the station and not before, today I was able
to continue my recordings of the banker
ritual with a banker joining on the back of
a freight at the north end of the station and
pushing it up Grayrigg Bank.

'For a change there were so many freights
that they were queuing up two abreast in
the loop sidings south of the station and
there were two bankers on the go instead of
the normal one – both Stanier and Fairburn
class 4 tank engines from Tebay shed.

'I rode Vintora north over the airy fells
to the cutting at Castle Green, just east of
Kendal, where I recorded a banked freight
under way up the fellside with twitching
sounds on the long, welded rails from the
wheels of the train long before and after

it passed by. Then I filled in the gaps I
had left in between the recordings with
announcements preceding the sound tracks.'

**Siesta on Oxenholme station
6 May 1967**

'In the afternoon I took Karl by bus up
to Oxenholme railway station to watch
the trains. Unfortunately most of them
were diesel-hauled but we saw the steam
banking engine running light down from
the fells, a southbound steam freight and
two northbound steam freights, one of
them banked. I recorded two Britannias
on fast freights: No 70021 *Morning Star*,
southbound, whistling down the fell and
hurtling though the station, then No 70051
Firth of Forth, northbound, storming the
gradient without banking assistance.

'All the other people on the station,
apart from the railway staff, were railway
enthusiasts. One of them was Guy Moser,
a Kendal solicitor I knew from reporting
cases in Kendal Magistrates' Court; he was
also secretary of the Ravenglass & Eskdale
Railway. He said he had "come to spend a
quiet hour" away from the office, apparently
to photograph trains. It certainly was
pleasant up there, sitting on the platform
in the warm sunshine, away from the noise
and fumes of the town, surrounded by green

hills and trees and the sounds of birds, cows
and sheep and the occasional steam train
passing through.'

**On Black Fives over Shap and back
10 and 11 May 1967**

In the morning mail I had a letter from
Watson Sowerby. It was dated May 9th and
read: "Just a line to let you know that we
have had some link changes since I saw you
and I am on Carlisle this week. I can't say
exactly what time I'll be at Oxenholme but
if you are there tomorrow night by 10.15 I
shall look for you. If I'm late as it is quite
possible, don't worry, I won't go without you.
See you tomorrow night. Watson."

'I waited by the water column at the
north end of the down platform and Watson
came through and picked me up at 10.30pm
on Black Five 44817 at the head of a freight
train from Stoke-on-Trent to Carlisle.

'A footplate ride by night is not as
interesting as by day because one cannot
see ahead along the track but there is more
atmosphere at night with the gas-lit stations,
the oil-lit headcode lamps on the engines
and the firebox glow on the underside of the
smoke. We plunged blindly into the black
night at speeds up to 50 miles an hour with
the silhouettes of the great fells around us
and nothing visible ahead but the steam and

rain swirling around the headcode lamps and the green signal lights looming up out of the darkness. When the fireman opened the firebox door the cab was aglow with orange light but when he closed the firebox the figures of the driver and fireman were scarcely discernible in the darkness. The only light in the cab was from the small oil lamp illuminating the water gauge and I had to grope my way across the cab.

'I absorbed and appreciated everything about this flight of a dying and almost historic form of locomotion. I could imagine this locomotive standing in a museum but no-one looking over it as a static exhibit could conceive what it was like when it was working, with all the noise and shaking and the fireman sweating as he swings heavy shovelfuls of coal into the hot and hungry furnace.

'At midnight we clanked and echoed through the border city, looking down on gas-lit back streets of wet granite setts. Our journey ended in Carlisle's vast, floodlit marshalling yard at Kingmoor on the flat no-man's-land about two miles north of the city. The crew changed engines in Kingmoor loco-shed, at this time the largest steam shed with the most numerous stud of steam locomotives on British Railways, but Watson told me that railfans are not too popular in Kingmoor shed so he dropped me

outside. I sheltered from the rain – which was accompanied by sheet lightning and thunder – in a shed housing a steam railway crane. I sat on the front of the crane while Watson raised steam in another engine and I passed the time by playing back my tape recording of the footplate trip and watching the silhouettes of steam locomotives moving slowly through the floodlit haze and rain along the rails leading to and from the loco-shed.

'After about an hour Watson emerged from the shed with another Black Five, 45394, picked me up and we backed on to another freight train in the yard. At 2.40am we left Kingmoor and headed slowly upgrade through Carlisle's complex network of freight lines. opened up in the country, stopped in Penrith station at 3.30am to fill up with water from the column, then headed over the fells. Dawn broke as we freewheeled, clanking rhythmically, down the long, steady descent from Grayrigg to Oxenholme, where the train stopped to drop me at 5am. I rode Vintora home and, after a hard scrub to get the grime off my hands and face, I went to bed at 5.30am and had two hours' sleep before getting up to go to work at the office.'

'The Long Drag' from Selside to Ribblehead'
24 May 1967

'I rode Vintora via Endmoor and Ingleton up to the head of Ribblesdale to start my tape programme "The Long Drag", featuring trackside recordings of steam trains and interviews with signalmen on the high reaches of the Midland main line over the Pennines from Selside to Mallerstang. From a window in Selside signal cabin I recorded a ballast train toiling up the 1-in-100 gradient up Ribblesdale from Settle. The locomotive, Ivatt Mogul 43119, with only 12 trucks, was beaten by the Long Drag and was gasping and panting like a human as it approached – "short o' puff" as the signalman put it – and stopped outside the cabin to raise more steam. There were exchanges between the driver and the signalman, who reported the position by telephone to "control" at Carlisle. As we waited, the electric bell tinkled mysteriously in the cabin but it was not a call from the next cabin and the signalman said it was lighting striking the overhead wires between the cabins. The hiss of steam became louder as steam pressure rose and, as it reached a crescendo, the train continued on its way north. That was a "scoop" to start "The Long Drag" programme!

'The signalman here, Bill Sharpe, was previously the stationmaster at Ribblehead for seven years until most of the stations between Settle and Carlisle were made unstaffed halts earlier this year. He turned down an offer to be assistant station manager at Appleby because he wanted to stay in the station house at Ribblehead. He had been a signalman for eight years before becoming the stationmaster so he reverted to signalman and became a relief at all cabins from Horton to Ais Gill.

'Much of the romance of the line is in its remote stations, all rugged, Victorian Gothic buildings in local stone, and its lonely, wooden, oil-lit signal cabins of traditional Midland Railway architecture. Ribblehead station 1,025 feet high, at the head of Ribblesdale, serving a short row of cottages and a widely scattered farming community, used to have a harmonium and Anglican service in the waiting room in the 1950s and the rough, stony, station approach road was used as a sheep market twice a year. Ribblehead station was also the highest meteorological station in England and, as stationmaster, Bill was also the weather observer, reading the instruments and telephoning regular weather reports to RAF Dishforth and Air Ministry headquarters and rainfall reports to the Yorkshire Ouse River Authority and the Lancashire River Authority. His wife, Faith, now sends the

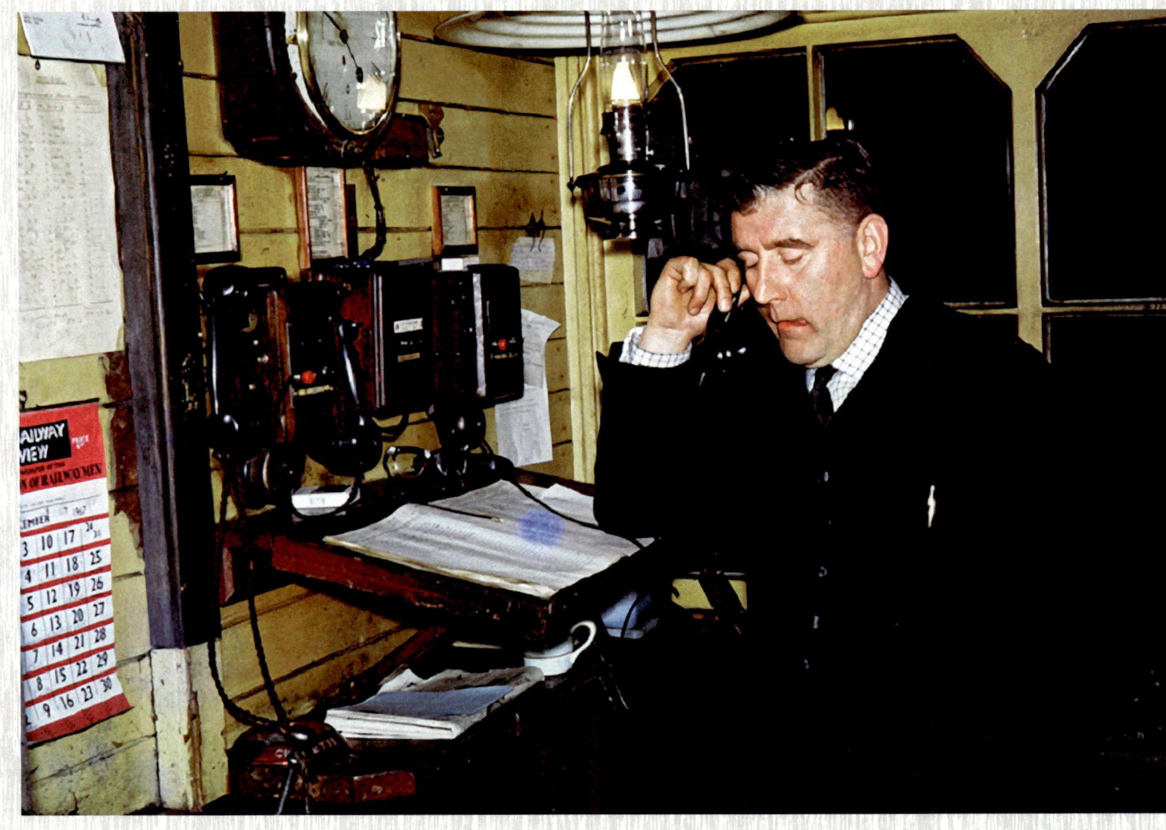

weather reports and doubles as lamp woman at Ribblehead.

'I recorded an interview with Bill about the wild weather up here. He said the average rainfall was 78in a year and the highest figure he ever recorded was 109in in

Bill Sharpe, formerly stationmaster at Ribblehead (1960-67), became a relief signalman at all cabins from Horton to Ais Gill after his and many other stations on the Settle and Carlisle line were relegated to unstaffed halts in 1967. He is pictured here in Ais Gill cabin on the telephone to 'control' at Carlisle on 7 December 1967.

At the head of Ribblesdale a Carlisle to Bradford stopping train calls at the remote moorland station at Ribblehead at 10.04am on 25 September 1963. The locomotive is 'Black Five' No 44898. On the left are sidings to a limestone quarry, which was a source of freight traffic on the railway, and in the background rises the great fell of Whernside, 2,419 feet, the highest peak in Yorkshire.

The rugged stone station, 1,025 feet above sea level, serves a hamlet and farming community and is used by fell-walkers. The station waiting room doubled as a chapel with a harmonium and Anglican services on Sundays until 1956, and the stony station approach was used as a sheep market twice a year. From 1938 to 1970 Ribblehead station was also the highest weather station in England and the stationmaster and his wife doubled as weather observers, telephoning regular wind and rainfall recordings to Air Ministry headquarters, RAF Dishforth and the Yorkshire and Lancashire River Authorities. During that time Ribblehead had an average rainfall of 78 inches a year, the wind blew up to 60mph, and in January 1963 the station was buried in a 30-foot snowdrift!

The quarry sidings and signal cabin closed in 1969, and the station closed in 1970, but the up platform reopened as a halt for southbound trains in 1986. The down platform was rebuilt south of the up platform and reopened for northbound trains in 1993. The Settle & Carlisle Railway Trust restored the derelict up-side buildings as a Midland Railway period station and visitor centre, which opened in 2000. Since 2004 an automated weather station has transmitted weather reports and given forecasts for hikers alighting here. The former quarry is now a nature reserve and new sidings have been laid opposite the up platform and behind the down platform for the shipment of timber from nearby plantations.

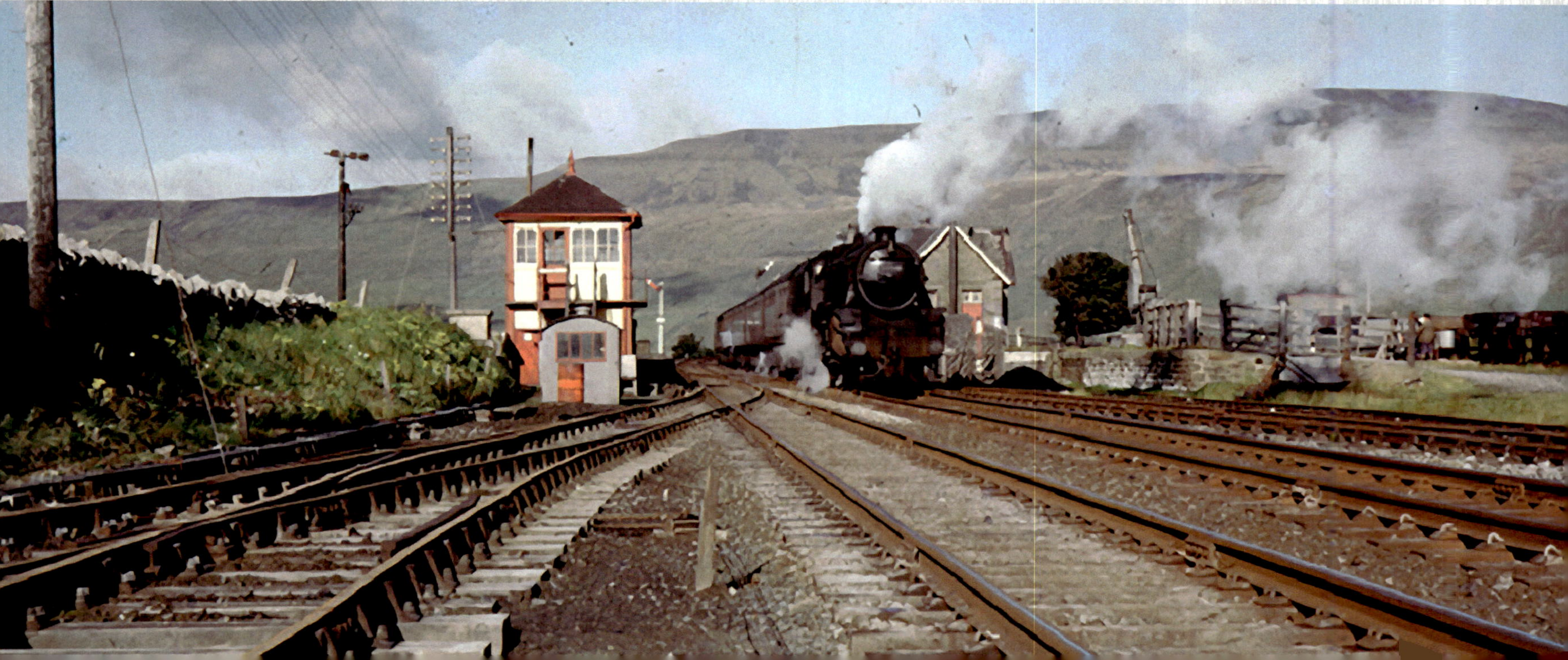

1954, when 5in fell one December day!
Winds often blew 30 to 40mph and his
highest wind speed recording was 96mph
on the night in December 1964, when it
blew eight new motorcars off a train of
flatcars on Ribblehead viaduct. The train
was stopped by the signalman at Blea
Moor when he noticed that some cars
were missing. Carlisle "control" asked Bill
to check his section of the line and as
soon as he stepped out on the platform
he could see immediately that the cars
had blown off the train on Ribblehead
viaduct, which was "completely
illuminated" by the saloon lights as the
car doors had been flung open!

'When the wind brought snow the
blizzard could be so thick that you
couldn't see the buildings on the opposite
platform. Once during a blizzard he had a
phone call from three men marooned in
the quarry office on the down side of the
station. They couldn't get home because
the road to Hawes was blocked with
snow and they dare not cross the railway
to get to the station house. Bill had to go
and lead them across the railway to the
station house and they had to stay there
for the night.

'The Long Drag is notorious for trains
being stuck in snowdrifts. Bill had to
measure snow with a ruler but this was
not easy in January 1963, when Bill said

Ribblehead station was buried in 30 feet of
the stuff and he had to dig a tunnel through
it from his house to the station office. The
line was blocked for a week, mainly by a
60ft snowdrift over the north portal of Blea
Moor tunnel. A freight train was stuck on
the climb between Mallerstang and Ais Gill
and the fireman had to drop his fire till the
line was cleared. Snow ploughs reopened
the line in two days but Ribblehead station
approach road remained blocked for a
further six weeks.

'That winter Bill was working on the
snow ploughs for 24 hours at a time. Two
engines would be coupled together with
a plough at each end and charge into the
drifts with the firemen shovelling hard and
the driver pulling the injectors well out. Bill
used to come home black with soot from
being on the engines and when he took off
his overcoat in the house it "stood up, frozen
stiff".

'Despite the wild landscape and weather
Bill still wanted to stay at Ribblehead
because of the peace, the birds and the
friendly people. How did he feel about the
passing of the steam train and the diesel
taking its place? He said: "I don't like it at
all. I'd sooner have the steam trains. I like
the steam trains and I always did. I don't

George Horner, signalman at Blea Moor cabin on the
Settle-Carlisle line, on 7 December 1967.

like the diesels; they don't appeal to me one
bit; they keep breaking down do these diesel
trains; they cause a lot of trouble."

'Next, from a trackside location at the
north end of Ribblehead viaduct, I recorded
a northbound freight train, headed by Black
Five 45075, crossing the quarter-mile span

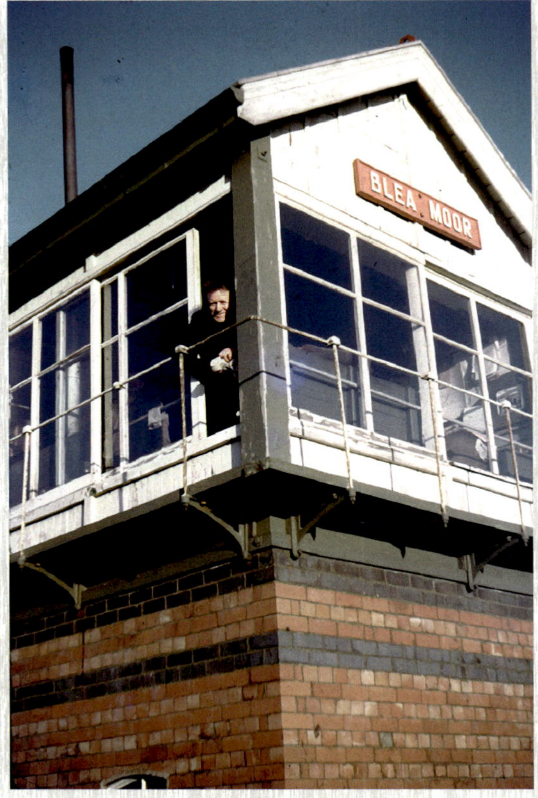

on 24 arches, the highest point 165 feet above the valley bottom where the river Ribble rises in Batty Moss.

'Then the northbound train passes Blea Moor signal cabin (the word 'blea' is from the Old Norse word 'bla', meaning dark). This is probably the loneliest signal cabin on British Railways. It stands 1,125 feet high on the edge of the moor, three-quarters of a mile from the nearest habitation, Winterscales Farm, a mile land a half from the nearest road, at the hamlet of Ribblehead, and seven and half miles from the nearest village, Ingleton. To get to the cabin from the motor road the signalmen have to ride their bicycles over a rough, stony track, riddled with large, deep puddles, then walk nearly a mile along a footpath to the cabin. When the wind howls over the moors, as if often does, the signalmen leave their bicycles at home and walk all the way.

'One of the three regular signalmen who man Blea Moor cabin round the clock is George Horner, who lives two miles away at Salt Lake Cottages, on the site of a railway navvies' shanty town called Salt Lake City. How did he feel about the loneliness of his eight-hour duty? He said: "We've always been used to it and I think we really like it. We are constantly in touch by telephone with control and various [signal] boxes as to the running of trains and we sometimes get the engine crews in for a few words when they stop in the loop. Sometimes we see hikers between the youth hostels passing behind the box and the shepherds with their dogs gathering up and that."

'For hours on end the signalmen at Blea Moor hear nothing but – on a fine summer's day – the bleating of lambs and the cry of the curlew or – when cloud is scudding off Whernside – driving rain flailing at the windows. I had heard of high winds up here. What effect did the wind have on the trains? George said: "The wind takes the sheets off the waggons and we don't know where they go. The lime train set off one day from Horton. It was a wild day. It had every waggon sheeted when it left Horton but there was only one in ribbons when it got to Blea Moor."

'In such an elevated and open place, was the cabin vulnerable to thunderstorms? He said that lightning struck the overhead wires and the trackside mechanism to the signals and "plays about on your bells and lever tops". It did put the instruments out of order at times but the lineman came and put them in order again.

'Lastly I asked George, if he had his time over again, what would he do? "Oh, I don't think I would swap it; I think I'd put in for Blea Moor again," he said.

'I rode back to Raven Scar, where I was visited in the evening by Richard Holloway, a 32-year old Kendal solicitor, who lives in Garsdale and is very interested in railways and tramways. He said his pet tramway system was Edinburgh's, which closed in 1956. I know from my mornings spent reporting cases in Kendal Magistrates' Court that he has a brilliant legal mind. He is the only solicitor in Kendal who specialises in criminal law to the exclusion of all other legal work and in March he became the clerk to Windermere Magistrates' Court and was the youngest magistrates' clerk in Westmorland – yet he said he would be prepared to give all this up to become a tram driver, if it were possible, in Edinburgh or on some similar, traditional city tramway system. He took a great interest in my museum in the attic, his favourite exhibit being the destination box off a Glasgow standard tram. I played him a selection of my gramophone records of tramcars in Sheffield, Glasgow and Toronto and interurbans in Los Angeles, which stimulated him immensely, and he borrowed my books *Branch Line Album*, *Tramway Heyday* and two books of cartoons by Rowland Emett: *Sidings and Suchlike* and *The Forgotten Tramcar*. Richard is also interested in Scotland, music and fishing.'

Dent Head to Ais Gill and the saga of snowdrifts
2 June 1967

'I rose at 4am and rode Vintora up the hills east through Sedbergh and Dent towards the rising sun and arrived at Dent Head at 6.50am to make an early start to another day of tape recordings for my documentary sound memorial to the "Long Drag" under steam. I recorded steam freights emerging from the north portal of Blea Moor Tunnel, thundering through Dent station and cresting Ais Gill summit from the north. There was not a cloud in the sky, not a breath of wind and not a sound but the continuous singing of the moorland birds. The peace was overwhelming. Dent station was the warmest and most peaceful place and the view down the dale from the station was wonderful and exhilarating.

'At an elevation of 1,145

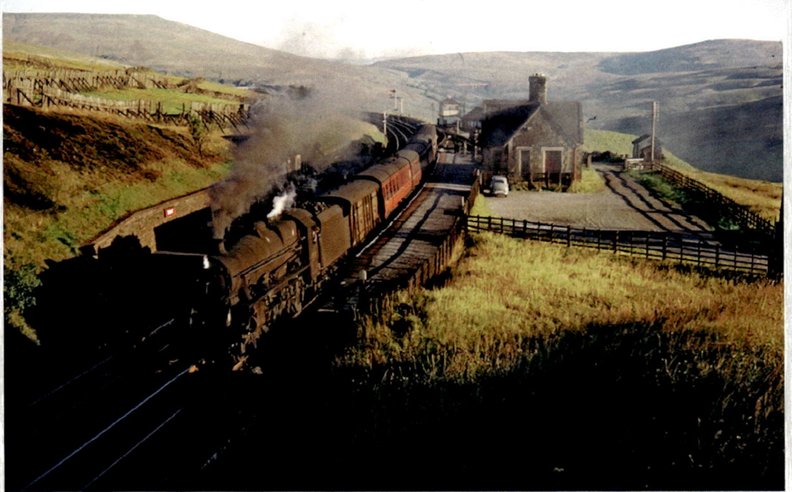

An ex-LMS 'Jubilee' Class 7P 4-6-0 locomotive, with a van and four coaches, stops at Dent station at 5.54pm forming a Bradford to Carlisle service on 20 September 1963. This station, at 1,145 feet, is the highest railway station in England; it is 5 miles from and 700 feet higher than the village of the same name and is reached by a road that climbs 450 feet from the valley bottom in three-quarters of a mile with successive hairpin corners on a gradient of 1 in 5 on the lower section. This road was first metalled in 1954. Dent signal cabin and Dent Head viaduct can be seen in the background, with Blea Moor on the right.

Jim Harper, signalman at Dent, with the station in the background, on 5 October 1967.

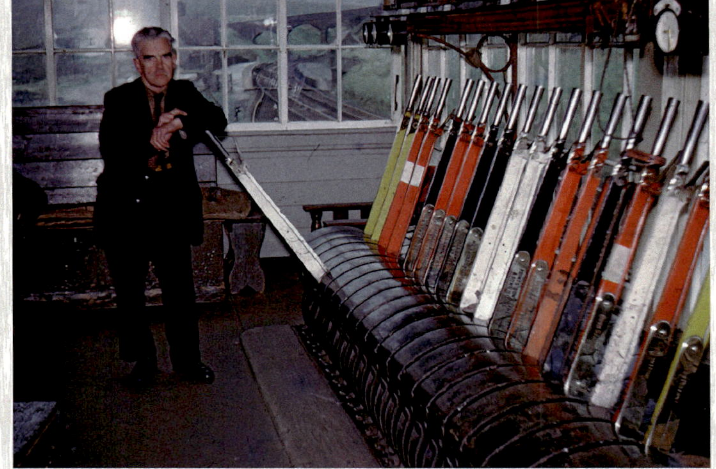

feet, Dent station is the highest railway station in England. It is five miles from and 700 feet higher than the village of the same name and is reached by a road that climbs 450 feet from the valley bottom in ¾ of a mile with successive hairpin corners on a gradient of 1 in 5 on the lower section. This road was not metalled until 1954. Some idea of the wildness of the weather up here at Dent station can be gauged by the fact that the stationmaster's house is sheathed in slates on three sides as well as on the roof and since its construction in the 1870s has had double-glazed windows, which must have been something of a pioneer experiment in house insulation. Dent station houses a canteen and rest room for men clearing snow from the neighbouring stretches of the line, which are prone to drifting.

'I recorded an interview with signalman Jim Harper in Dent cabin and asked him to tell me about the snow on the railway at Dent. He said the worst blizzard he could remember was in 1947, when strong night gales constantly caused deep drifts that blocked the railway and the station approach road for weeks on end. The railway sent three trainloads of German and Italian prisoners of war under the supervision of track gangs from Leeds to clear the snow every day. The weather was fine each day but as soon as the sun went down the wind got up again and undid all the work the men had done.

'"Within an hour you couldn't tell they'd been. They came next morning and cut it all out again but the same thing happened the next night. The drifts were up to about 12 feet high and the prisoners of war used to scratch their names on the keystones of the bridges over the line."

'Trains and snow ploughs were stuck in the snow, sometimes for weeks, and the locomotive superintendent virtually lived up here for the duration. Heavy freight trains were more vulnerable than passenger trains and once a train came to a standstill for 10 minutes it became snowed up in the wind. The drifts might range from 8in on one side of a train to 8ft on the other side. Ploughs got stuck and other ploughs sent to dig them out got stuck as well. When they tried to get a plough out, the spinning driving wheels overheated the rails, causing uneven expansions and cracked rails. The nocturnal gales were so wild that one night six or seven railway maintenance men were stranded in Dent Head signal cabin. The wind was shaking the cabin and one man said: "I've been 10,000 feet up in the Himalayas but I never saw anything like this!"

'Like all the other signalmen I interviewed on the Long Drag, who live in remote places and work lonely duties, Jim said he would not swap it for life in a town. He preferred the snow to the soot. As he was born in the country he was used to it and he would always prefer it. Jim Harper died six months after I recorded him; he collapsed across a lever in Dent cabin.'

Recording inside Blea Moor tunnel 9 June 1967

'Again I rose at 4am and rode Vintora up the hills east of Sedbergh and Dent and arrived at Dent Head at 6.40am to make another early start to a day of tape recordings on the Long Drag. Inside the north portal of Blea Moor Tunnel I recorded the ghostly, rather muffled sound of a northbound freight train emerging from the darkness and the north end of the tunnel. The train had crested the top of the long climb from Settle while inside the tunnel and had begun to run downgrade to Dent. As Black Five 45131 emerged from the darkness the driver gave a short blast on the Stanier whistle.

'Then I rode on the old Coal Road over Widdale Fell to Garsdale and on to Mallerstang at the head of the Eden valley to make the last few recordings of the programme. Next I wanted a northbound train running down Mallerstang. While I was waiting I re-recorded the verbal introduction to the programme and some of the announcements to the sequences I had recorded and, when a train came, there was no time to spin the tape forward to the place where I wanted to record it. So I

Opposite top left: 'Black Five' No 44900 spouts columns of smoke and steam as it pulls out of Garsdale station at 6.20pm on 20 September 1963. Garsdale station once had its own loco-shed at this former junction with the Midland branch to Hawes, connecting with the North Eastern branch down Wensleydale to Northallerton. The station now serves only a row of former railwaymen's houses and a remote farming community. It once had a library in

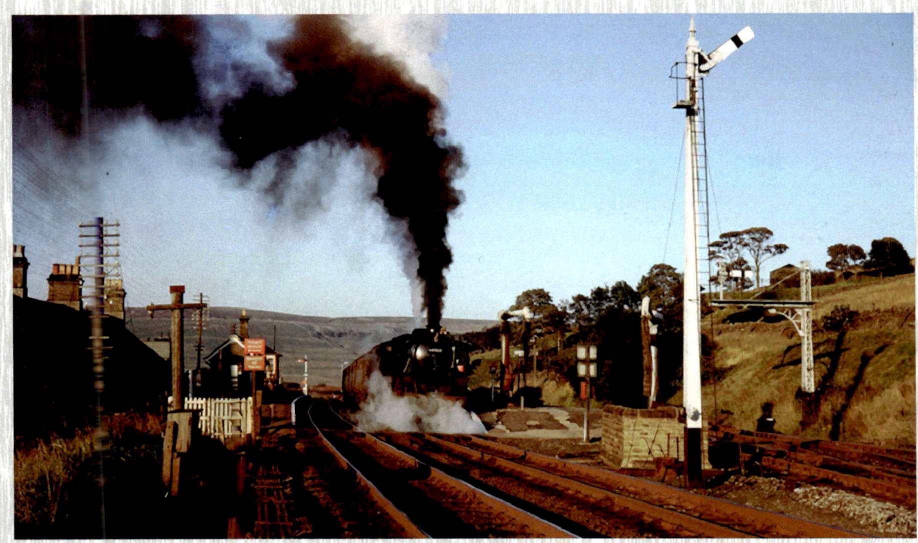

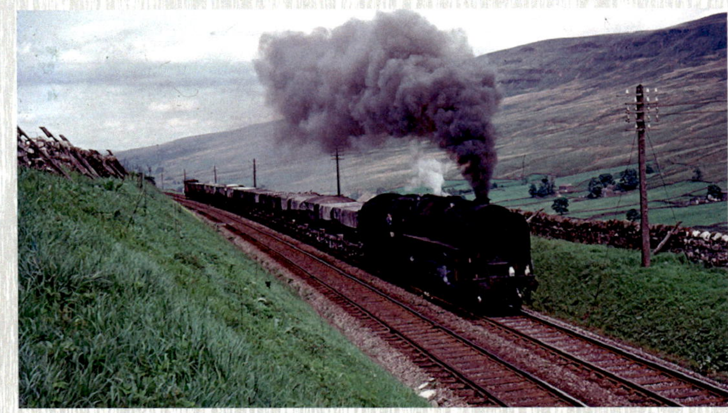

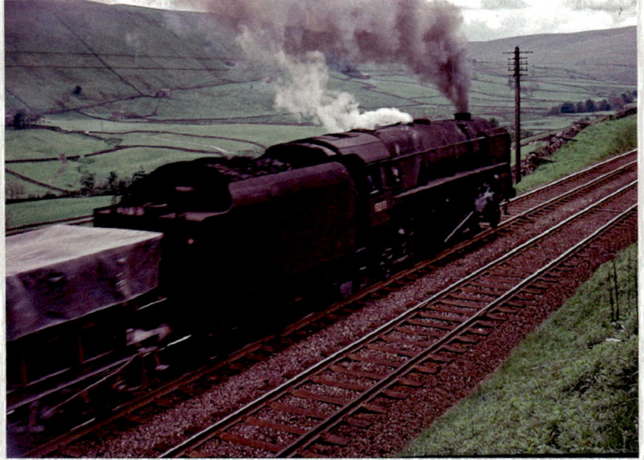

its waiting room and the stone building supporting the water tank (off right) housed the social centre of the district with a stage, a piano and upholstered seats.

British Railways relegated the remote stations over the high reaches of the Settle and Carlisle railway to unstaffed halts in 1967 and closed them in 1970. Passenger services were cut and freight was diverted with the intention of closing the line. BR appointed Liverpool district manager Ron Cotton as project manager to close the line but, as a professional railwayman, he attracted more passengers to use the line and in 1975 he started hikers' special trains. Then in 1981 BR declared that Ribblehead's quarter-mile-long, 24-arch viaduct was unsafe.

Thanks to a concerted promotion campaign by the Friends of the Settle & Carlisle Line, the Settle & Carlisle Railway Trust, the Yorkshire Dales National Park and transport user groups, many more passengers rode the line for sightseeing and hiking and many halts reopened in 1986. The Government dropped the threat of closure in 1989 and, after an independent inspection, Ribblehead Viaduct was restored at a fraction of the cost that BR had estimated. Diesel multiple units now serve all stations and halts between Leeds and Carlisle and the line is used by long-distance fast freight trains, steam-headed excursions and as a diversion route from the West Coast Main Line.

Top right and above right: 'Long Meg' on the 'Long Drag'. British Railways Standard Class 9F 2-10-0 No 92208 climbs the 1 in 100 gradient up the glaciated valley of Mallerstang in Westmorland towards Ais Gill summit with the anhydrite train from Long Meg quarry to Widnes chemical works on 9 June 1967. Mallerstang is the source of the River Eden and the railway follows the river down by Kirkby Stephen and Appleby to Carlisle, below which the Eden issues into the Solway Firth.

missed the only down steam train before I had to leave in the middle of the afternoon to help Ruth with the shopping in Kendal. The frustrating thing was that 3pm, the time I had to leave, is just the time steam freights start coming through to the north.'

Mallerstang
10 June 1967

'I rose at 4am again and rode up to Mallerstang, arriving at 6.15am, and got my recording of a down steam freight. With the Long Drag behind it and Britannia 70035 *Rudyard Kipling* on front, the fitted, fast freight hurtled down Mallerstang in a whoosh that was so quick it was hardly worth recording. Then I started to get some of the sounds of nature I wanted, such as the sheep and curlew, before leaving at 8.30am to start work in Kendal at 9.15.'

'It's better by bus'
11 June 1967

'I took Karl by bus via Milnthorpe and Burton to Beaumont Hospital at Lancaster for his scheduled ear, nose and throat surgery to try and improve his hearing. We went there on one of Ribble's newest buses and I returned on the same bus. It doddered along, jolting violently over every bump

and drain cover in the road and vibrating terribly as it ticked over at each stop. It was confined to a top speed of 20mph to keep to a long out-of-date timetable. I found the experience – combined with the thought that this was the form of transport to which tramway and railway passengers were forcibly being transferred – most depressing.'

'It's better by bus' was a slogan of the time. The diary does not record what kind of bus it was but it was probably one of Ribble's 15 Leyland Atlanteans with BET design Northern Counties bodies of 1967, as route 555, Lancaster-Keswick, was worked entirely by these buses when they were new.

Council chairman is another steam buff
14 June 1967

'After reporting Sedbergh Rural District Council's Development Committee meeting in the evening, the council chairman, Jack Dawson, a coal merchant in Sedbergh station yard on the Ingleton-Low Gill line, invited me to his home for supper and to see the large scale model of a Black Five railway locomotive he is building.'

Steam ends on the Southern
9 July 1967

'The last BR steam operation south of Crewe ran today on the Waterloo-Bournemouth service following the electrification of the route, thus leaving the north-west of England as the final theatre of steam traction on the national railway system.'

Steamy carnival, Grange-over-Sands
22 July 1967

'I reported the annual summer carnival at Grange-over-Sands. The events were held on a field sloping down to the sea with the Furness Railway coast line across the foot of the field. The highlights of the carnival were two steam freight trains and one steam passenger train, all drawn by Black Fives.'

Anglo-American railway picture show,
Kendal
31 July 1967

I had volunteered to arrange the concert venues and newspaper and poster publicity for two American choirs from Michigan visiting the southern Lake District for the American Festival in Britain, organised by Mr James Jones of Detroit.

'As Mr Jones had said that the festival company would include a number of railfans. I arranged a picture show for them in the Bindloss Room of Kendal Town Hall this evening. I asked Percy Duff, the borough treasurer, and Harry D'Arcy, of Westmorland Hobbies Centre, to contribute to the show with me and the three of us invited our railway friends to see the show and act as hosts to the Americans.

'About 25 Englishmen and 15 Americans came to the show. I was the master of ceremonies and started the show with a selection of 90 lantern slides of British tramcars, followed by 35 slides of British steam trains. Then Percy showed about 35 of his slides of British steam trains, Harry showed his movie films of Southern and LMS steam trains and I ended the show with 35 slides of American streetcars and interurbans and 30 slides of American steam trains on the Norfolk & Western and the Rio Grande systems. Tea and biscuits were served in the interval and two of the Americans, Jack Herr, the bass-baritone soloist, and Mr Jones, made the speeches of thanks.'

**Liverpool to Carlisle
4 August 1967**

'Karl was 3½ years old when I took him with me to record a steam passenger train journey from Liverpool to Carlisle. We went to Liverpool by diesel multiple unit train from Kendal to Oxenholme, diesel locomotive-hauled train to Wigan North Western and diesel multiple unit to Liverpool Lime Street. The line from Wigan to Liverpool was full of character with steep gradients and small, wooden, gas-lit stations, through a fascinating landscape of derelict coal mines surrounded by lovely, rolling, idyllic countryside, stern, black, 19th-century factories crowding the lineside and steaming Black Fives standing in weed-overgrown sidings or emerging from dark places.

'The entry into Liverpool Lime Street was the most dramatic and Wagnerian entry into any station I have ever seen. The four-track railway plunged down through a mile long cutting 20 feet wide between sheer cliffs of soot-blackened, red-sandstone, covered with large patches of moss and dripping water. As the railway descended on a gradient of 1 in 93 and 1 in 83, the cutting rose to a height of nearly 80 feet and some 25 bridges and short tunnels came in an ever quickening succession of graceful, black, stone arches, high enough to accommodate four-decker trains, and the railway seemed entombed in a long, gloomy chasm descending into some underworld like Niflheim [of Norse mythology]. Through a short tunnel we entered Lime Street station, which, despite its modernisation, retains its majestic, wide-span, glazed, twin-arched trainshed on massive, cast-iron columns to form a suitably dramatic terminus and a light, spacious contrast to the dark gulf of the approach. The diesel and electric locomotives that used this cavernous corridor looked very insignificant and unbecoming. Only steam locomotives, which no longer used it, could fill the stage with their rugged grandeur and plumes of smoke.

'Outside Lime Street station Karl and I became embroiled in the hellish nightmare of road traffic hurly-burly and congestion as we rode a corporation bus on its frustratingly slow, stop-start journey to Pier Head. I took Karl on the ferry to Seacombe and back to show him the Mersey shipping but I don't think he appreciated it with the wind and rain in his face and from his stand high above the water on the top deck of a vessel lurching through the swell.

'From Pier Head we walked up to Exchange railway terminus and there was Britannia 70029 *Shooting Star*, waiting to back on to our train, the 1.27pm to Glasgow Central, which ran on Fridays and Saturdays only in the summer. It was a great experience to ride behind a steam locomotive again, especially with the distinctive Britannia chime whistle. The first coach was full of Merseyside railway enthusiasts, who apparently rode this train every Friday throughout the summer. There were several other tape recordists like myself. One of the fans was a Liverpool schoolmaster with a bushy, red beard and wearing an engine driver's cap. He made a practice of standing on the platform ahead of the locomotive, taking a photograph of it starting off with plumes of smoke and steam, then jumping aboard the first coach as the train was moving out of the station!

'I recorded the train (1) leaving Liverpool from Exchange through Sandhills, Kirkdale and Walton Junction, (2) galloping across the flat, open countryside of the south Lancashire plain through Burscough, (3) entering Preston, (4) leaving Lancaster, (5) climbing Shap Fells with the aid of a banker and (6) entering Carlisle Citadel station.

'Karl thoroughly enjoyed the ride and took a great interest in all the steam engine activity, joining in with the other enthusiasts as if he was one of them – as, indeed, he was. As the next train from Carlisle to Oxenholme was late for Karl's bedtime, we went by express coach back to Kendal.'

Part 3 Isle of Man interlude, 1967

I set off on a week's holiday to the Isle of Man to make tape-recordings for a programme called 'Isle of Man Journey': the ship from Liverpool, Douglas horse tramway, the Manx Electric Railway, Ramsey pier tramway and the Isle of Man Railway. Although Karl was only 3½ years old, I took him with me because I thought it would interest him – and I couldn't have been more right. We travelled by Ribble coach to Liverpool and the Isle of Man Steam Packet to Douglas.

Liverpool to Laxey
14 August 1967

'We walked along Liverpool landing stage to the Isle of Man ship *Manx Maid*, of 1962. This is one of the new car ferries and, although it was a steamship, like most modern things it did not make such interesting sounds for my recording as its elder sisters, but the Liver clock, "Great George", chimed in nicely for the 10 o'clock departure. I recorded the steam whistle blasting to signal casting off and the winches hauling in the mooring ropes but the engine room was totally enclosed so that there was no point from which I could record them. As they were steam turbines, not the slightest sound or vibration could be heard or felt as the ship sped through the sea. Although there was a strong wind, it was a following wind and we had a smooth passage.

'On arrival at Douglas pier, Karl wanted me to carry him – but not when he saw the horse trams at the pier entrance. I intended we should have dinner before we went on the trams and, after a sojourn at the horse tram terminus in the middle of the road at Victoria Pier, I had to carry him, struggling, up Victoria Street. After dinner at a restaurant, Karl ran back to the promenade and wanted to run along the 3ft gauge tramlines, fearless of the busy traffic on each side. We rode on a bench next to the driver on a horse tram along the 1½-mile promenade and I recorded it clip-clopping and grinding, from Victoria Pier to Broadway, on the 3ft gauge tracks. The horse tramway ends in a large, Victorian, iron, Dutch barn kind of structure at Derby Castle. Here Karl wanted to get back on a horse tram and ride back – until his interest was diverted by the arrival of a trolley-car and tr iler on the Manx Electric Railway, which erminates alongside the horsecar termin s.

'T e Manx Ele tric Railway is a 3ft gauge, double-trac , electric interurban railwa which run s for 18 miles through the hi ls and woo ed glens along the east coast c the island for 18 miles to Laxey and Ramse . The line was built between 1893 and 1899 and its 25 trolleycars date from 1893 to 1906, so the Manx Electric Railway today bears a remarkable resemblance to the pioneer interurbans of North America of that period with its roadside and cross-country route, its wayside passenger shelters, its former freight service, its mail contract and in its rolling stock: the wooden trolleycars with their clerestory roofs, arched windows, big headlamps, cowcatchers and long wheelbases, the open-sided, cross-bench trailer cars and the mail/freight vans occasionally coupled on the tail end of the trains. [Freight service ended in 1966 and the mail contract in 1975.]

'The line retains a late-Victorian atmosphere and charm with its rustic wooden buildings and seats at some of the

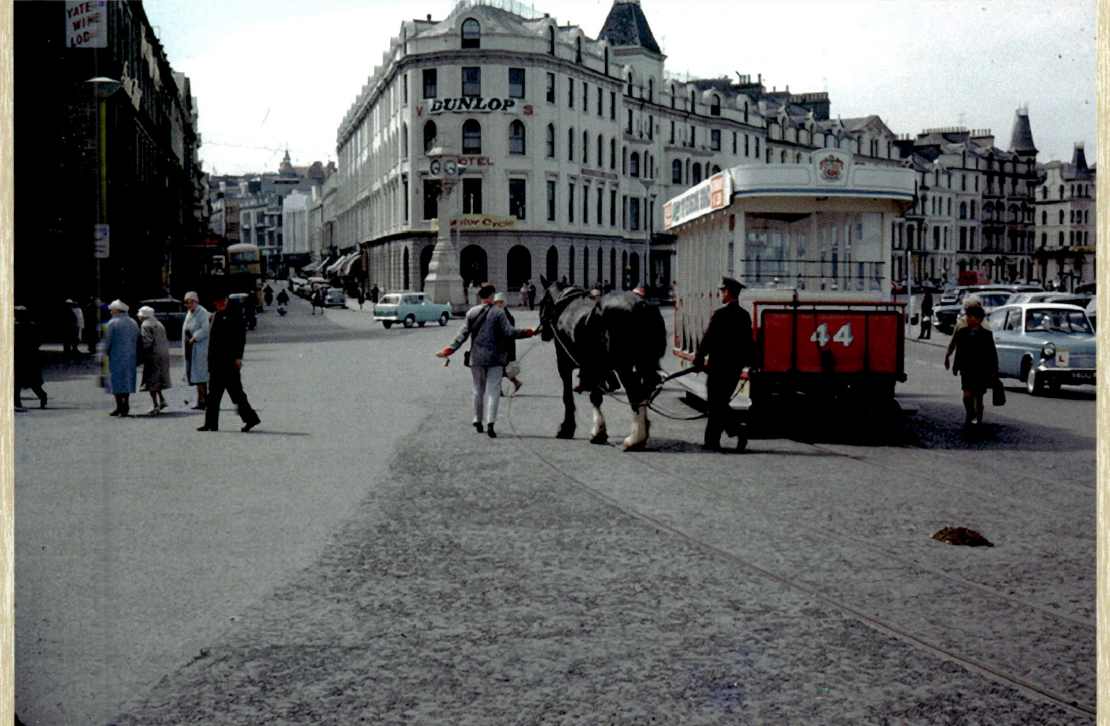

The conductor leads the horse around the tram with the driver holding the drawgear at Victoria Pier terminus, Douglas, on 15 June 1964. Cross-bench car 44, of 1907, carried Queen Elizabeth, the Queen Mother, from Summer Hill to Villa Marina on 5 July 1963, hence the Royal coat of arms on each end of the roof. Victoria Street, the main street of Douglas, is on the left, with a Corporation bus on route 12. The Corporation-owned 3-foot-gauge horse tramway bears right along the promenade for 1¾ miles around Douglas Bay to Derby Castle, where it connects with the Manx Electric Railway.

A horse tram ticket from Victoria Pier to Derby Castle on 22 September 1964, fare 9d.

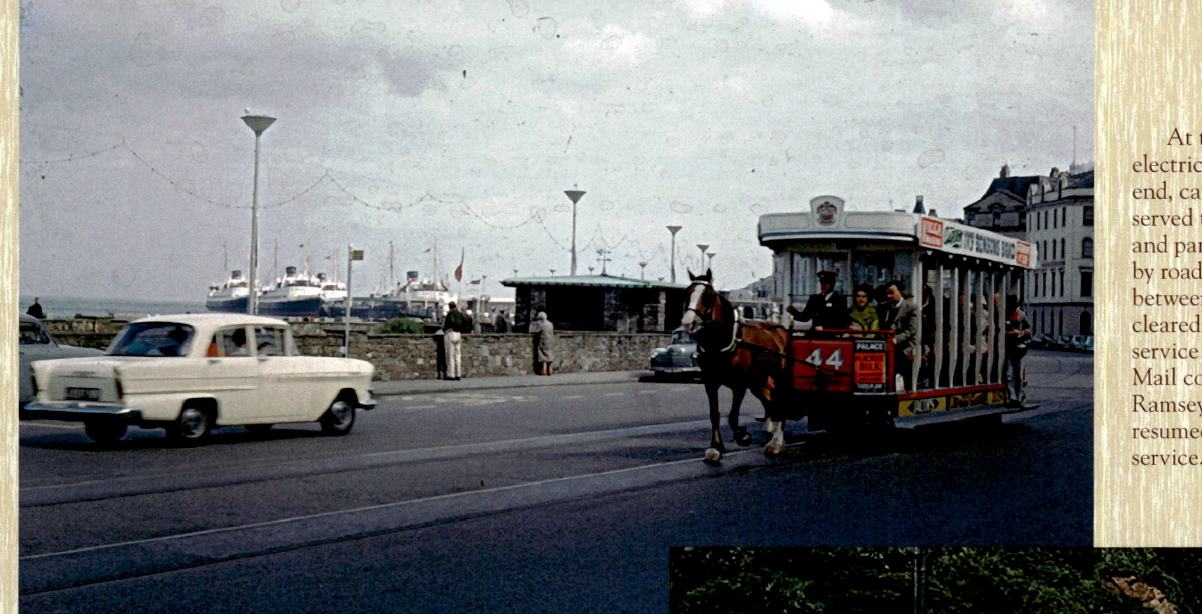

At the time of this photograph, 9 June 1961, electric trains to Ramsey still towed a van at the tail end, carrying goods, mail and parcels. The MER served the east and north of the island with goods and parcels, with off-line collection and delivery by road vans. It also carried GPO locked mailbags between Douglas and Ramsey and conductors cleared lineside postboxes for the GPO. The freight service ended in 1966 and the MER lost the Royal Mail contract in 1975 with the closure of the Laxey-Ramsey section, although service to Ramsey was resumed in 1977 and the railway still offers a parcels service.

Above: Four handsome turbine steamers of the Isle of Man Steam Packet Company are berthed at the pier in the background as horse tram 44 clops and grinds along Loch Promenade on the first stage of its run around Douglas Bay on 15 June 1964.

Right: Derby Castle was the joint terminus where the Douglas Corporation horse tramway met the Manx Electric Railway. An electric train, comprising an 1899 trolley car, a cross-bench trailer and a van, stands at the southern limit of the rails. The large, cast-iron, Dutch barn behind it, known as the Great Canopy, sheltered only the horse trams. It was built in 1896 by the Isle of Man Tramways & Electric Power Company (1894-1900), which bought the horse tramway and built the 18-mile electric railway to Ramsey. All the trolley cars and most of the trailer cars for this line were built by G. F. Milnes at Birkenhead from 1893 to 1903.

stations, the faded blue photographs of the tramway in the waiting room at Laxey, the tall, globular lamps at Laxey and Ramsey stations and the station nameboard at Garwick Glen: "for the beach, smugglers' caves and tea gardens".

'I recorded a ride on board trolleycar 9 of 1894, towing a trailer car, climbing out of Douglas up to Onchan Head with the droning motors resounding against the rock cliffs on our left-hand side and close past the front of a row of shops at Port Jack as it swung into the curve around the headland. The car slumped to a stop at Onchan Head station which was nothing more than a green hut on a grass bank, then we moved on, continuing to climb, though more gradually, past open fields and piecemeal residential development, with beautiful large houses and bungalows overlooking Douglas Bay. We alighted at Howstrake and walked on the road alongside the railway. Karl wanted to get on every tram that passed, whichever direction it was going and

North of Baldrine the MER deviates from the roadside along its own private right of way, still roughly paralleling the main road to Ramsey. A southbound electric train pauses at Garwick Glen station, 'for the beach, smugglers' caves and tea garden'. The date is 16 June 1964. The wooden station buildings, dating from 1895, were demolished in 1979, when the glen and the hotel were closed to the public. Trains no longer stop here.

whether or not we were at a stop, and he tried to push our heavy suitcase across the road towards the tramlines.

'We left the tramway and descended a steep lane down to Port Groudle, a rocky cove. The lane led on to a track, which crossed a wooden footbridge over a rushing river and then narrowed to a footpath, up which we climbed to the overgrown

1ft 11½in gauge line of the Groudle Glen Railway. The line runs for ¾ of a mile through the woods on the north side of the glen and round the top of the sea cliffs to Sea Lion Cove. The railway was built in 1896, last worked in 1962, and is now derelict. The glen terminus is a ramshackle Dutch barn kind of trainshed on timber posts with ornate iron spandrels, half tiled,

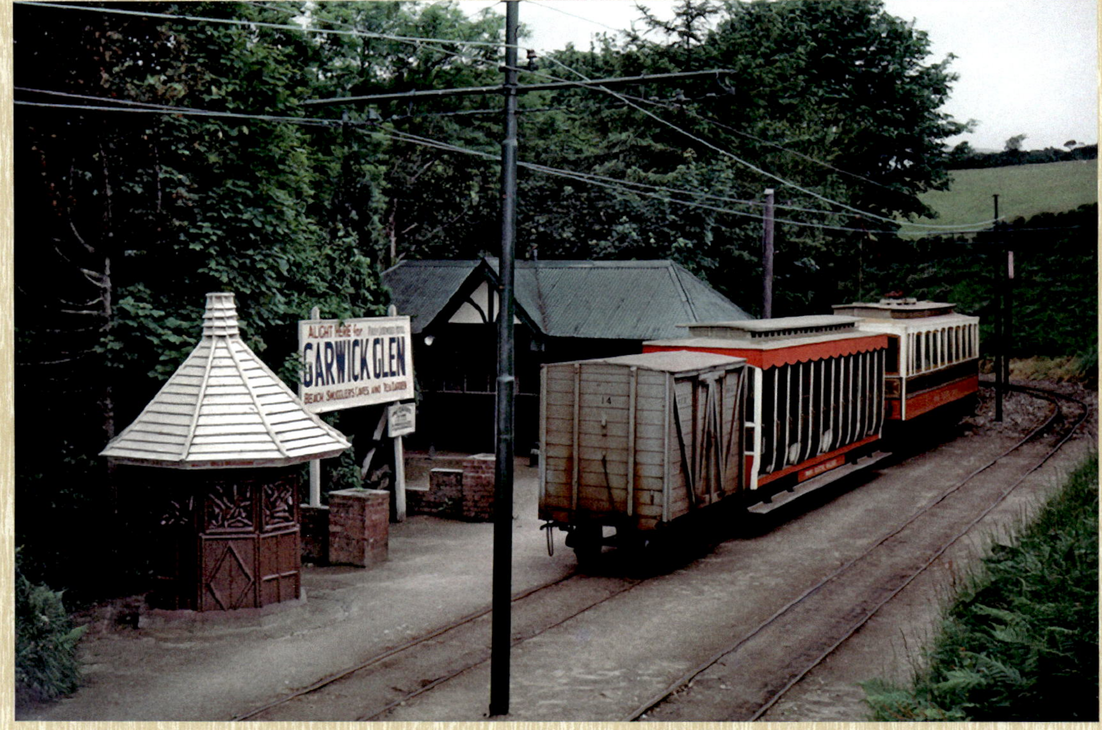

timber-framed gables and spindly bench seats for waiting passengers. The locomotive *Sea Lion* of 1896 stands rusting on rails in a miry pool in a natural shed of bushes and trees. All was intact on my last visit in 1964 but now the carriages, also of 1896, with open sides and tramcar type reversible seats, have been wrecked by vandals, who have burnt down the shed in which most of them were stored and tipped two coaches down the side of an embankment. The railway looked as if it had been sabotaged by an enemy army. [The Groudle Glen railway infrastructure and rolling stock was restored and reopened in 1982-92 with the locomotive *Sea Lion*.]

'We walked up the glen by the footpath alongside the rushing river with roaring waterfalls back to the electric railway at Groudle Glen station. Karl was obviously thrilled to see the railway and overhead wires again and, though tired from his travels, livened up again. I recorded a tram coming through from the north: car 20 of 1899 with a trailer car, with that characteristic groan and clatter, hoving into view

The Groudle Glen Railway is a 1ft 11½in-gauge steam railway that runs for three-quarters of a mile through the wooded glen to the top of the sea cliffs. Two Bagnall 2-4-0 tank engines, *Sea Lion* of 1896 and *Polar Bear* of 1906, were named after main attractions in the original menagerie of animals enclosed in the sea-washed rocky coves, viewed from footbridges. The polar bears were released when this tourist railway closed for the 1914-18 war and the performing sea lions too when the 1939-1945 war closed the railway again.

The quaint charm of this railway was not appreciated by vandals and thieves, whose depredations postponed post-war reopening till 1950 and put the railway out of action again from 1959 till 1961, when it reopened for two seasons. In this photograph on 17 August 1961 we see the locomotive *Polar Bear*, in green livery, arriving at the glen terminus with its train of cross-bench coaches built in 1896-1905 by G. F. Milnes of Birkenhead, the same company that built most of the cars on the Manx Electric Railway.

Advanced decrepitude and havoc closed the glen railway again after 1962 and the two engines went to England. The railway was restored for reopening in 1986. The locomotive *Sea Lion* is back, in its original yellow livery, supplemented by other restored engines, as *Polar Bear* is now working in Amberley Chalk Pits Museum in Sussex. The original Milnes coaches have been rebuilt and accompany both engines at Groudle and Amberley.

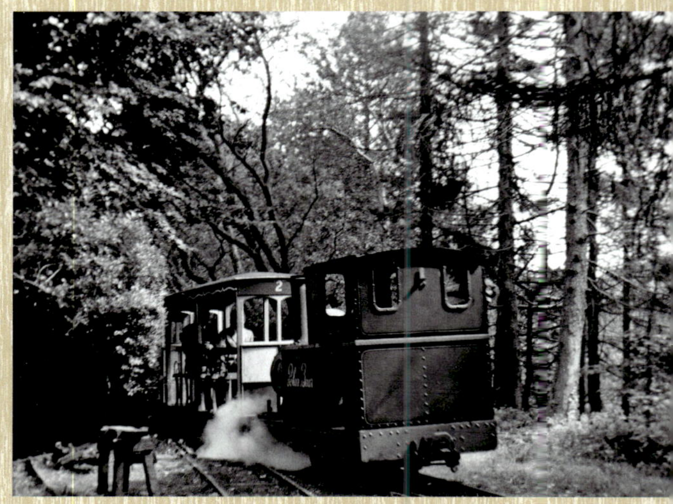

This is the original trainshed at Llen Coan, the inner terminus of the Groudle Glen Railway, on 15 June 1964, two years after closure. It was later demolished to save it from collapse. A replica shed was rebuilt in 1991-93. As before, it doubles as a passenger terminus and carriage shed.

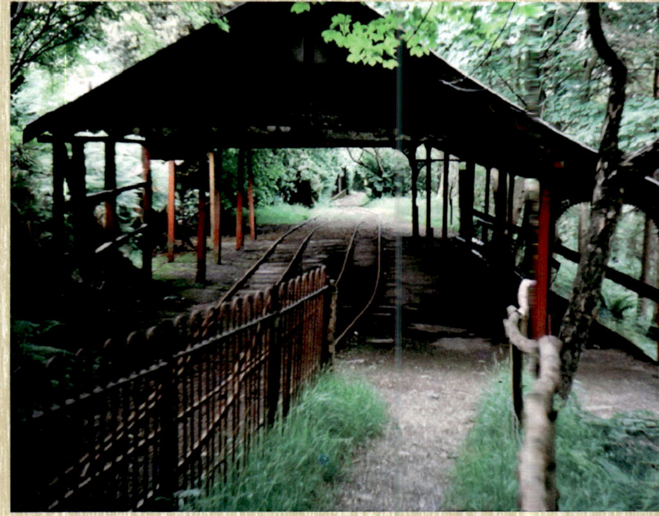

across the crenellated viaduct, stopping with a hiss of brakes at the large, wooden waiting shed, air brake pump churning, then leaving into the distance. We rode the next train north to Laxey, trolleycar 19 of 1899 with a trailer car, and I recorded it winding through Baldrine, stopping at Garwick Glen and climbing up to the next crossing. I was lucky to catch the conductor calling out "Garwick Glen" and a conversation between two elderly Manx passengers.

'Laxey was where I intended we should stay while we were on the island and we found bed and breakfast accommodation in a tall, grey house on Laxey New Road right behind Laxey tram shed. The accommodation was pleasant, clean, comfortable and hospitable with unrivalled views of the tramway around Laxey Glen, and every evening and morning I could hear the hiss on the trolley wire, the clatter of wheels on the rail joints, the droning motors and the squeal of flanges as the tramcars passed below and negotiated the bends through the village and climbed the far side of the glen. I later found that the landlady's husband was a tram driver!'

Laxey village nestles in Laxey Glen with Snaefell (2,034 feet) in the background in this classic Manx Electric Railway view with car 22 of 1899, towing a cross-bench trailer and van, droning up the 1 in 40 gradient to South Cape on 18 June 1964.

Snaefell to Ramsey
15 August 1967

'Next morning, from our bedroom window, I recorded the first northbound train, the 7am 'boat car' from Douglas, passing through Laxey at 7.30. This was trolleycar 20 of 1899 with a cross-bench trailer car and a mail van in tow. Above the sound of the rushing Laxey river the train could be heard distinctly in the otherwise still, early morning air with no motor traffic about. It stopped at Laxey car shed request stop below our bedroom window with a hiss of air brakes and moved on across the viaduct into Laxey station with a characteristic electric

traction drone. Next the glen was filled with the echo of the train clattering over the rail joints as it began its ascent along the far side of the glen.

'Laxey station, with its clumps of stunted palm trees and rustic wooden waiting room and café, is set in a glade of tall trees of cawing rooks. This is the junction for the branch line up Snaefell. Karl was fascinated by the electric tramcars. He smiled and pointed at each one that passed and waved it goodbye. He was particularly fascinated by the short-working reversal ritual at Laxey station, where the trolleycar uncoupled from the trailer, moved forward beyond the upper crossover, the conductor swung round

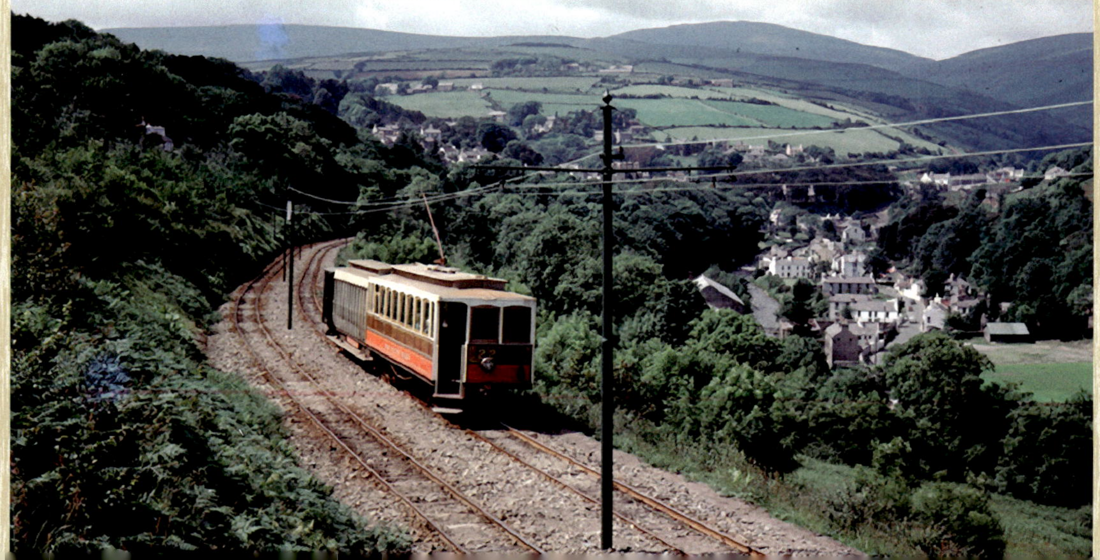

the trolleypole, the car then reversed over the crossover and down the opposite line beyond the lower crossover, the conductor released the brakes on the trailer car and let it run by gravity over the lower crossover and the two cars were coupled up again. Sometimes Karl lay flat on this tummy to watch the wheels go round.

'From Laxey station we rode in a tramcar on the 3ft 6in gauge, 4½-mile branch line up Laxey Glen and Snaefell to a terminus at 1,990 feet, 44 feet below the summit, with wonderful views of hills, glens, plains and coasts over the length and breadth of the island. This highest point on the Isle of Man is disgustingly littered with a scruffy restaurant, café and gift shop, surrounded by crates of empty bottles. Karl didn't like the wind up here so we went in the restaurant for dinner but I didn't subscribe to the restaurant because it did not display a menu nor anything to say how much the one set dinner would cost, so we took the next tram down the fell. While we were queuing for it, patches of cloud passed close over and around the summit and the woman in front of us in the queue asked her husband where all the smoke was coming from!

'My on-board recording of the Snaefell tramcar starting the ascent suffered from some kind of electrical interference so I replaced it with a trackside recording by the

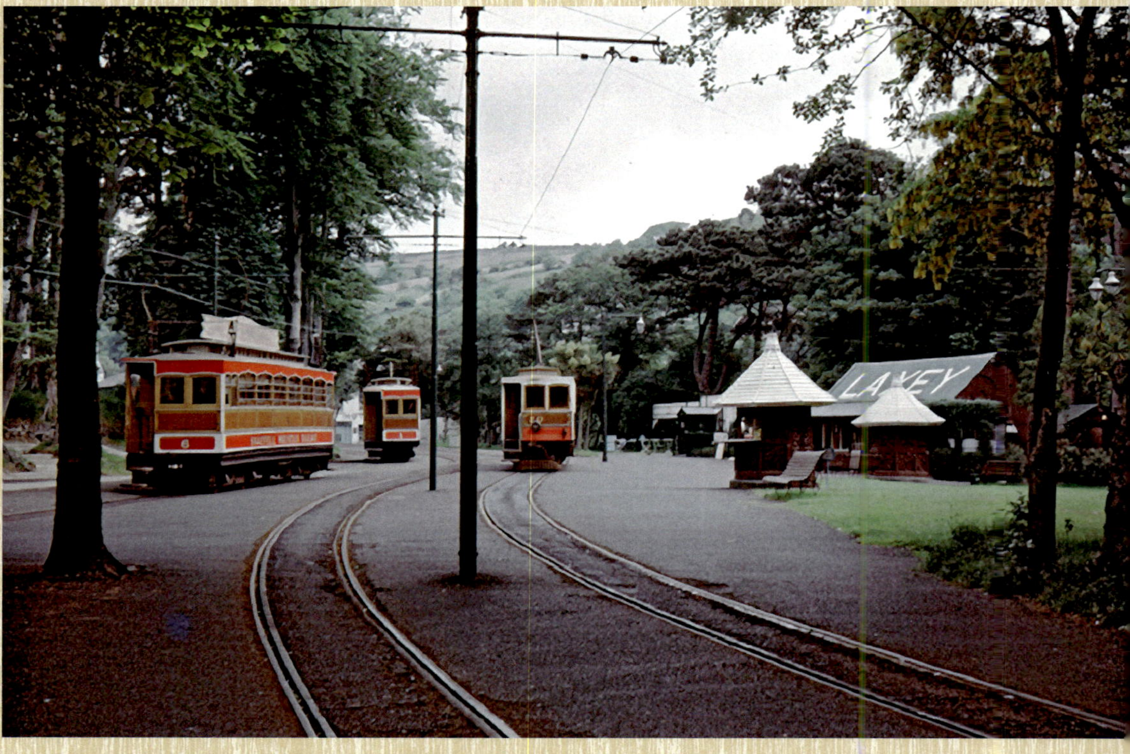

Laxey station, with its rustic wooden buildings of 1899 in a glade of cawing rooks, is the junction for Snaefell. Passengers can change here from the 3-foot-gauge MER tracks in the centre to the 3ft 6in-gauge depot of a car starting the ascent from Laxey station until it was out of earshot up the fell. While the Snaefell tram climbs up into bleak, windy moors and low clouds, to me

Snaefell Mountain Railway on the left. Here on 16 June 1964 is MER car 20 of 1899 and Snaefell cars 1 and 6 of 1895.

the Manx Electric main line between Laxey and Ramsey is more scenic and interesting, leaving the road and winding through beautiful, rich-green countryside, past great, cloud-capped hills and through wooded glens with wide views of the sea from high elevations.

'We rode an open-sided, cross-bench trailer car, No 40, of 1930, behind trolleycar 19 of 1899 from Laxey to Ballaskeig Beg and I recorded the run from Dhoon Glen to Dhoon church at Glen Mona. At Ballaskeig Beg I made a trackside recording of a passing northbound train, trolleycar 6 with a trailer car. Then we rode the next train to Dreemskerry, where I recorded a southbound car 6 of 1899 and a trailer car stopping at this halt on a steep lane crossing among trees. We rode on the front bench next to the motorman on an open-sided cross-bench trolleycar from Dreemskerry to Ballure, where I recorded the next northbound train crossing the steel truss viaduct and the adjacent main road into Ramsey.

'We walked down the road into town and, while we were eating sandwiches on a seat in Queen's Drive, I recorded trolleycar 20 of 1899 and a trailer

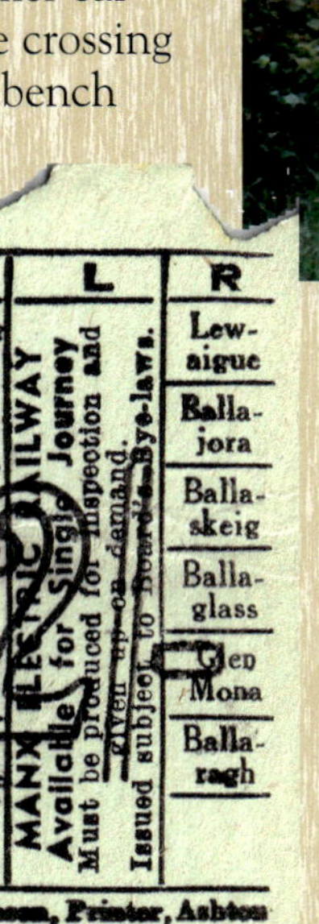

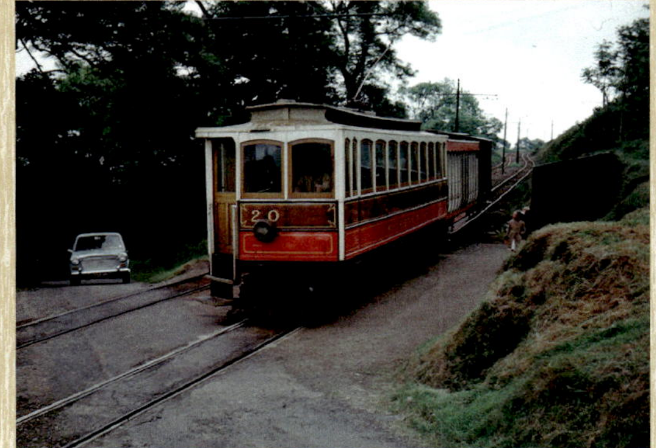

Above: A northbound MER train passes the crossing and request stop at Ballasholaigue between Dhoon Glen and Glen Mona on 17 June 1964.

Right: A Manx Electric Railway train stops at Dreemskerry to drop home-coming school children from Glen Mona on 17 June 1964. Winter saloon trolleycar 20 of 1899 is heading an 1899 cross-bench trailer car and a mail/parcels van.

Left: A Manx Electric Railway ticket from Ramsey to Douglas on 21 September 1964, fare 2s. The fare stages are printed on each side.

car traversing the only grooved rail section on the whole line, on a grass reservation alongside Walpole Road. [When the track was laid in 1899 the Ramsey Commissioners wanted to pave the full width of the road to include the tramway but this has never been done.]

'Then we caught the next tram back to Laxey and as we walked into the boarding house the landlady's husband recognised us as the front seat passengers he drove from Dreemskerry to Ballure. He said he enjoyed his work as a tram driver even though he often had to work long hours in summer, sometimes from 7am to 10pm. He used to be a freight train guard on British Railways at Garston, Liverpool, but he said he would not go back to the mainland because here he had the railway, the countryside and the sea and he couldn't wish for anything more.

'That night I sat by Laxey tram shed watching the late trains passing through the wooded glen. Each train was a small oasis of dim light and Victoriana, like a ghost from the past, hissing along the overhead wire between the dark trees.'

Electric, petrol and steam railways at Ramsey
16 August 1967

'I took Karl on an electric train from Laxey to Ramsey, where I recorded the reversal ritual in the terminal yard, concluding my recordings of the electric railway and the first side of the tape. Trolleycar 20, of 1899, uncoupled, moved forward and reversed

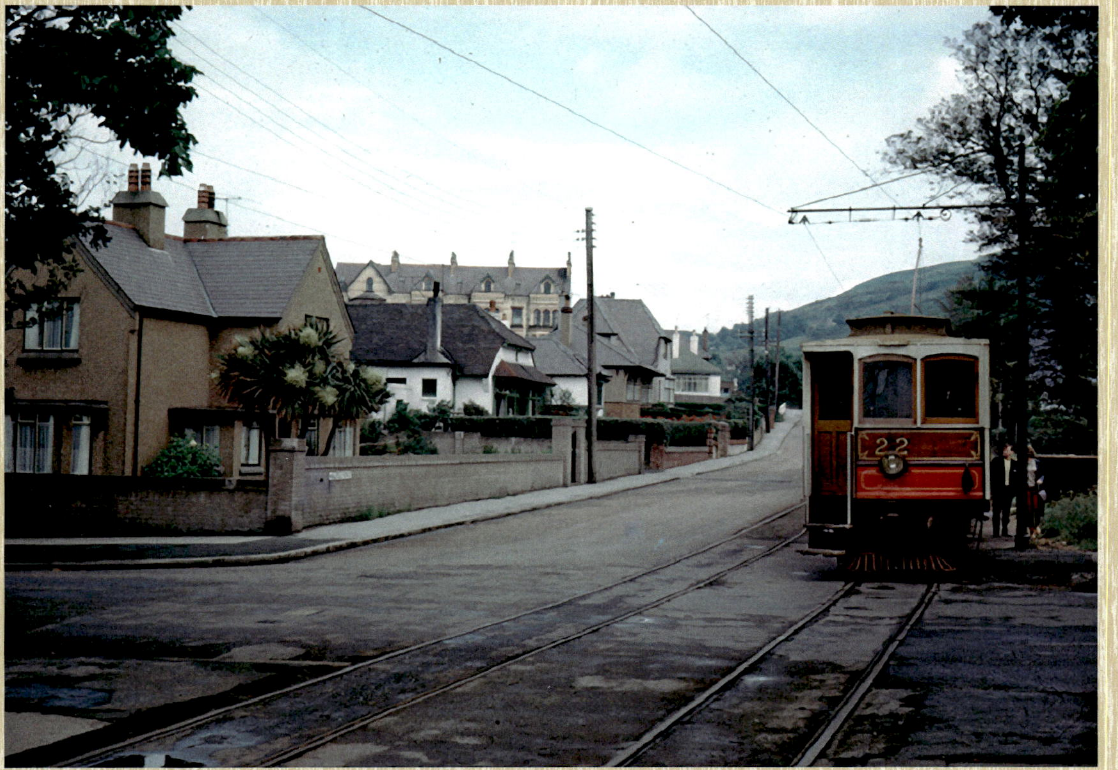

The only conventional tramway section on the 18-mile Manx Electric Railway is the 100-yard stretch of grooved rail with side traction poles alongside Walpole Road and across Queen's Drive in Ramsey. Trolley car 22 of 1899 stops on the corner of Queen's Drive on 17 June 1964. When the line was laid in 1899, Ramsey Commissioners planned to pave the full width of Walpole Road but the rails still run along a turfed roadside reservation. A private right of way behind the houses on Waterloo Road led to the terminal yard at Ramsey (Plaza), beside the cinema, now gone, on Albert Street.

through the crossover, the trailer car rolled by gravity past the crossover and the trolley car ran down through the crossover and coupled up to the trailer car.

'I started the second side of the tape with a short recording of the 3ft gauge tramway on Queen's Pier, Ramsey, operated by the Isle of Man Harbour Board. I recorded the small, 10-seater, Wickham petrol tramcar from the trackside shelters at the passing loop halfway along the pier, where it has to slow down to take the curves. There is also a Planet diesel locomotive that draws a passenger car, four flatcars and a van for the luggage along the ¼-mile pier in connection with the Belfast and Ardrossan ships. [The steamers ceased to call at Ramsey after 1970 and the tramway closed in 1981. The pier is now closed and derelict.]

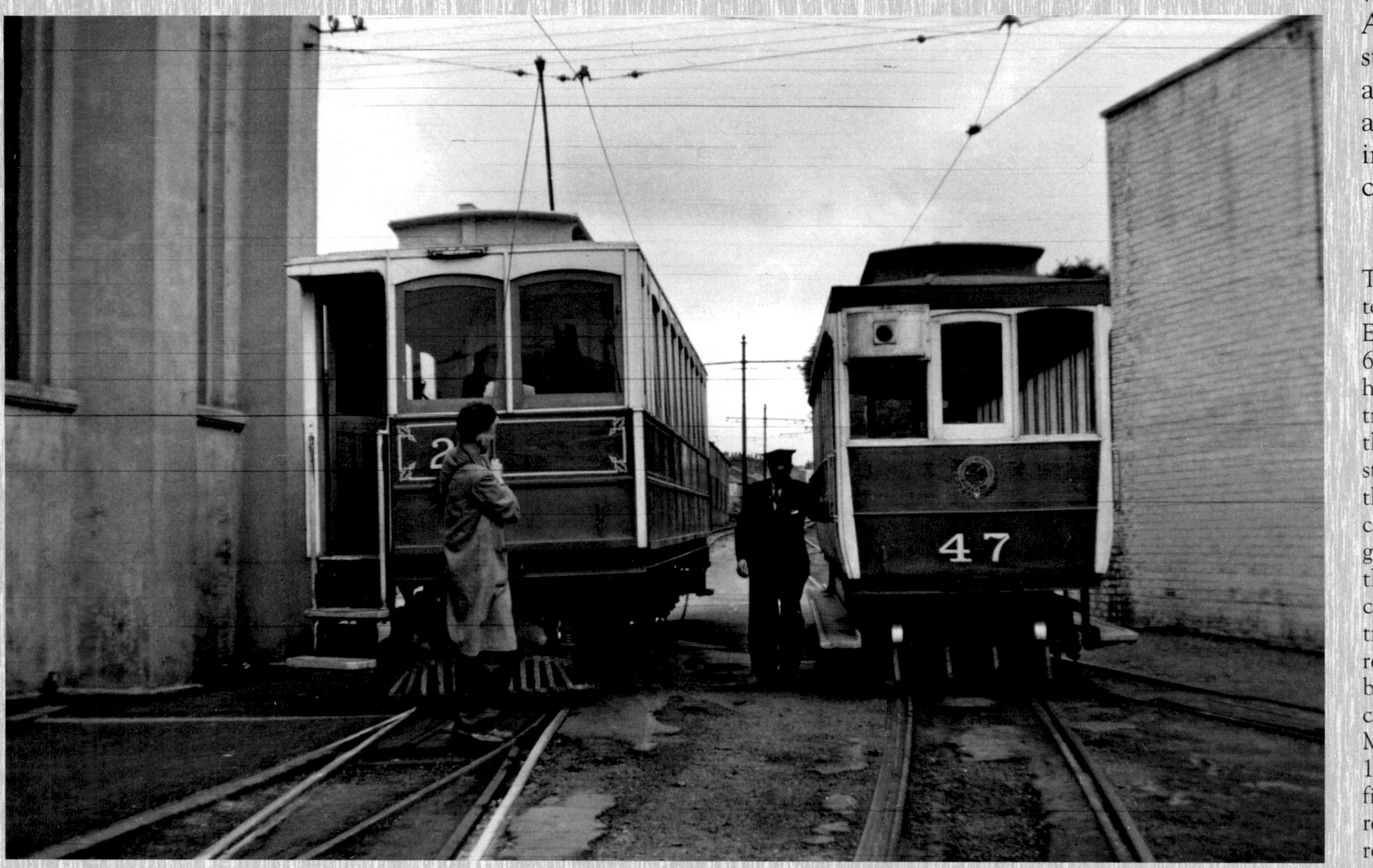

The reversal ritual at Ramsey terminus of the Manx Electric Railway is seen on 6 June 1961. Trolleycar 22 has uncoupled from the trailer car and crossed to the southbound track. The stationmaster has released the handbrakes on the cross-bench trailer to run by gravity down the slope to the end of the line while the conductor waits to turn the trolleypole from car 22 to reverse on the crossover and back down on to the trailer car. Both cars were built by Milnes at Birkenhead in 1899. Car 22 was gutted by fire in 1990 and completely rebuilt as an exact replica to return to service in 1992.

'The rest of the programme on the second side of the tape was on the Isle of Man Railway. We went to Ramsey railway terminus to see the timetable. The station looked derelict but a train was expected.

Incredibly, there appeared a cloud of steam in the distance along the 3ft gauge single line and a quaint locomotive, beautifully restored in the original IMR green livery, with full lining-out and shining brass dome

and nameplate, materialised at the head of a short train of archaic, hobbling, wooden carriages and came trundling slowly into the station. I'd missed the Irish narrow gauge but this was just as good.

Queen's Pier, Ramsey, was built by the Isle of Man Harbour Board in 1881-86, projecting from the foot of Queen's Drive, and reaching 717 yards – nearly half a mile – out into the bay to meet the Isle of Man company's ships plying between Douglas, Belfast

and Ardrossan. The 3-foot-gauge pier tramway was worked by a 1937 Planet diesel locomotive with a passenger coach (on the left of this view), four flatcars and a van. augmented in 1950 by a 10-seat Wickham petrol tramcar, which also provided the

residual service at quieter times between ships to carry promenaders and anglers. The Wickham car is seen at the pier tollhouse carrying the headboard reading 'Isle of Man Harbour Board tram to pierhead, singe fare 4d, children 2d'. Ferries ceased to call at Ramsey after 1970, the tramway continued in service till 1981, and the pier closed in 1991. Restoration work on the derelict structure began in 2011.

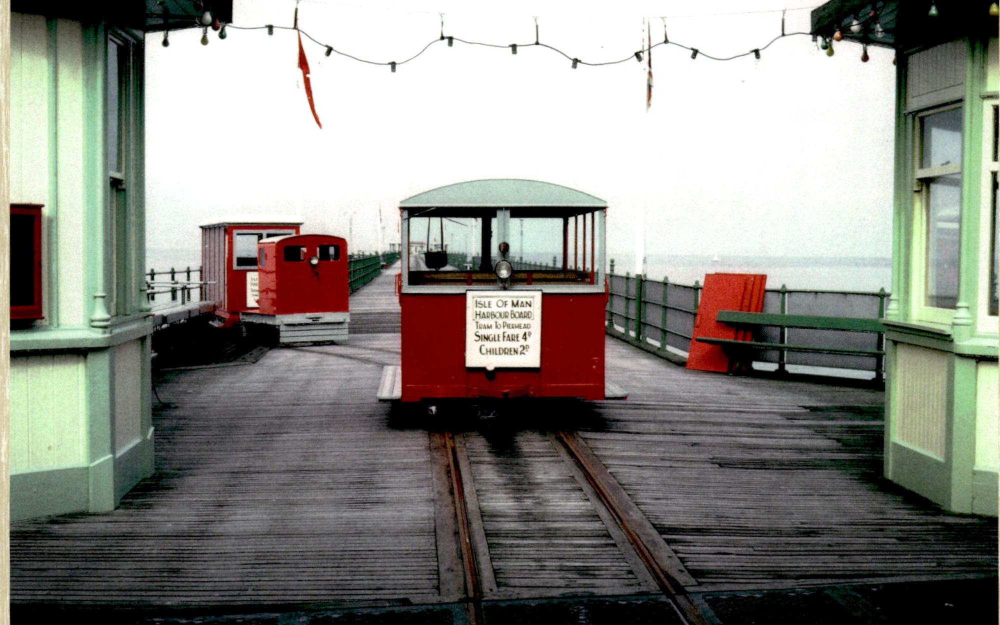

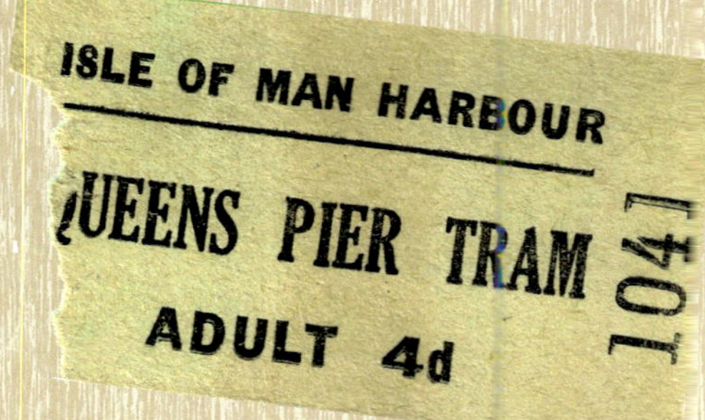

A ticket for the Queen's Pier tram from pier toll to pier head on 17 June 1964, fare 4d.

Opposite: The afternoon train hobbles slowly into Ramsey terminus, Isle of Man Railway, behind 2-4-0 tank engine No 11 *Maitland* on 16 August 1967. The IMR is 3-foot gauge, like the MER, but there was no connection between the two. Karl, then 3½, is on the left. The Ramsey line closed in 1968.

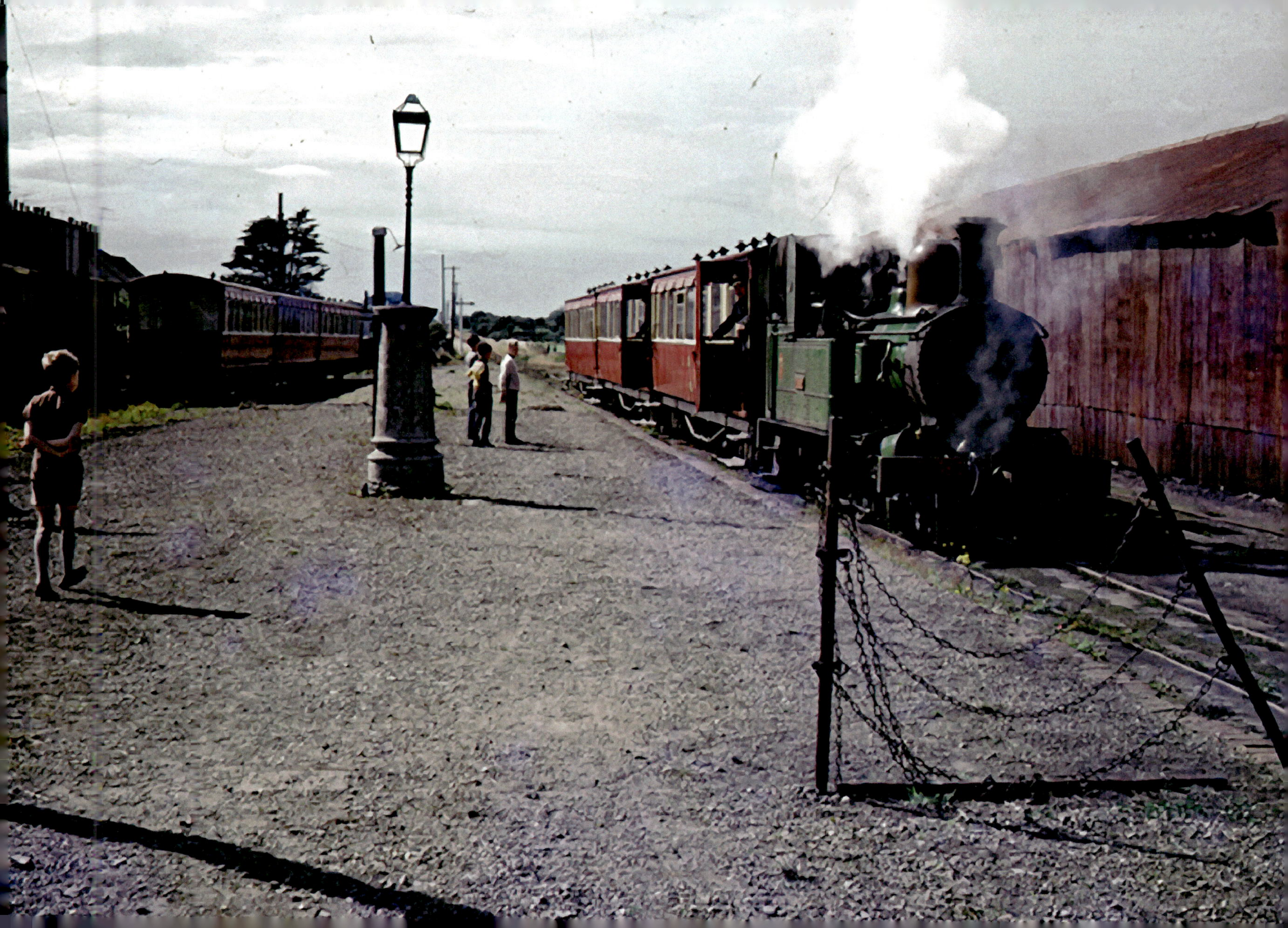

Maitland, built by Beyer, Peacock in 1905, stands outside the slate-stone engine shed at Ramsey on the same day. At this time the locomotives were restored in the original IMR green livery of the period 1873-1944. The domes were always of polished brass.

Until the 1950s the Ramsey train engine used to shunt the harbour sidings during the lay-over between passenger trains. A siding in Ramsey station yard extended across Bowring Road on the level and along Derby Road and West Quay. The Ramsey harbour extension was used to export lead from the Foxdale mines branch and import Cumberland coal, building materials and animal feed. The harbour line closed in 1954.

'We then went by bus from Ramsey to Sulby to record the same engine – No 11 *Maitland*, a 2-4-0 tank engine, built in 1905 – returning with the afternoon train from Ramsey to Douglas, stopping in Sulby Glen station with clanking, loose couplings and loose rail joints, then chuffing off into the distance. We returned by bus to Ramsey and by tramcar to Laxey.'

Douglas to Port Erin
17 August 1967

'I took Karl by electric tramcar from Laxey to Douglas (Derby Castle), by horse tramcar from Derby Castle to Victoria Pier and, after dinner in Douglas, we went on the 2.05pm steam train from Douglas to Castletown, which I recorded all the way.

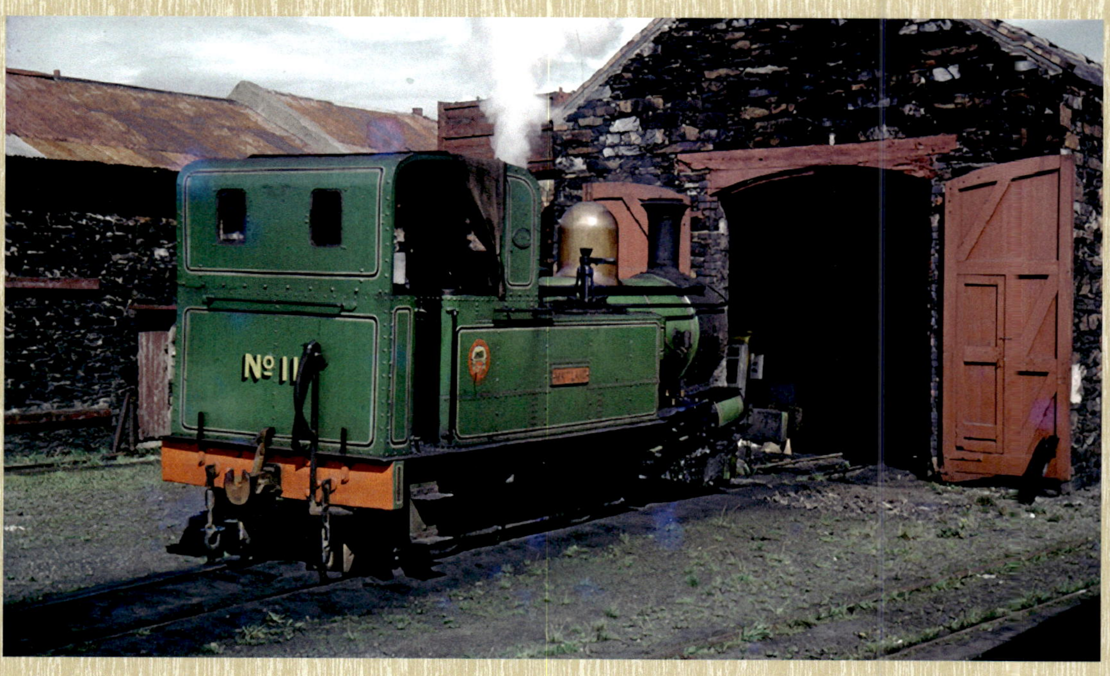

'Apart from when we were on the horse tramway, Karl seemed rather tired and bored in Douglas but as soon as we entered Douglas railway terminus we became animated and happy. The station was a haven of peace after the busy traffic in the streets of Douglas. There were eight or nine lines of carriages in the platform bays and sidings and three shiny green locomotives coaling-up and raising steam outside the loco-sheds. This was the year when the

railway enthusiast the Marquis of Ailsa took a lease of the IMR, re-engaged the staff and reopened the lines from Douglas to Castletown, Peel and Ramsey, a total of 39 miles, over a year after complete closure at the end of the 1965 summer season. Things were very different at Douglas station under the new regime. Whereas under the strict regime of the old company the railway enthusiast was almost arrested if he stepped off the end of the platform to take

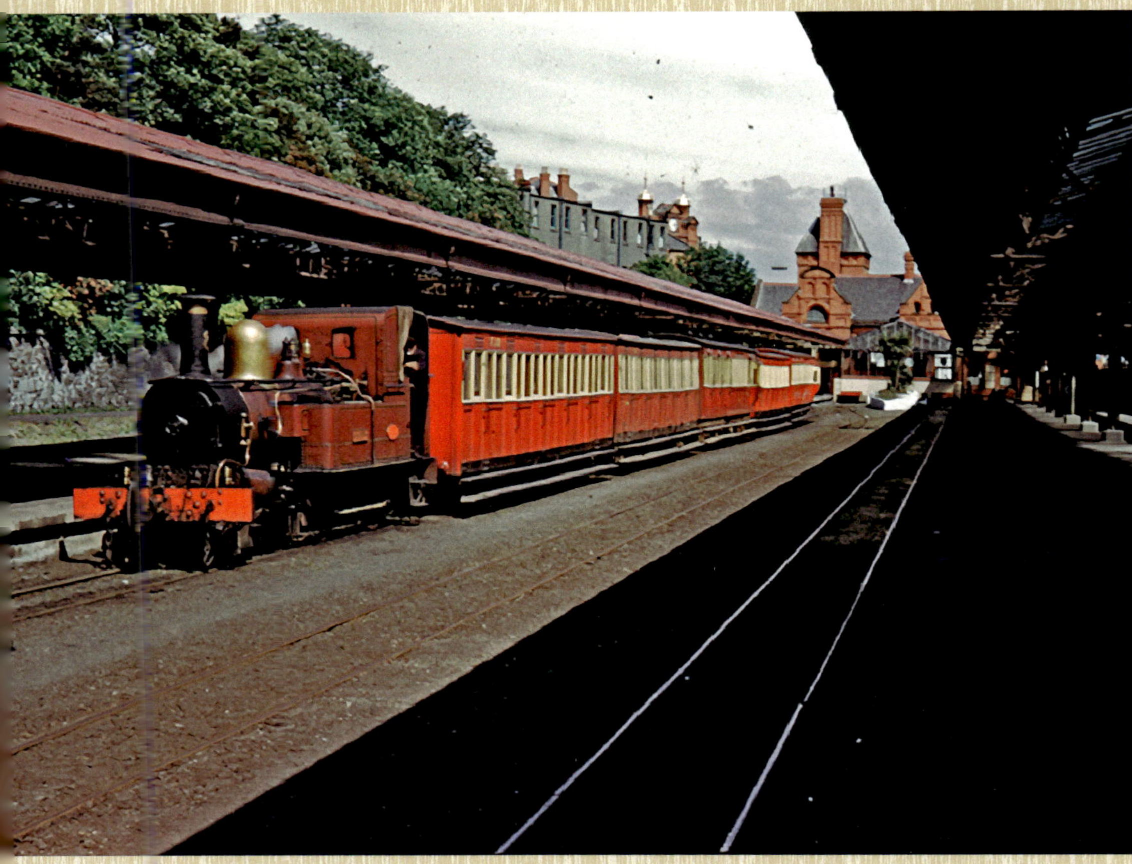

Douglas station, with its substantial glazed-redbrick buildings, golden cupolae and extensive canopies, was the central terminus of the Isle of Man Railway's three lines to Peel, Port Erin and Ramsey. The train in the station is headed by 2-4-0 tank engine No 11 *Fenella* of 1884, in the Indian red livery of the period 1944-65, with copper-capped chimney and brass dome. The date is 7 June 1961. Since the closure of the Peel and Ramsey lines the number of platforms at Douglas has been reduced and they have lost their canopies.

a photograph, now we were free to wander anywhere across the tracks and into the loco-sheds and workshops.

'Locomotive No 10 G. *H. Wood*, a 2-4-0 tank engine of 1905 [named after the General Manager and Secretary of the railway company from 1876 to 1903], backed on to our train for Castletown. I recorded the journey from an open window of the first carriage behind the locomotive. We stormed up the 1 in 65 gradient out of Douglas, the exhaust echoing in the surrounding woods. The archaic, wooden carriages rocked and clattered along the undulating, overgrown 3ft gauge at a cracking pace with long whistles, making the herds of grazing cattle stampede as if the trains were so rare they had never got used to them. Although it was running late, the train sojourned unnecessarily long in intermediate stations at Port Soderick and Ballasalla while the guard chatted to the driver.

'We clanked into Castletown's ground-level station in a glade of trees and a special bus was laid on to meet the train and take passengers on to Colby, Port St Mary and Port Erin, where the railway used to extend beyond Castletown. Karl and I were the only passengers on the bus and we were going to Port Erin so the bus went straight there. I verbally concluded my "Isle of Man

Journey" programme on the sandy shore at Port Erin with the gentle waves and the gulls. We returned on the special bus back to Castletown and the train – this time the ex-County Donegal diesel railcars with clanking coupling rods on the driving wheels – back to Douglas. We rode Corporation buses to Victoria Pier and Summer Hill and an electric train back to Laxey. In the evening I recorded my verbal introduction to the Isle of Man programme on Laxey shore with the waves crashing on the shingle.'

Next day Karl and I left the island by bus from Laxey to Douglas and by the 1927 steamship *Ben-my-Chree* from Victoria Pier to Liverpool. It was a rough passage for the first 2 hours or more but smooth into Liverpool Bay and the Mersey under lowering skies.

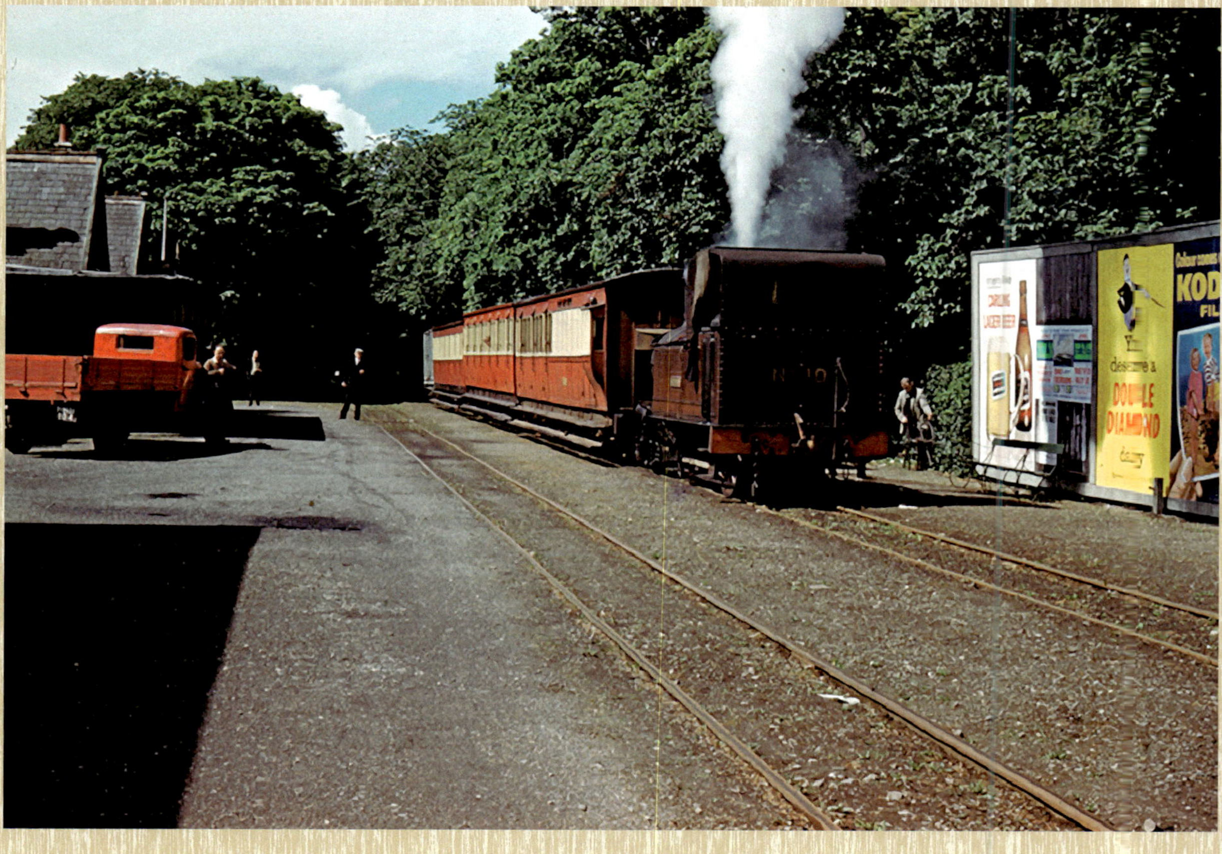

Castletown station on the Port Erin line had no platforms when this photograph was taken on 8 June 1961, with an up mixed passenger and freight train for Douglas, headed by 2-4-0 tank engine No 10 G. *H. Wood* of 1905. The train and the stationmaster are awaiting the late arrival of the down train to Port Erin to pass on the loop. An IMR lorry is standing by for onward delivery of freight and parcels. The locomotive was named after the IMR Manager and Secretary from 1873 to 1903.

The Douglas-Port Erin line is now the only survivor of the former IMR system and Castletown station now has low-level platforms.

Part 4 The demise of steam, 1967 – 1968

As diesel and electric traction progressively took over, it became clear that steam's last role, like its first role, was as a freight hauler. British Railways kept extending the deadline for steam-rostered passenger trains, month by month, owing to the shortage of serviceable diesel locomotives and multiple units, until March 1968, but even then, up here in the remote north-western fells, far from Euston, steam soldiered on. The last steam passenger train on the Windermere branch ran on 29 July 1968, only five days before the end of steam on freight.

In the last months of steam traction there were only six classes of steam locomotive extant: the British Railways Standard Class 4, Class 5, Class 7 ('Britannia') and the heavy freight Class 9 2-10-0, and two ex-LMS classes, the 'Black Five' mixed-traffic 4-6-0 and the Class 8 freight 2-8-0. These two LMS types, dating from the mid-1930s, were a tribute to their designer, Sir William Stanier, who also designed the recently retired 'Jubilees', 'Princess Royals' and 'Princess Coronations' and the rebuilt 'Royal Scots'.

Oxenholme to Windermere
30 August 1967

'I re-recorded the journey by steam passenger train from Oxenholme to Windermere. A previous recording I made on August 25th was perfect but the locomotive did not whistle once and no station names were called. This time I asked the porter at Oxenholme to do his traditional call in his stentorian voice as the down train rolled into the station. He put on a wonderful performance for me: "Windermere train… Kendal, Burneside, Staveley, Windermere … Oxenholme … Oxenholme … Oxenholme … Oxenholme, next stop Kendal."

'I was recording continuously from the entry of the train into Oxenholme to the arrival at Windermere, so before joining the train I walked up to the engine, Black Five 45331, and handed the driver a note asking him to give me some good whistles in the right places on the way. He did blow the whistle – the deep, gruff, Stanier whistle – before starting from each station and for the level crossings but they were brief, restrained whistles – in contrast to the long North American steam whistles.

'I recorded the journey from the first windows in the vestibule of the leading carriage. Here were all the traditional sounds of a journey by steam train with the clickety-clack of the carriage wheels on the 60ft lengths of track and the engine puffing and snorting. There was a lengthy stop in Kendal for parcels [foreshortened on the CD] and quiet pauses at rural Burneside and Staveley. As we slowed for the descent into Windermere terminus, with the panorama of fells in the background, my recording picked up the shrill whistle of a shepherd to his sheepdog in an adjacent field. As we slid into the platform the porter called "Windermere" and I continued the recording until it was completed by the porter saying "Thank you" as I handed in my ticket.'

Last steam passenger trains on the Windermere branch?
1 September 1967

'This was said to be the last day of steam passenger trains on the Windermere branch, the last country branch line on British Railways with steam traction. After the summer services finished the following day there were to be no more steam passenger trains on British Railways, apart from railway enthusiasts' specials. Trains which were drawn by steam locomotives on the Windermere branch from Mondays to Fridays were usually drawn by diesel locomotives on Saturdays, when the reduction in freight traffic made more diesels available. Today the last steam train on the Windermere branch was the 9.20am from Oxenholme, returning from Windermere at 11am. I watched it stopping at Staveley station at 11.06am. In the afternoon I recorded the last steam passenger train from Liverpool to Glasgow rushing north on the main line through Oxenholme station, headed by Britannia 70045 *Lord Rowallan* without banking assistance for the fells ahead.'

**A 9F on the yard and a railfan signalman
8 September 1967**

'When I went down to Kendal goods yard to record some steam freight movements, I found a large class 9F 2-10-0 doing the honours and I got some good recordings of its wheels slipping and flanges squealing and the wagons creaking and moaning and groaning and squealing. Then I went up into the signal cabin and found that the

signalman, John Gardner, of Sedbergh, was a railway enthusiast, who photographed steam trains, sometimes abandoning his cabin to do so, then dashing back to his post. He was formerly signalman at Grayrigg and Ais Gill. His wife ran a boarding house and a great many of their guests were railway enthusiasts from south-east England who came up here photographing and recording the last of steam traction on the Leeds-Carlisle and Lancaster-Carlisle lines.'

**Another last steam train on the
Windermere branch
9 September 1967**

'I saw what was again said to be the last steam passenger train on the Windermere branch. As the official deadline for steam passenger workings had passed and it was a Saturday, most people expected that the 11am from Windermere to London would be diesel-hauled to Crewe. I was sitting on Oxenholme station writing the draft of an article on the Windermere line for the *Evening Post* when the signal went off and up from the branch line appeared Britannia 70045 *Lord Rowallan* at the head of the train, the same locomotive as I had recorded hauling the last steam train from Liverpool to Glasgow through Oxenholme eight days before. In the 90 minutes I was there I also

saw two up steam freights and two down on the main line.'

**Finalising 'The Long Drag' programme
12 October 1967**

'Another day up on the Settle-Carlisle line, this time to conclude my tape programme "The Long Drag". I had so far recorded northbound trains from Selside to Ais Gill. Today I recorded a southbound freight, "Long Meg", climbing the 1 in 100 gradient up Mallerstang. "Long Meg" was the heaviest train on the "Drag", a twice-daily load of anhydrite from Long Meg quarry in Cumberland to Widnes chemical works. In latter years it has always been hauled by a BR standard class 9F and this one was 92208. As it approached the exhaust echoed against the scar on Wild Boar Fell, high above the line on the west side. In the still air I was able to record the train far into the distance towards Ais Gill summit.

'Then I took more photographs at the north end of Blea Moor tunnel, Blea Moor sidings, Ribblehead viaduct and Selside signal cabin. I also took pictures of George Horner at Salt Lake Cottages and Bill Sharpe at Ribblehead station.'

Railway wreck on Grayrigg bank
19 October 1967

'At night I went to see a railway wreck that blocked the LNW main line at Docker. A BR standard class 4 tender engine, 75043, on banking duty and returning light, tender first, from Grayrigg to Oxenholme, had run into a stationary engineers' coach, which was crushed between the banker and the 8F, 48381, to which it was coupled, and reared up on one end. A man in the engineer's coach was badly injured and the two locomotive tenders were derailed. When I went to the scene, between 10 and 11pm, a steam crane and five steam locomotives – the two involved in the accident and three Black Fives in attendance – stood hissing quietly in the darkness; one would not have thought steam traction was dying out on British Railways. Workmen went quietly about their business in the light of lamps.'

'My Merseyside' no more
31 October 1967

I originally bought the tape recorder to capture the sounds I remembered of my boyhood on Merseyside. I recorded the second steam train into Birkenhead Woodside on 4 March as an introduction to a new tape programme to be called 'My Merseyside'. On 4 May I rode Vintora from Kendal to Birkenhead to continue the programme. Owing to many inconceivable technical difficulties and re-recording sequences several times to get what I wanted, I only succeeded in recording the sounds of buses turning and unloading outside the station and ferry entrance, the echoes of tramping feet and clicking turnstiles inside the ferry tollhouse and the clattering gangways and churning wake of the diesel ferry crossing to Liverpool. There was no time to venture into the city before I was due to visit Allan Clayton at New Brighton in the evening and return home to Kendal that night.

On 31 October 1967 I wrote:
'I've decided not to proceed any further with "My Merseyside" tape programme because there are now hardly any sounds of my Merseyside left to record. I recorded steam into Woodside a few days before steam finished on that service but the buses don't sound as guttural as when I lived there in 1949-52, the ferries are no longer steam but diesel, the streets of Liverpool are much noisier with motor traffic and there are no longer any tramcars on the Pier Head or main streets nor any horse waggons, steam lorries or saddle-tank engines trundling along the dock road – only diesel buses, diesel lorries and diesel dock engines, and these engines no longer run along the central and southern sections of the dock road because the southern docks are now served by lorries.

'The traditional sounds of Liverpool streets, with the street newsvendors shouting "Echo, Express!" against the ringing tramcars, can no longer be heard. All the newsvendors have kiosks or stands and don't shout any more – and, of course, the tramcars have gone. In the residential back streets and bombed sites of the inner suburbs the children no longer play traditional street games with songs and chants on chalked flagstones.

'The old wooden electric trains no longer thunder along the Liverpool Overhead Railway or through the Mersey tunnel to Birkenhead. The Overhead Railway has gone and there are more modern, quiet electric trains on the Mersey Railway [although I did record these in 1969 for my 'Vintage Voltage' programme]. The traditional dramatic bus exodus from Seacombe ferry every 10 or 15 minutes is no longer dramatic; several bus services to the ferry have been withdrawn so that there is now only half the number of buses in the exodus and they no longer leave together in line astern. The location where I was going to record birds, cows and rural peace only 2½ miles from the centre of Birkenhead now reverberates to the sound of building contractors' plant and new roads are being laid and rows of new houses and towering blocks of flats are going up.

'The only sounds that haven't changed are the Mersey lapping against the river wall, the gulls, the dock drawbridges, the sea at New Brighton, the wind rattling the shutters of the hibernating fairground and cafés, the seaspray splashing across the promenade and, of course, the local accent.

'Merseyside has lost its individuality and is too much like other conurbations now, with too many people, too much built-up area, too much road traffic and too much noise, but if we look at the Georgian, Victorian and neo-classical architecture apart from the new Liverpool it is still a wonderful place. I never cease to marvel at the beautiful architecture of Dale Street, Castle Street and Water Street, which is imposing in its presence on a Sunday morning when the streets are almost empty of people and motor traffic. Despite its visual heritage it is no longer an aural experience.'

Requiem for Woodside station and steam at Birkenhead
25 November 1967

'I was shocked to learn, in a letter from my friend Allan Clayton of Wallasey, that Birkenhead Woodside terminus, my favourite station, had closed on November 4th. Main-line passenger trains were now curtailed at Rock Ferry. On the same date Birkenhead loco-shed went over from steam to diesel traction and steamers – the big 9Fs – finished on the iron ore trains between Birkenhead docks and Shotton steelworks. It all seemed like a nightmare to me. It was bad enough when steam locomotive-hauled trains into Woodside were replaced by diesel multiple units on March 4th, but it seemed inconceivable that Woodside station was closed and there were no steam locomotives in Birkenhead; these were the last links with my Merseyside.'

Woodside station, built in 1878 to the design of Robert Johnston, the engineer of the LNWR/GWR joint line from Chester, was the only station on Merseyside to be listed for its architecture in the early 1950s, when Victorian railway and industrial buildings were not in vogue. BR demolished it shortly after closure. Pevsner's guide to *The Buildings of England: Cheshire* (1971)

described Woodside station, posthumously, as 'one of the few post-1847 buildings of any note in the town centre and one of the few really good main-line termini outside London.'

Long Drag round-up
7 December 1967

'I rode Vintora via Sedbergh and Garsdale up to "The Long Drag" to take the last few photographs I needed to illustrate my tape recordings of the line. I took four shots of Britannia 70045 *Lord Rowallan* storming up Mallerstang with a parcels train, throwing up voluminous clouds of white steam in the cold air. I had dinner at Hawes and rode up Widdale to Blea Moor and photographed George Horner leaning out of his signal cabin. He told me that Jim Harper, one of the signalmen at Dent, had died three weeks earlier. I had recorded an interview with Jim on June 2nd, 1967, and photographed him in his cabin on October 5th 1966. Lastly I rode via Appersett to Ais Gill to photograph Bill Sharpe in the dimly oil-lit signal cabin. A hulking, grimy 9F with an extra "Long Meg" was standing in the up loop when I arrived, waiting for a diesel express passenger train to pass. Then I rode back down Garsdale via Sedbergh to Kendal.'

On a 'Britannia' over Shap
14 and 15 December 1967

'On a visit to Carnforth loco-sheds two weeks earlier I learned that no slow steam freight were now allowed over the Lancaster and Carlisle railway between 10pm and 5am to leave the road clear for diesel express passenger, freight and car trains. The only steam-hauled night freight over Shap now was the 7.55pm from Carnforth and this would be dieselised from Christmas week. I was told that the only driver who would be likely to take me on the footplate on that run before then was Harry Bush so I asked my driver friend Watson Sowerby to arrange me a trip with Mr Bush to get a longer and more comprehensive programme of recordings than I did the first time, in May. I received a telephone message from Watson two days earlier to say that Mr Bush would take me tonight.

'I went by bus to Carnforth. Watson met me on the down platform and led me along and across the tracks to the siding where Harry Bush was waiting with a Britannia class locomotive, No 70012 *John of Gaunt*.

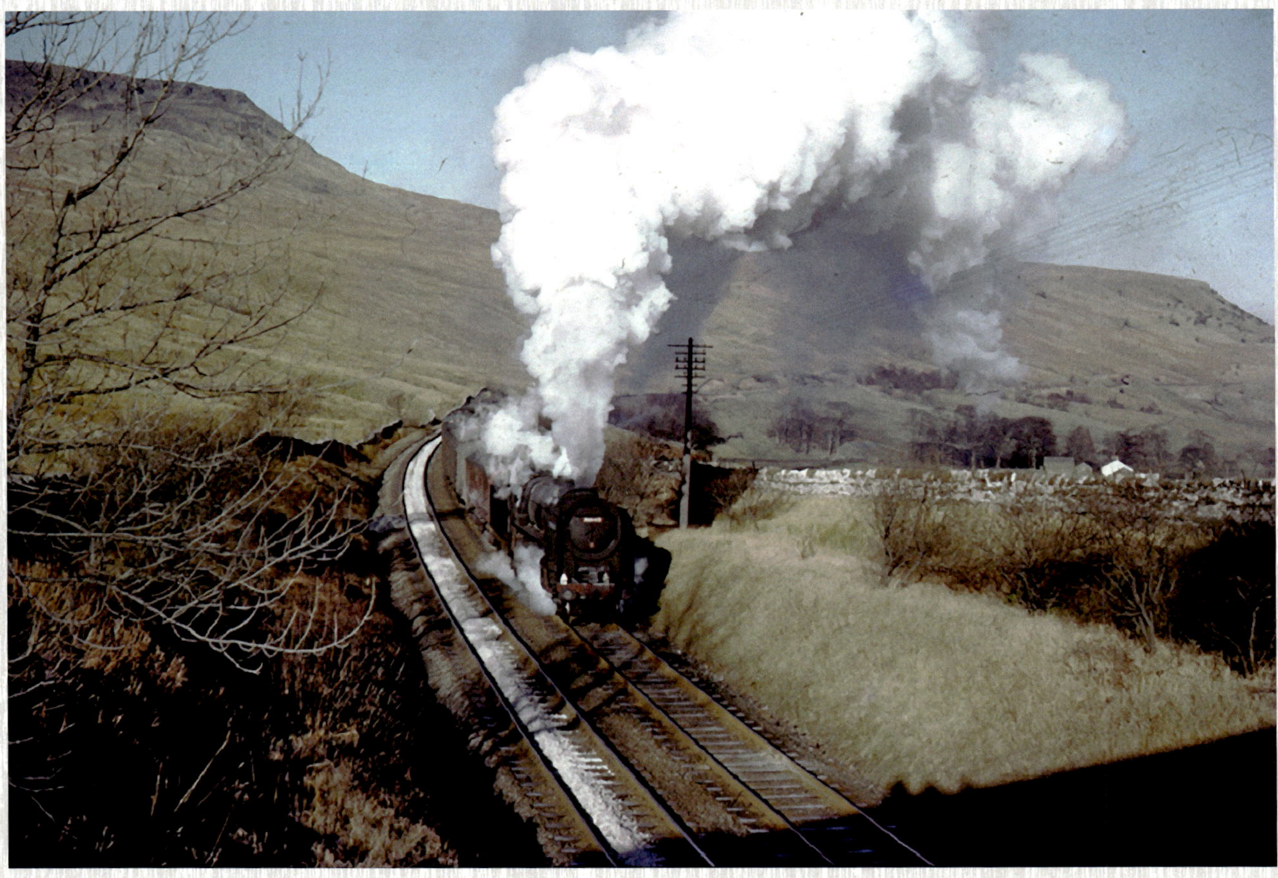

Piling steam and smoke into the cold air, 'Britannia' No 70054 *Lord Rowallan* climbs the 1 in 100 gradient up Mallerstang with a train of vans on 7 December 1967. Wild Boar Fell (2,324 feet) is on the left.

The height and shape of the cab and the view from the cab along the massive, rugged boiler made me feel as if I was riding a North American steam locomotive more than a British one. There is no doubt that there is some American influence in the design of these locomotives and the impression was completed by the beautiful wailing chimes from the whistle, which was slung at a jaunty angle on the right hand, upper side of the boiler up front behind the smokebox. Harry Bush was a master exponent of North American Wild West whistles and he gave me some wonderful recitals for the recording, particularly through Carnforth and Penrith stations, where it echoed loudly around the empty, canopied platforms. The recordings I made on this journey were a great improvement on those I made in May. I entitled this programme "Riding the Iron Horse".

'We left Carnforth at 8pm, echoed through the station and headed north on our night ride over the fells with the fireman shovelling hard for the long climb ahead. We whistled for a banking engine as we passed Oxenholme sidings, echoed through the station at 8.30pm and stopped beyond the platform to wait for the banking engine to join on behind for a push up Grayrigg bank. After a long wait, with the fireman shovelling for the next climb, we got two "crows" from the banker, the standard signal

it was ready to go, our engine whistled "cock-a-doodle-doo" back, and off we set together up the side of Hay Fell and Lambrigg Fell.'

'At the top of the climb, at Grayrigg, the banker [which was not coupled to the train] cast off astern to return to Oxenholme and we gathered speed as we descended into Lunesdale. At Tebay we had to pull into a siding between 9 and 9.30pm for two diesel expresses to pass and while we were waiting the crew had a wash. The driver wedged the fireman's shovel flat among the coals on a ledge under the tender doors, the fireman squirted it with steam to clean it and then put some hot water into it from the boiler. The driver got out a bar of soap, the fireman produced some paper towels and they proceeded to wash in the shovel.'

'We had to get another banker from Tebay shed to assist us on the four-mile climb at 1 in 75 up Shap Fells to the summit at 914 feet above sea level and I recorded from the start at Tebay as far as Scout Green. At Shap summit we reversed into a siding to let another express pass and thence we had a clear road down to Penrith. From a signal stop just before Penrith our loud, wailing whistle was enough to rouse the dead in the churchyard as we echoed through the station and past lineside buildings at 10.40pm.'

'From Penrith we continued to descend, more gradually now, to Carlisle. At 11.30pm we threaded our way through Carlisle's network of freight lines and I recorded from Upperby to the Eden bridge. The fireman pointed out where we converged with the Long Drag from Leeds. Our journey ended in Carlisle's vast, floodlit marshalling yard north of the city at 11.45pm and I stepped down from the locomotive on the approach road to Kingmoor loco-shed at 12 midnight.'

15 December 1967

'Kingmoor loco-shed is near Carlisle's youth hostel at Etterby, where I had stayed a few times, so I knew the way to walk through Stanwix into Carlisle city. As I walked up Lowther Street through the empty streets at 12.30am I realised what a fine city it is. It has wide streets and sidewalks, fine, sturdy, stone buildings and grand old wooden shop fronts. I stood at the top of Botchergate and thumbed a lift in a lorry back to Kendal, where I was dropped at Miller Bridge around 3am and walked home.'

Watson Sowerby told me later that the train I had recorded was the last steam freight over Shap, and *John of Gaunt* was retired for scrap before the end of the month.

**Carnforth loco-shed
20 December 1967**

'This, the third consecutive evening I spent standing by the water column and the coaling plant at Carnforth loco-shed, I got the recordings I wanted of a steam locomotive filling up with water and coal as it runs into the shed at the end of a day's duty, ready for the next day. The previous two nights the locomotives came in twos and threes and made a confusion of sounds: while the locomotive I was recording was quietly filling up with water, another would start coaling noisily in the background. I waited to record just one locomotive going through the procedure alone.

'I did not mind spending two evenings standing in the icy cold darkness waiting in vain. It was a great experience to be so close to the grimy iron monsters at home "on shed", to see them standing outside like creatures of the night, their black bulk merging with the sky and steaming with hushed and reverend quietness, to see them moving around the yard silhouetted in the haze of the yard lights, see them half hidden in their own steam, see the light glinting on their oily rods and valve gear as they moved slowly about the yard, to hear them puffing stealthily or barking loudly, their rods clanking, their flanges squealing and binding on the curves. The yard was full of pictures to photograph and sounds to record if only one had enough film, tape and time to capture them before the beauty and poetry of it all was shattered by the repulsive ugliness, noise and smell of the succeeding diesel locomotives.'

**Last steam passenger train over Shap
26 December 1967**

'Percy Duff called for me at Raven Scar – Karl came too – and he drove us in his car via Grayrigg to Low Gill, where we waited to photograph what he thought would be the last steam-hauled passenger train over Shap Fells: a Carlisle United football special to Blackpool, headed by Britannia 70013 *Oliver Cromwell*, the last steam locomotive to be overhauled by British Railways. The weather could not have been more perfect; the sky was clear and blue and the sun shone brilliantly.

'With the impetus of a run down Shap Fells, *Oliver Cromwell* came storming up the side of the Lune valley from Tebay towards Grayrigg so fast that I only had time to take one photograph. Specially cleaned and polished for the occasion, it looked a magnificent spectacle, shining and gleaming in the sunlight and snorting plumes of white smoke.

'Then we drove on to Tebay to see the loco-sheds but all five engines were dead: four BR standard class 4 tender engines and one condemned Black Five. This short extension of our excursion gave us a glimpse of the dreary, bleak future: the inactivity here when the loco-sheds close with only diesel-headed expresses roaring through and the desecration of the Lune gap with the motorway, then under construction.'

Oliver Cromwell returned with the football special after dark. That was the last BR steam train over Shap. 'Oliver' was stabled at Carlisle Kingmoor shed, last home of the 'Britannias'. *Lord Rowallan* took a freight from Carlisle over 'The Long Drag' to Skipton on 30 December, then Kingmoor shed closed, to be replaced by a new diesel shed at Carlisle on 1 January 1968. Tebay shed turned over to diesel traction the same day but only briefly as there was no call for banking duties now that steam over Shap was a thing of the past and the shed closed in March 1968. The football special was not quite the last steam passenger train over Shap; five days later, on 1 January 1968, *Oliver Cromwell* headed a relief passenger train from Preston to Glasgow.

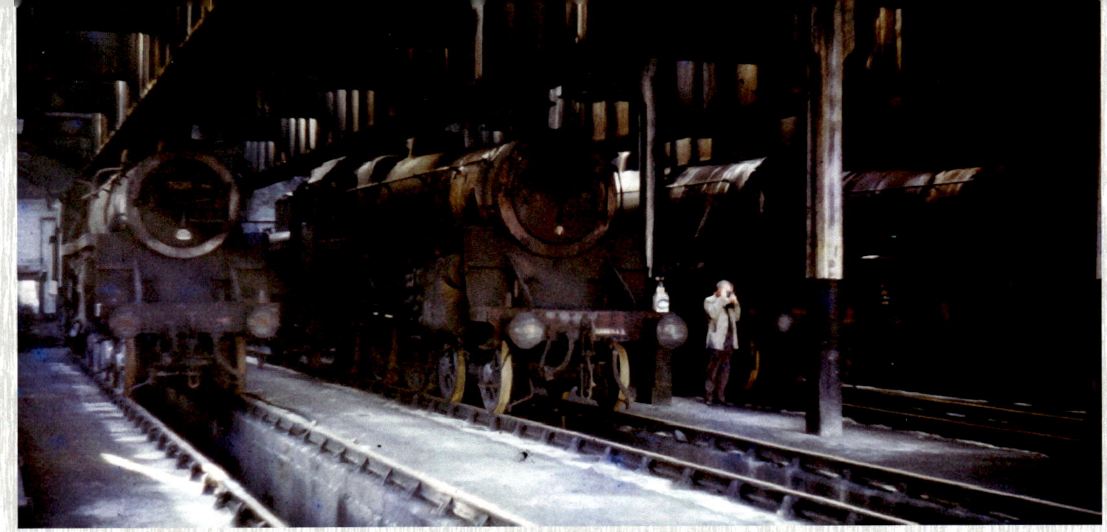

Three BR Class 4MT 4-6-0 banking engines and an ex-LMS 'Black Five' appear in this shed scene at Tebay on 26 December 1967, shortly before closure following the total dieselisation of the main line north of Oxenholme. The second engine from the left carries the shed name Bank Hall (Liverpool) on its buffer beam. Percy Duff, the Kendal borough treasurer, is seen taking photographs too.

Steam review
9 January 1968

'Steam is now extinct in Scotland and north-east of England, and in the north west between Oxenholme and Carlisle. The remaining steam sheds in Lancashire work freight to Windermere and Barrow, and the three or four daily steam freights over the "Long Drag". We still get an occasional steam passenger train on the Windermere branch when the diesel multiple unit breaks down. Northwich shed is still open.'

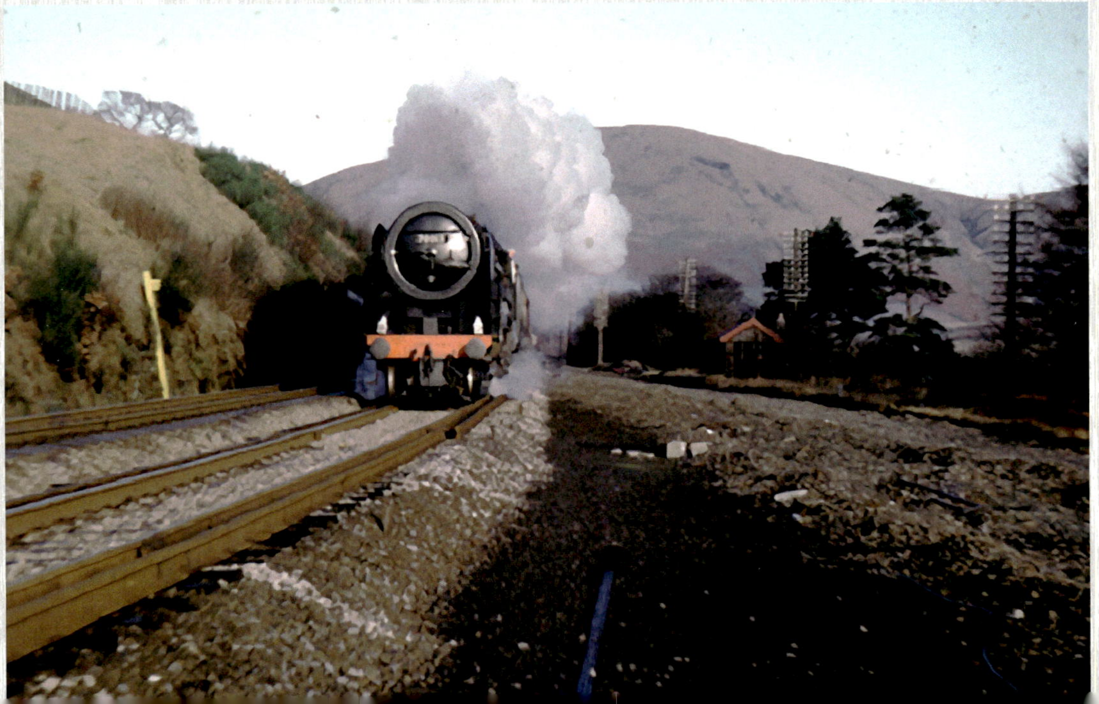

'Britannia' No 70013 *Oliver Cromwell* storms up the side of Lunesdale with the last steam passenger train over Shap, a football special from Carlisle to Blackpool on 26 December 1967, returning to Carlisle after dark.

This was the site of the former Low Gill station at the junction with the single line to Ingleton and Clapham, which closed in 1964. The track was lifted in the spring and summer of 1967, leaving the ballasted trackbed we see on the right.

Kendal freight yard
12 January 1968

'I tape-recorded 8F locomotive 48167 shunting and making up a train in Kendal freight yard and taking it away to Carnforth for my programme 'Steam's Last Duty'. Besides the bark, clank and squeal of the locomotive and the clangour of shunted waggons, I got close-up sounds of the shunters uncoupling and coupling-up the waggons, the crossover points being changed, the fireman coupling the tender to the first waggon and the signal cabin bells in the background.

Engine drivers come to listen to the sound of steam
14 January 1967

'We had a surprise visit to Raven Scar from Watson Sowerby with two friends, another Carnforth engine driver and a young Kendal school teacher, who came to listen to my railway tape recordings. I played them "Riding the Iron Horse" [Carnforth to Carlisle] and the freight side of "Smoke Over Kendal". They seemed enthusiastic about them and I surprised myself – I hadn't realised they were so good.'

The 'Belfast Boat Express'
20 and 21 January 1968

'As Watson Sowerby was driving the down Belfast Boat Express (Manchester Victoria-Heysham Harbour) to meet the night ferry, he invited me to travel on the footplate with my tape recorder. This was the very last regular steam passenger service on British Railways and Watson was driving it from Preston to Morecambe, then running light back to Carnforth shed.

'I rode Vintora to Carnforth and parked it outside Watson's home. Then I caught a Glasgow to Manchester coach, which went along the same route as I was to return by train in the evening: via Morecambe, Lancaster, Preston, Chorley and Bolton. I bought a coach ticket to Bolton because I wanted to travel the railway between Bolton and Manchester to note landmarks on the Manchester side of each station so that I would know when to turn the tape recorder volume down to zero to provide a space in which to announce each station when I added the narration afterwards.

'I alighted from the coach at Bolton's Moor Lane bus station. Boltonians are made very conscious of the moors around their town. Bolton's full name is Bolton-le-Moors and the town has a Moor Lane bus station and a Great Moor Street railway station. I walked through characterless streets of modern shops with large display windows and neon-lit names towards Trinity Street railway station. However, when I turned into Trinity Street it was like entering an Edwardian picture postcard scene. The tall black tower of Trinity Church merged into the black night sky. I could almost see double-deck tramcars round the tight curve in the narrow street south-west of the church tower. The Victorian bulk of Trinity Street station, with its short clock tower and its massive colonnade covering a third of the width of the road, dominated the street. Part of the carriageway around the station was paved with granite setts and just outside the station, almost in the middle of the road, stood a large, wooden hut for cab drivers. The opposite side of the street was lined with former tramway passenger shelters of iron and glass. Trinity Street seemed an oasis of the old, forgotten by the municipal modernisers.

'Likewise, Trinity Street station seemed to have been forgotten by British Railways' modern image "brooms". I was in ecstasy at this grand piece of Victoriana, spacious and dignified, built on a theme of beautiful arches. Its grandeur and spaciousness was unspoiled by BR's modern clutter. The north end of the station looked just like the setting of an old photograph in a railway book. The lines curved sharply away north-east and north-west, lorded over by a dimly lit, wooden signal cabin. The only sound was the quiet hiss of a Standard class 5 at the head of a parcels train at the Manchester end of the station. Alas, most of the trains that now use this station are two-car diesel multiple units, which look incongruously small and lost in the Victorian grandeur and make the most repulsive "blatt" noises.

'I travelled in one of these diesel multiple units from Bolton to Manchester, taking notes of landmarks where I should have to provide spaces on the tape recording to announce each station. The line went through a corridor of heavy industry [which has since disappeared] and the train rushed headlong down the gradient to Manchester, echoing loudly at various pitches against the walls of factories and rows of waggons in sidings.

'At Manchester Victoria I had nearly two hours to kill before the departure of the Belfast Boat Express. I went for a high tea in the cafeteria, a large room with white marble pillars, green tiled and mosaic walls and relief friezes of fruit and flowers around the ceiling. Victoria was an appropriate name for this station. This was another station British Railways so far seemed to have forgotten. Some of the platforms were still of timber and the station furniture, such as the train departure boards and the parcels weighing machines, were museum

pieces. When I emerged from the subway on to platform 13 for the Belfast Boat Express, it was like walking on to the platform of a haunted station as it was dark and dimly lit and the station furniture and architecture was Victorian and stern. The black framework of the ruined overall roof looked as if it had been left like that since the blitz and was open to the Manchester night.

Bolton Trinity Street station was the setting for the classic repertoire of traditional station sounds in the recording of the 'Belfast Boat Express' when it stopped there at 9.20pm on 20 January 1968.

In this daylight picture on 6 June 1968, 'Black Five' No 45318, built by Armstrong Whitworth at Newcastle in 1937, chugs slowly through the station with a short freight from Bolton yard to Blackburn. By that time all passenger trains were diesel multiple units.

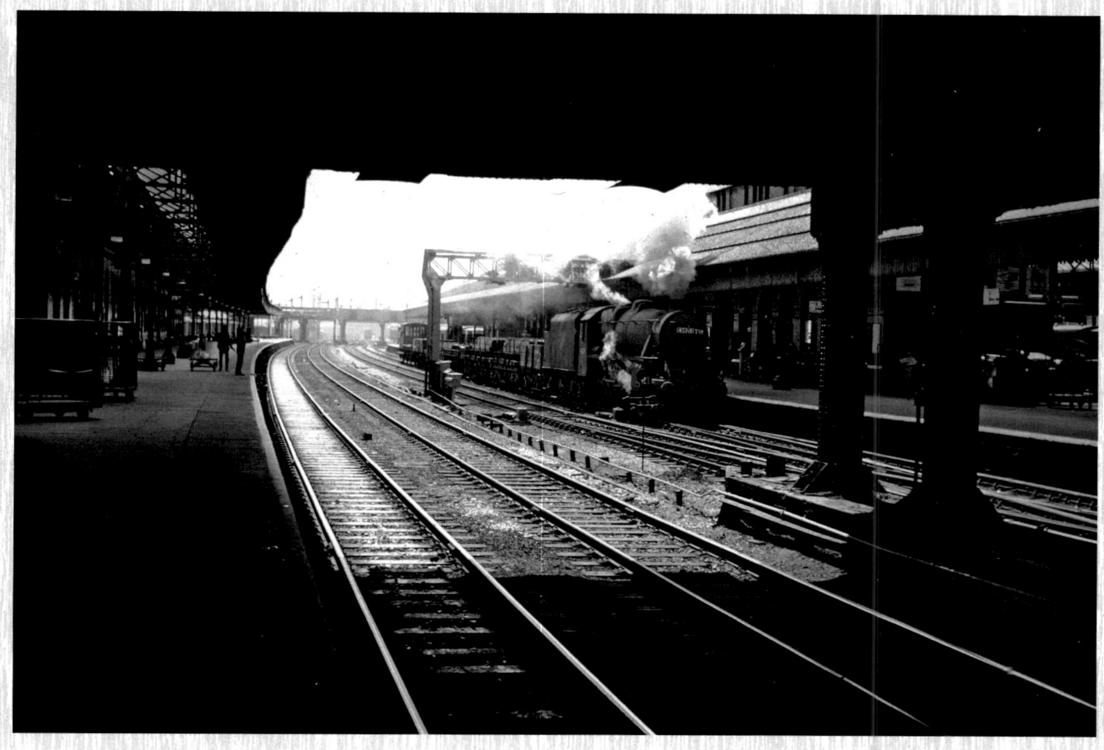

The lights of the city made a ruddy glow in the sky rather like the blitz fires. Black Five steam locomotives stood steaming quietly in the shadows and clanking around with parcels vans.

'Black Five 45390 headed the Belfast Boat Express into the station and I boarded the first passenger coach, which eventually filled up with railway enthusiasts, including three or four other tape recordists, but most of them got out at Bolton to return home to Manchester. I got some good sounds of the wheels clattering and echoing through the industrial corridor to Bolton and at Trinity Street station I captured all the traditional sounds of a stop in a large station: echoes of the steam and coupling rods as we entered, doors slamming, the deep, Boltonian voice of the station announcer over the loudspeaker, men talking on the platform, a mail trolley on four iron wheels trundling by along the platform, the heavy sound of the mailvan doors being opened and closed, the

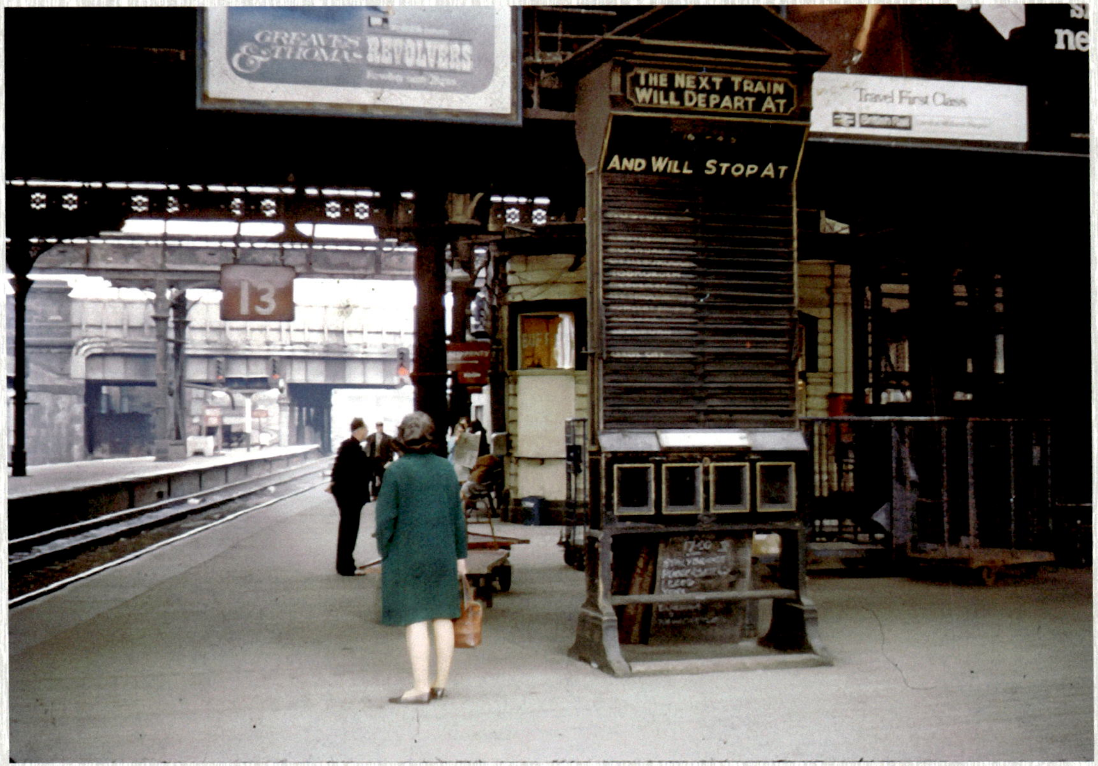

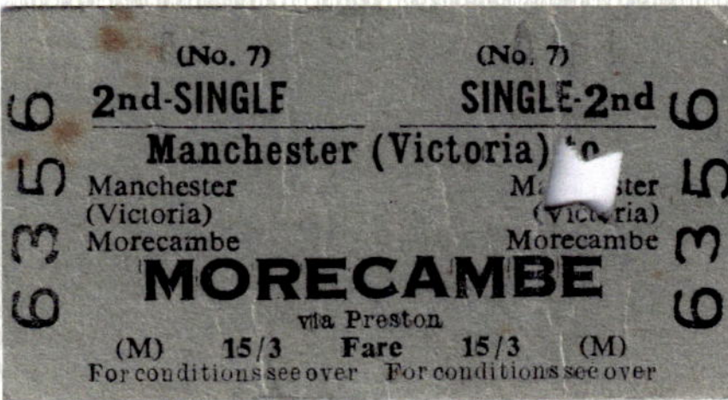

Platform 13 at Manchester Victoria station (LYR) was the period setting for the starting point of BR's last regular steam passenger train, the 'Belfast Express', and described in some detail in the diary extract for this journey on 20 January 1968.

This photograph was taken on 9 April 1969, showing the wooden platform, the weatherboarded buffet building and the old departure board listing a stopping train to Moston, Castleton, Rochdale, Littleborough, Todmorden, Hebden Bridge, Mytholmroyd, Sowerby Bridge, Halifax, Bradford and Leeds City. Other nameboards are stored underneath and a chalked blackboard is visible marking the 17.00 to Stalybridge, Huddersfield, Leeds, York, Darlington, Durham and Newcastle.

The ticket for the journey from Manchester Victoria to Morecambe, dated 20 January 1968, fare 15s 3d.

porters loading mailbags, the guard blowing his whistle, porters shouting "Right away", the masculine Stanier whistle from the locomotive, the echoes as it snorted out of the station and the squealing flanges on the tight curve at the north end of the station.

'The rest of the Manchester railway enthusiasts went only as far at Preston, where they reluctantly caught a diesel multiple unit back home. I disappeared into a cloud of steam around the front end of the train and groped my way up on to the locomotive footplate. Watson and his fireman took over from the Manchester crew here and, after a long wait with the enthusiasts looking on sadly, we forged north into the night, reaching a crescendo of ear-splitting noise as we sprinted along the straight and level track between Barton & Broughton and Brock at 70 miles an hour.

'I reverted to the first coach at Lancaster Castle station for the run to Morecambe, recording a spirited departure from Lancaster. The train reversed at Morecambe Promenade terminus and I recorded another Black Five, 45394, taking the train out towards Heysham and the ride on 45390 running light, tender first, to Carnforth shed and filling up at the water column and under the coaling plant in the shed yard.

'At midnight Watson took me to his home in a black terrace of railwaymen's houses on a cliff overlooking the railway and sidings. His wife plied me with a big supper before letting me leave to ride home and Watson gave me some railwaymen's books he had no further use for: "The Steam Locomotive: Its Failures and How to Deal With Them", published by the LNER in 1927 [Watson hailed from Kirkby Stephen East shed], a "Book of Instructions in Connection With the Working of Electric Trains, Lancaster, Morecambe and Heysham Section" (LMS, 1937), a "Handbook for Railway Steam Locomotive Enginemen" (BTC, 1957) and a book of operating instructions on LNW lines north of Crewe for 1966.

'I rode Vintora from Carnforth to Kendal and Raven Scar, arriving around 1.30am.'

Shunting at Ulverston and on the Conishead branch
8 February 1968

'I rode Vintora via Levens Bridge, Lindale and Newby Bridge to Ulverston to record a steam locomotive, Black Five 45394, shunting a level freight yard [as distinct from shunting by gravity in Kendal's sloping yard]. It was a more aural experience on a level yard because the engine had to work harder and barked louder.

'I had an interesting ride in a brakevan on a short freight down to Plumpton Junction and along the old Conishead branch to the bridge over the Ulverston Canal. The bridge was too weak for locomotives heavier than class 2 so we shunted a tank waggon over the bridge into the factory sidings and returned via Plumpton Junction to Ulverston. We stopped in Ulverston station, where the down line is sandwiched between the main platform and the island platform, both with ornate iron and glass canopies. The platform seats have ornate iron armrests and legs with squirrels and bunches of grapes, ex-Furness Railway. The train moved on up the line and shunted the brakevan on its own into the yard. It was fascinating as we bowled along at an ever-increasing speed through a succession of points, switching from track to track, to the far end of the yard. After more shunting, I rode Vintora the same way back to Kendal.'

Oxenholme by gaslight
16 February 1968

'In the evening I had a lift on the footplate of Black Five 44394 from Kendal yard with the evening freight to Carnforth and got off in Oxenholme station to take some photographs of the station by gaslight. I returned in a two-car diesel multiple unit to Kendal.'

On the footplate with the borough treasurer
27 February 1968

'In the afternoon I took Percy Duff on the footplate of Black Five 45095, with Watson Sowerby in charge from Kendal freight yard up to Oxenholme station. I recorded the trip for Percy on his tape recorder while he took photographs. His wife, Margaret, was waiting at Oxenholme station with Percy's car for him to drive us back to Kendal.'

Ex-LMS 'Black Five' No 49394, built by Armstrong Whitworth in 1937, was pictured and recorded while shunting Ulverston freight yard on 16 February 1968.

Another trip on the footplate
29 February 1968

'I rode on the footplate of Black Five 45134 with Watson Sowerby from Kendal freight yard up to Oxenholme station.'

A freight train leaving Kendal yard
1 March 1968

'After it had shunted Kendal yard, I recorded 8F 48666 panting rhythmically through the curves and points to couple up to the freight train it had made up in the warehouse.'

Oxenholme station by gaslight, looking north along the down main platform on 16 February 1968. The picture shows the grimy limestone buildings, the wooden inquiry kiosk that doubled as a porter's hut, and the destination boards for 'Penrith & Carlisle' and 'Kendal & Windermere'. The up platform is on the right.

In 1965 this platform was the scene of a midnight murder. The gaslights were doused after the last passenger train and a gunman on the run hid in the empty waiting room. When cornered, he escaped by shooting three policemen, killing an inspector and seriously injuring a sergeant. He ran south along the main line and was caught next day in a police chase on the open fells.

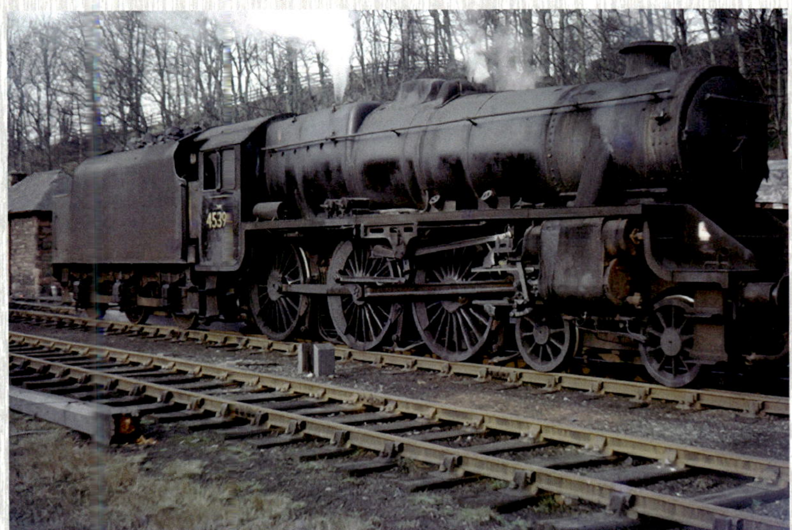

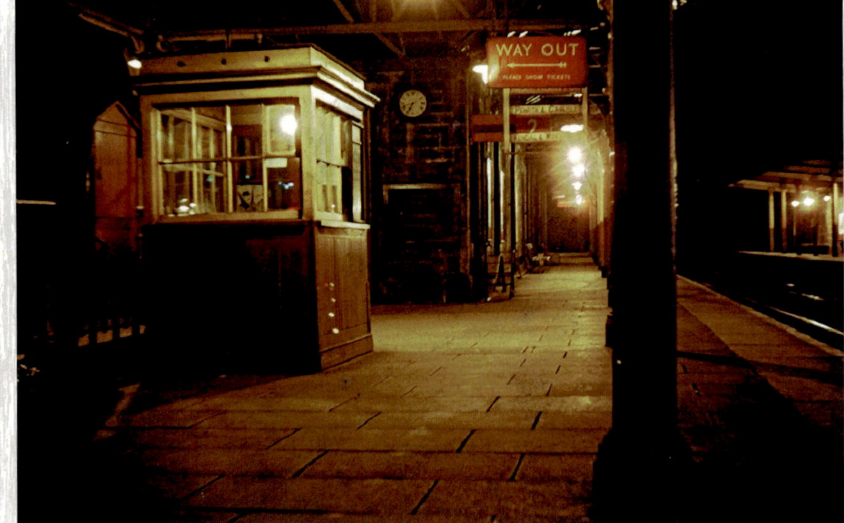

Then, with flanges binding and squealing on the curves and barking "stack talk", 48666 pulled the train, tender first, out of the yard. Next, with a flurry of rods and a whistle, 48666 ran past the train. We heard the crossover points being switched and signal being cleared, the locomotive backing down on to the train, the fireman coupling the tender up to the first waggon and the locomotive heading the train away south to Carnforth.'

Exclusive pictorial memorial to steam over the fells
8 March 1968

'Kendal signalman John Gardner invited me along with Percy Duff and Richard Holloway to his house, Farfield, near Sedbergh, to see his lantern slides of steam trains. He showed us 600, all taken in one year, on the Settle and Carlisle line between Ribblehead and Long Marton and on the Lancaster and Carlisle line between Oxenholme and Shap summit. Here was a magnificent and worthy pictorial memorial to steam over the fells. Strange, stormy, wintry sunlight at sharp angles picked out the voluminous columns of smoke and the autumnal colours on the fells, and his telephoto lens brought up the snow-capped fells in the background in great majesty. My favourite pictures were of Britannias and 9Fs on the Midland line. It was a highly ecstatic and enjoyable evening, rounded off with superb catering by Mrs Gardner.'

More young footplate inductions
15 and 16 March 1968

'I took eight-year-old budding railway enthusiast Trevor Atkinson, son of a family friend in Kendal, for his first ride on the footplate of a Black Five on the evening freight from Kendal yard. The driver dropped us in Oxenholme station and we walked back down the track to his home in Castle Oval.

'In the morning [next day] I took Karl, now aged four, on the footplate of Black Five 45445 shunting in Kendal freight yard, pulling the train out of the yard and running round it. He watched the driver's every movement with the controls but was still a little apprehensive when the locomotive was moving.'

Borough treasurer arrested
16 March 1968

'My friend, Percy Duff, the borough treasurer, told me he was arrested by railway police for trespassing in Carnforth shed yard to take a picture of a 9F in the afternoon and was told he would be prosecuted in court. I'm afraid I laughed my head off when he told me.'

I did not follow up the result of this incident.

Coal railways at Philadelphia, County Durham
28 March 1968

'I rode Vintora via Tebay, Kirkby Stephen, Stainmore Common, Barnard Castle, Bishop Auckland and Durham to Philadelphia to tape-record the National Coal Board 0-6-0 saddle-tank locomotives with North American style chime whistles that worked trains from the collieries to BR exchange sidings.

'I had only been to County Durham once before, in 1959, hitch-hiking south down the A1 road, from which it looked rather prosaic and scruffy. This time, from Barnard Castle to Durham, it looked very pleasant and interesting. The rolling moors and foothills on the flanks of the Pennines, the ancient stone town of Barnard Castle, the pleasant village of Staindrop around its wide greens, the bustling market town of Bishop Auckland with its architecturally interesting buildings, Durham city with its steep, narrow streets – all this made me glad and proud to live in northern England. Only beyond Durham were the drab, scruffy, colliery villages that one usually associates with County Durham – villages of small, plain, terraced houses straggling over the skyline of the low, bare hills, looking strangely out of place in a landscape that was still largely rural.

'Philadelphia was just such a village but it turned out to be a paradise of quaint steam railway operations. Philadelphia was the loco-shed and workshop on the NCB railway from Herrington colliery to Penshaw marshalling yard (BR) and at Philadelphia Bank Top was a triangular junction with the line from Houghton colliery at the top of the steep gradient up from Penshaw. The sheds and workshops at Philadelphia were old and dark and the roof of one engine shed was in ruins and let shafts of sunlight through on to the rusting locomotives, most of which looked derelict. The track had some remarkably steep gradients and tight curves, which made the railway look as if it was just built without any planning, surveying or civil engineering. The short, wooden signal posts stood dozing at various angles out of perpendicular with their ball and spike finials leaning over at crazy angles and I could never make out whether the signal arms were meant to be up or down, off or on.

'I recorded several trains and light engines at Bank Top junction and then recorded a ride on the footplate of an engine through Philadelphia simply by putting up my hand and stopping a train as it approached and climbing up into the cab! Unfortunately I later found that most of the recordings I had made at Bank Top were marred by wind in the microphone. Nevertheless it was a pleasant day's adventures and I got some photographs of the railway.

'I rode Vintora home to Kendal in two and a half hours as against three hours for the outward journey.'
Black Five

National Coal Board railway 0-6-0 saddle-tank locomotives stand at the coaling plant on the Lambton colliery railway at Philadelphia, County Durham, on 28 March 1968. The drop-bottom wagons on the ramped pier dropped coal down chutes to the locomotive bunkers in the same way as ships were loaded at the coaling staithes on the Durham coast and the Tyne.

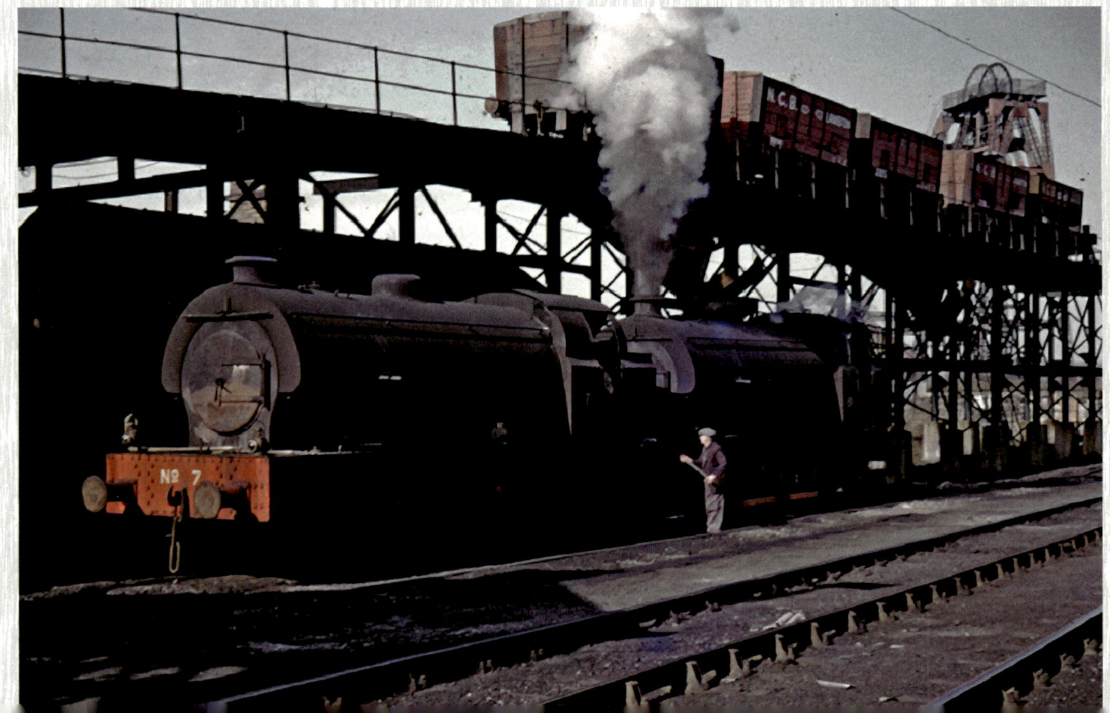

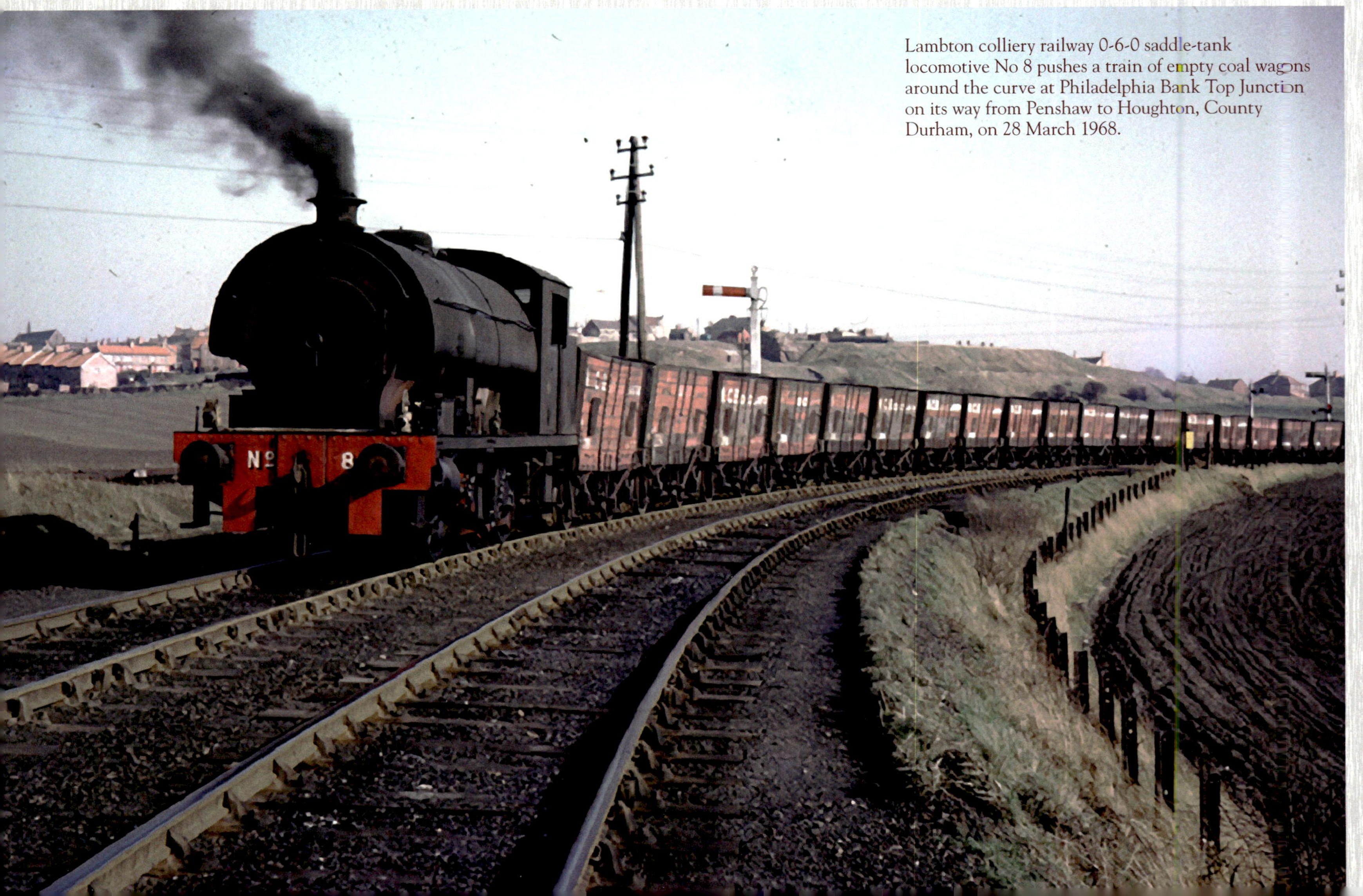

Lambton colliery railway 0-6-0 saddle-tank locomotive No 8 pushes a train of empty coal wagons around the curve at Philadelphia Bank Top Junction on its way from Penshaw to Houghton, County Durham, on 28 March 1968.

29 April 1968

'Ruth's mother and brother Tony, from Folkestone, were staying with us at Raven Scar for eight days. I got Tony a ride on the footplate of a Black Five on the afternoon freight from Kendal yard to Burneside and back. It was his first trip on the footplate and he stayed on board while the locomotive shunted Kendal yard.

'In the meantime I was in the shunter's hut interviewing Paul Barnes, producer, director and cameraman of a sound, colour film for the British Film Institute and television about Carnforth enginemen working the last steam operations in this area.'

The film, called *Black Five*, is a 22-minute classic, available on DVD. It features the images and sounds of steam and the only commentary is by the enginemen, quite unlike any other railway film. Paul recorded many of the enginemen's comments and stories in the shunter's hut in Kendal yard.

The afternoon freight from Kendal to Oxenholme
May 1968

Two of my favourite recordings were of the afternoon freight up the 1 in 80 gradient from Kendal to Oxenholme on two afternoons in May 1968, not recorded in my diary. I picked a still day with not a breath of wind to record the birdsong and the train approaching and disappearing in the distance. In this recording we can hear 'Black Five' No 44963 for a total of 2½ minutes as it lifted the train out of Kendal and snorted through the trees of Castle Grove on the east side of town as it climbed steadily into the hills.

I never turned up the volume, as some recordists did, when a train was approaching or disappearing in the distance because it gives a better impression of the train passing if you keep the volume on a constant level and I like the distant sound of a steam train. If we adjust the volume to maintain a constant level of sound it gives

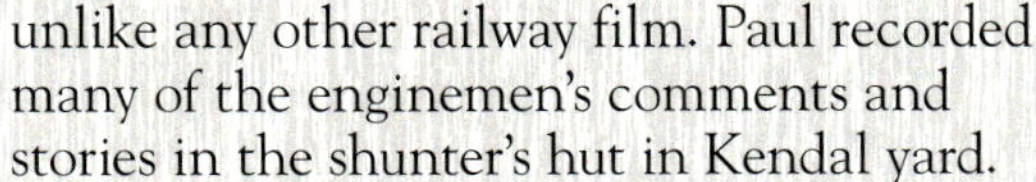

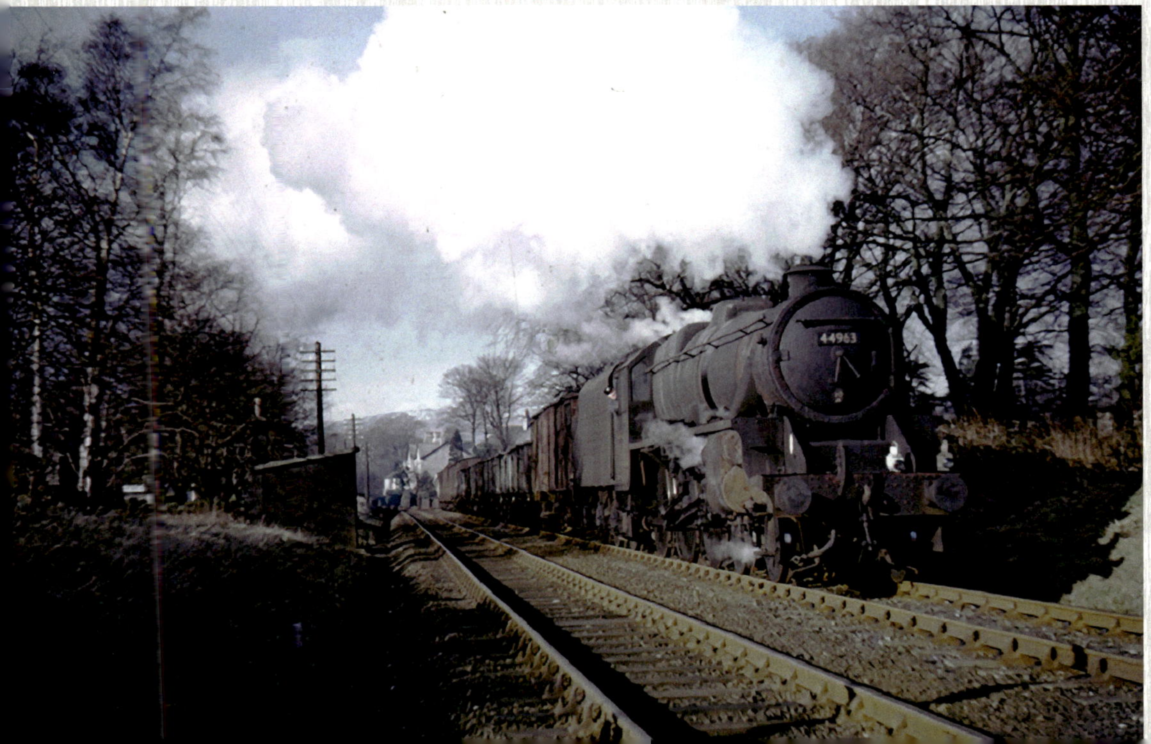

Climbing the 1 in 80 gradient out of Kendal towards Oxenholme is 'Black Five' No 44963 with the early-afternoon freight to Carnforth on 14 February 1968.

the impression that the train is constantly passing the microphone or running on the spot. It's like films that zoom in to trains for a telephoto view as they approach and again

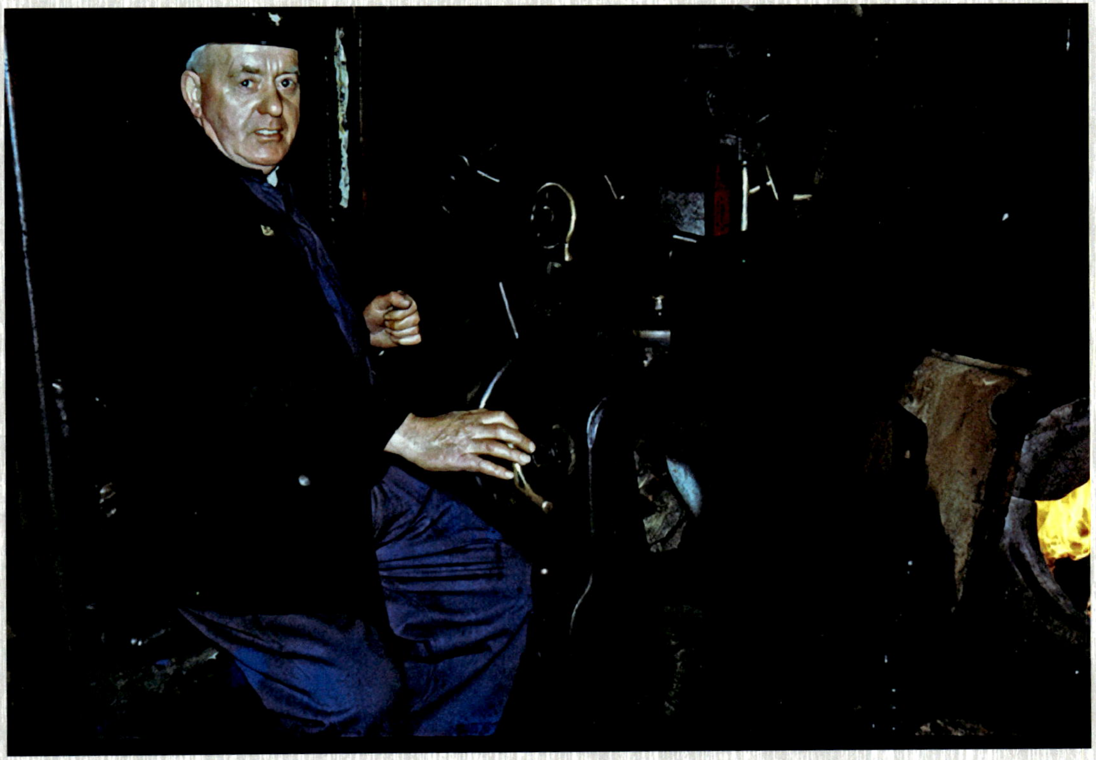

Driver Joe Wilson, aged 64, from Carnforth shed, in the cab of BR Standard Class 9F No 92009 in Kendal freight yard on the evening of 15 February 1968.

as they disappear; it gives a false impression of the progress of the passing train.

My second recording of the afternoon freight from Kendal about that time was taken from the dark cavern of the single line bay platform at Oxenholme. As the train staggered to the top of the bank you could hear the beat of the exhaust

change tempo as the train levelled off and thundered through the station, the sound of its exhaust and rods echoing loudly against the sounding board of the overall roof and retaining wall. As the train disappeared south the home starter signal bounced several times as it dropped with a clatter into the horizontal position. Then I went into the signal cabin to record the levers and bells as the next southbound freight cleared the station on the main line.

Communing with the engines
19 May 1968

'Now that steam haulage has finished on the main line through Oxenholme, I have stopped attending that "temple" and now attend daily "worship" of the steam locomotive in the open air in Kendal freight yard, where we get two steam engines each day, one on the morning shunt and the Windermere coal train and the other on the afternoon shunt and the Burneside mill coal train, both engines bringing and taking general freight as they come and go between Carnforth and Kendal.

'Most of the engines are Black Fives dating from 1934 to 1951. Every day I visit the yard, wander at will across the tracks, commune with the engines, inspect the more elderly parcels coaches – inside as well

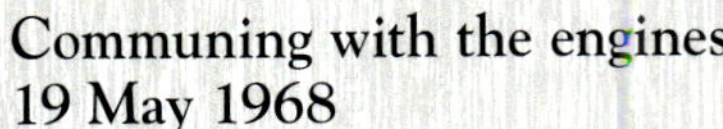

as out – and talk with the shunters, drivers, firemen and guards, who give me all the latest railway "intelligence".

'I feel completely satisfied and at one with the world as I wander about the yard, sniffing the steam and listening to the squealing flanges of the locomotives, the 'dank-donk' of their driving rods and the 'clink-clank' of the shunted waggons. This is a very valuable experience to me and something I must make the most of because there are, incredibly, only 11 more weeks of steam on British Railways. I shall, inevitably, feel lost for a while after that but steam railways will take their place with tramways in the hall of memory.'

Rods and flanges in Kendal freight yard
18-20 July 1968

'Today and the next two days I went down to Kendal freight yard between 7.30 and 9am, between 12 noon and 2.30pm and between 4.15 and 6 30pm, sometimes playing truant from the office or from the magistrates' court, to record side two of my tape "Steam's Last Duty". My object was to commune with the locomotives and catch their many intimate sounds, especially the clanking rods and squealing flanges of Black Fives working in the yard, from the trackside, from the brakevan and from the locomotive footplate.'

The clanking of the connecting rods and coupling rods to the driving wheels was actually the sound of worn 'big ends' on the eccentrics as they converted the reciprocating motion of the pistons to the rotary motion of the wheels. Flange squeal was caused by flanges of the large driving wheels binding on curves, turnouts and crossovers at speed. When this was done in slow motion the sound was broken down to a succession of very short, deep, bass grunts and the ground trembled underfoot as I stood alongside.

Classic wheel-slipping, Kendal yard
23 and 24 July 1968

I was down at Kendal freight yard almost every day during this last month of steam traction. About 8 o'clock in the morning of 23 July I noticed that the shunting engine had a prolonged period of wheel-slipping when lifting a heavy coal train upgrade out of a siding, so next morning I went back at the same time to record it. With early morning dew on the rails 'Black Five' No 44735 took nearly 4 minutes to move past the microphone with a short train of trucks 150 yards out of the coal yard before it got to grips with the rails. I had never witnessed such a classic sequence of wheel-slip. The locomotive was running on the spot most of the time.

A fireman's shovel
26 July 1968

'The crew of the afternoon freight brought me a fireman's shovel from Carnforth loco-shed. I had requested this artefact as a representative souvenir of the steam locomotive that I could keep in my museum at home. They threw it out on the trackside by arrangement and I hid it in the undergrowth at the side of the track until I could collect it on the motor scooter in the evening.' [It still resides in my workshop museum.]

The last steam passenger train on the
Windermere branch
29 July 1968

'The official last steam passenger train on the Windermere branch ran in September, 1967, but there have been many more since, owing to diesel failures. The last steam passenger train along the branch ran today from Preston (dep 8.15am, Kendal dep 9.28am) to Windermere (arr 9.47am) behind Black Five No 45110, which returned with the 11am train from Windermere to London, departing Kendal at 11.16am and Oxenholme at 11.25am' [This was only five days before the end of BR steam on freight.]

Last week steam activity in Kendal freight yard
1 August 1968

'This afternoon I took Karl down to Kendal freight yard to watch the 2.25 freight depart. The locomotive, Black Five 44894, had been cleaned up on one side – the side the sun shone – by a band of railway enthusiasts during the morning. The fireman put a lot of coal dust on the fire to create black smoke for the photographers. There was quite a bit of activity to interest Karl with the teatime freight engine, another Black Five shunting the yard, two diesels in tandem moving a parcels train and the freight yard crane at work.'

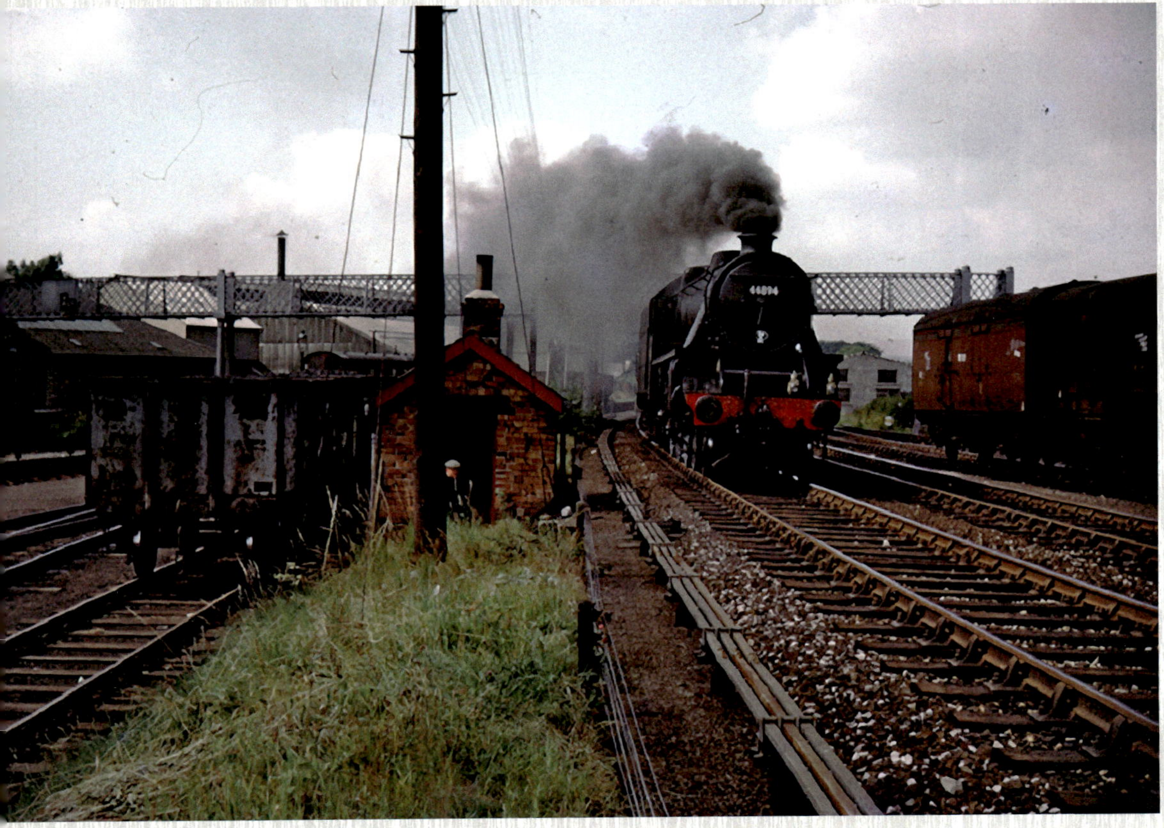

The last steam freight to Windermere
2 August 1968

'In the morning I drove Karl on Vintora to Ings railway bridge on the Windermere branch and we walked back along the track about half a mile to a scenic location to photograph the last steam freight to Windermere. It was the most beautiful location I had ever found on the Windermere line, framed between two clumps of fir trees with a flush of mauve wild flowers in the foreground, great hills on each side in the background and the

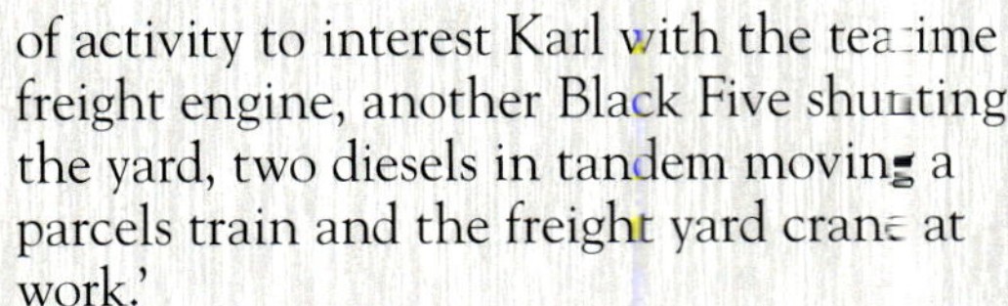

Left: Two days before the end of steam on BR 'Black Five' No 44894 runs around its train (just out of sight) on the running lines at Kendal before taking the afternoon freight to Carnforth on 1 August 1968. The freight yard, on the left, was on a gradient for shunting by gravity. The parcels van sidings are on the right.

Opposite: Cleaned up by a band of railway buffs, 'Black Five' No 44894 pulls out of Kendal at 2.25pm with a freight to Carnforth on 1 August 1968. The smokebox door carries the 24K shed plate of the then closed Preston shed.

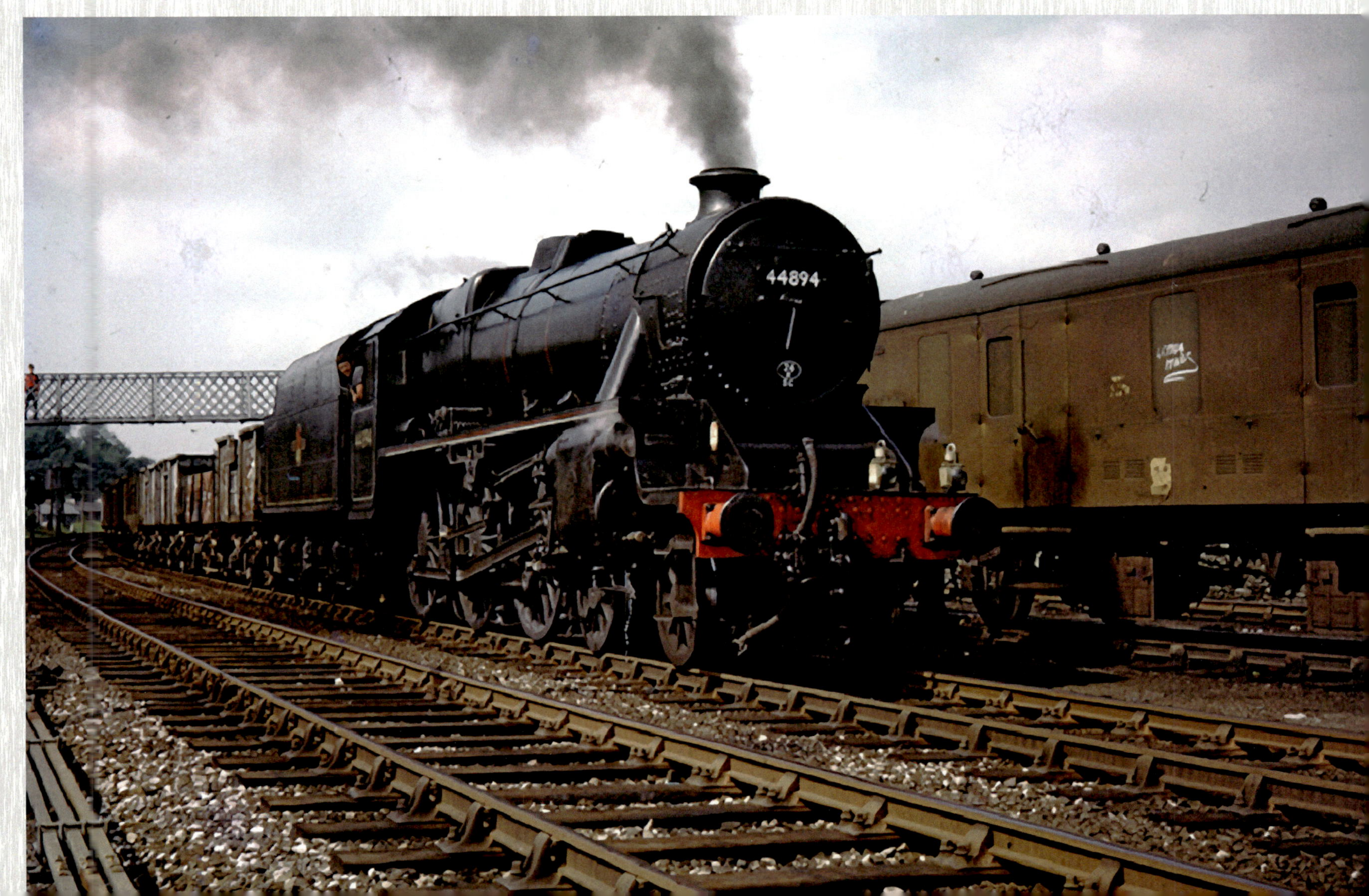

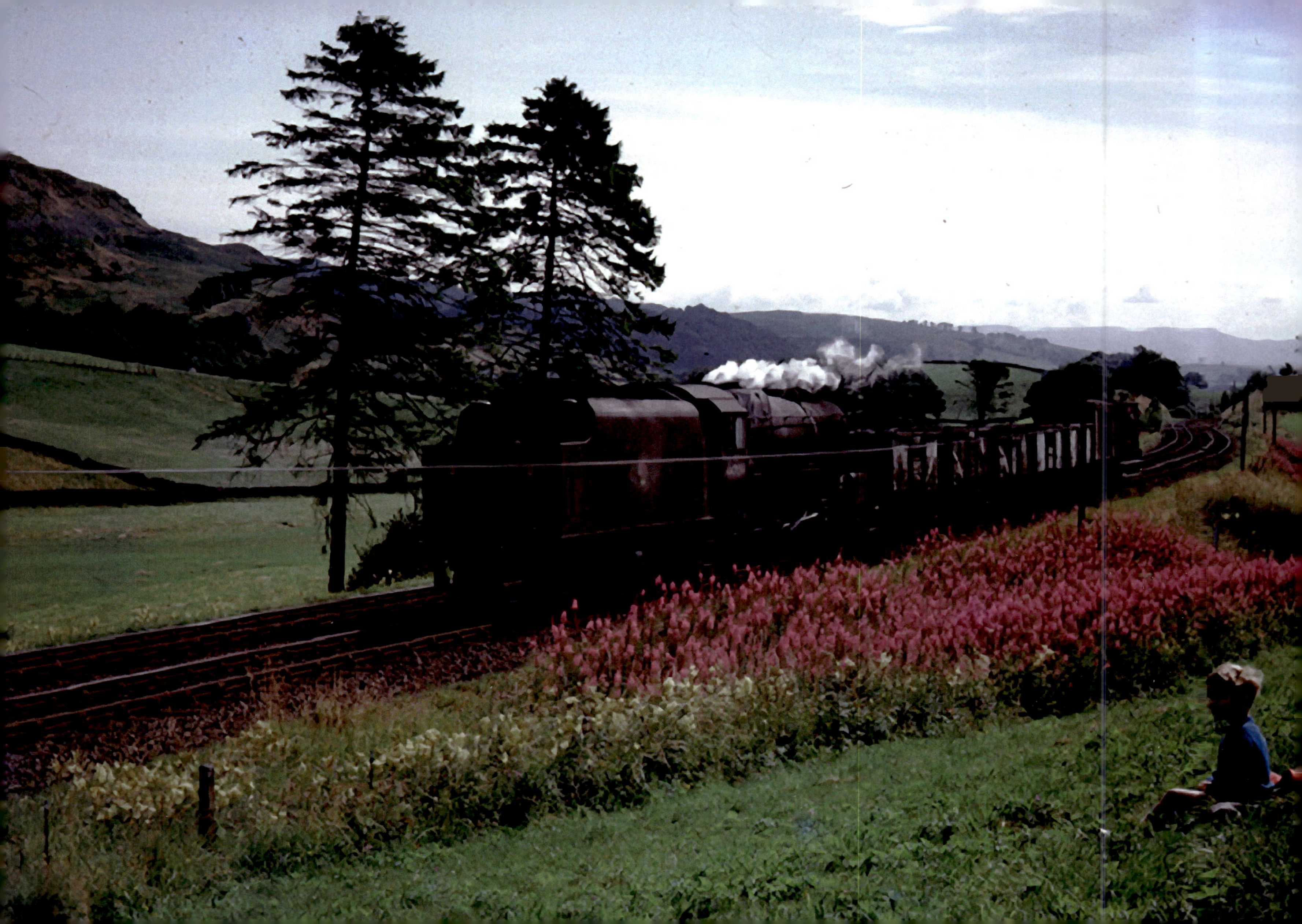

line curving through the rich green rolling countryside into the foreground.

'Karl spotted the first puffs of smoke from the train in the distance. The smoke weaved from side to side following the line winding through the hills and then the historic black monster, Black Five 44709, snorting steam, clanked slowly by, tender first, with a short coal train. It was a sight that had been common for the last 100 years or so but which we should never see again.

'A former British Transport Commission chief, General Sir Brian Robertson, vowed to get rid of "Emmet style steam locomotives clanking through the countryside" when he announced the British Railways modernisation plan in 1955. Now steam locomotives were due to finish on the morrow and local freights and rural branch lines were following them. Tomorrow's railways were a harsh and depressing world of miserable, smelly diesels, concrete stations and bridges, scruffy overhead electric catenary, continuous welded rail and trains that streak through the countryside, air horns sounding, never deigning to stop until they reach the next large town.

'In the evening Karl and I went with my friend John Proctor, of Kendal, in his

The last steam freight to Windermere is headed by 'Black Five' No 44709 running tender-first west of Staveley on 2 August 1968.

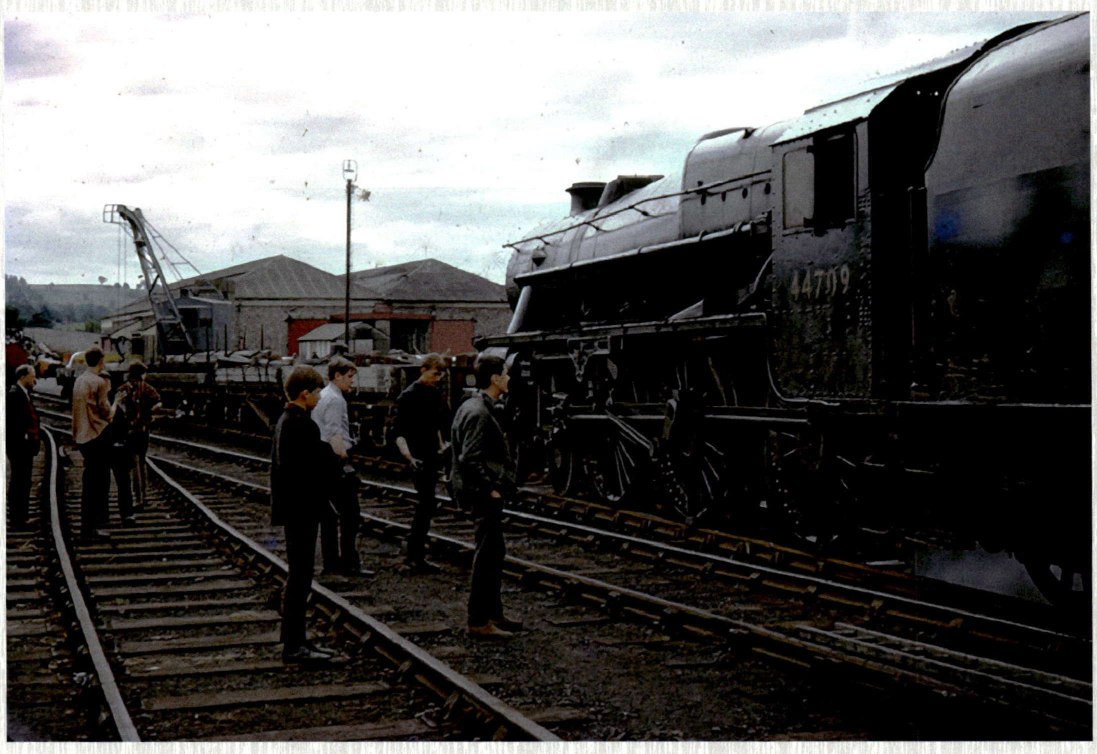

car to the last Railway Correspondence & Travel Society visit to Carnforth loco-shed, which served the Windermere branch and provided the banking engines for Grayrigg bank. Carnforth was one of the last three steam sheds on BR along with Lostock Hall near Preston and Rose Grove near Burnley. I recorded the variety of sounds of

No 44709 was the last steam locomotive on the Windermere branch, and is seen here on shunting duty in Kendal freight yard on the morning of 3 August 1968. Again the locomotive had received the attention of volunteer cleaners.

locomotives ambling around the shed yard, barking, clanking, hissing, the pulsating valve motion and the flanges binding on the curves. It was sad to see every steam locomotive that came in having its fire raked out for the last time but there was a good deal of steam activity considering this was the last working day for most of them and the last day but one for the rest of them.'

After closure, Carnforth shed reopened as 'Steamtown' railway museum. It is now the workshops of West Coast Railways, where locomotives and carriages are restored for steam excursions and preserved railways.

'We drove back to Kendal via Arnside to see the last up steam parcels train cross the 700-yard-long viaduct over the Kent estuary. The shore was lined with railway enthusiasts waiting to witness it and many to tape-record it. Two of the recordists had come from Weymouth and London on a last steam week visit to the north-west. We joined them at the water's edge. There was a beautiful red sundown glow in the sky over the hills of the Cartmel peninsula on the far side of the estuary. Then there was a puff of smoke at Grange-over-Sands. An onrush of staccato exhaust reverberated on the still air across the tranquil estuary scene as the engineer opened up to full throttle and the train thundered across the iron viaduct with its whistle blowing wildly, no doubt for our

benefit. That was a dramatic and memorable moment. Steam was going out like a lion.'

Last day of regular steam working 3 August 1968

'My heart was heavy overnight with the thought that maybe the last steam train had already gone from Kendal and that I would commune no more with the rods and wheels of the steam locomotive nor smell its steam and hot oil. The tenders were being allowed to get low on coal so that at the end there was not too much coal to shovel out and the crew of the Friday evening freight thought that might be the last steam train out of Kendal as there was a 50:50 chance that a diesel might be put on the duty on Saturday.

'When I was sitting at my desk in the office in Stramongate and heard the familiar clank of a steam locomotive entering Kendal about 10am my heart leapt and I could no longer concentrate on my work. I had to get down to the freight yard to join it.

'Frank, the shunter, and Paul Barnes, who had been filming Black Fives and local steam working for the British Film Institute, came into the office to collect me and together we walked to the yard. Who should be driving the last steam locomotive at Kendal but Watson Sowerby, my driver friend I usually travelled with on

the footplate! [That was the last time I saw Watson. He died in 2000, aged 76.]

'A band of railway photographers with ladders and oily rags was busy cleaning the sunny side of the locomotive and tender and it looked a handsome sight gleaming in the sunshine, black with a red buffer beam and white Southern Railway headcode discs fans from the Southern Region had brought with them. I recorded and photographed its historic departure from Kendal from a trackside location in the ballast box near the bridge over Sedbergh Road.

'Tonight the last steam passenger trains in regular timetable service on British Railways' standard gauge with Black Fives doing the honours: 45212 took the 8.30pm from Preston to Blackpool South (arr 9.22pm) and 45318 headed the 9.25pm from Preston to Liverpool Exchange (arr 9.58pm)'.

The steam age was over. The last three steam sheds, Rose Grove, Lostock Hall and Carnforth, closed that weekend. The new age of diesel traction soon saw the

The last steam train out of Kendal consisted of 'Black Five' No 44709 and brakevan only at midday on 3 August 1968. The engine sported Southern Railway white headcode discs added by visiting railway enthusiasts. The 'Auld Grey Town' Les in the background in this picture taken near the bridge over Sedbergh Road.

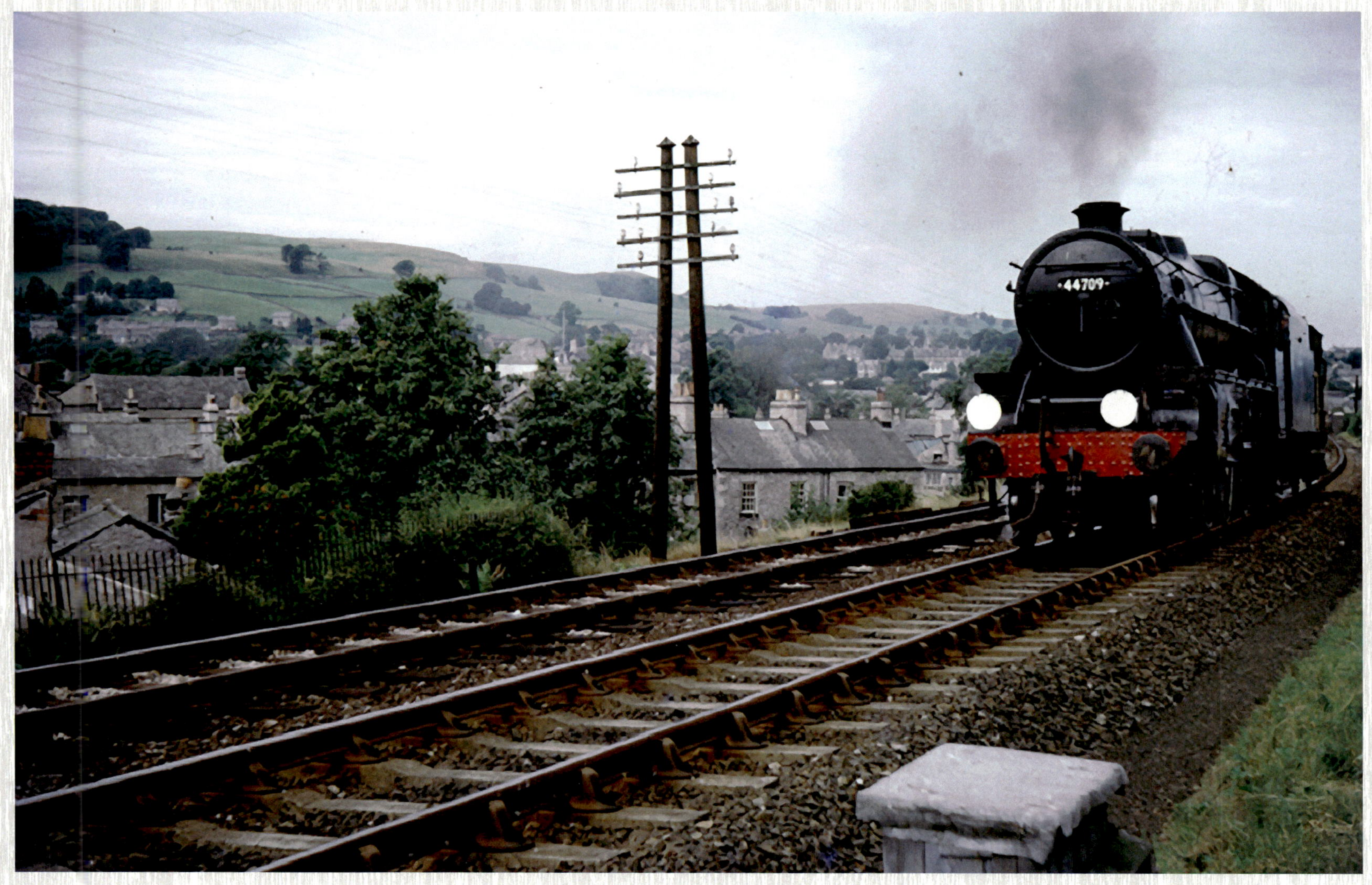

rundown of the Windermere branch: freight services ended in 1972 and the double track was singled in 1973 together with the electrification of the main line, the signal cabins were demolished and there could be no more excursion trains to Windermere.

The next 20 years saw something of a recovery for the railways as a result of traffic congestion on Britain's roads, particularly in the Lake District, and the high cost of motoring. In 1994 through trains began running again between Windermere and Manchester and in 2014 the branch line was scheduled for electrification as a spur of the 'West Coast' main line together with the Manchester, Liverpool and Blackpool feeder lines in 2016.

A steam evening with Sedbergh Council chairman
7 August 1968

'After reporting a Sedbergh Rural District Council meeting in the evening, by prior arrangement I followed the chairman, Jack Dawson, to his home in Highfield Villas to entertain him to my slide-illustrated tape programme "The Long Drag". Jack was Sedbergh's coal merchant in the old station yard on the former Clapham-Low Gill line and he was very interested in railways and steam locomotives. As I was packing up and

we were having supper I played him my tape programme "Riding the Iron Horse" (on a Britannia from Carnforth to Carlisle). He was absolutely transported by it all and I think he was the most appreciative audience I have ever had.'

The final curtain
11 August 1968

'British Railways' last steam train on the standard gauge was a railfan excursion known as "the 15-guinea special" to mark what was then thought to be the end of steam traction on the national railway system. It ran from Liverpool Lime Street to Carlisle Citadel and back, routed both ways via Manchester Victoria, Blackburn and Settle.

'I went up to the "Long Drag" to see it and took Ewan Preston, of Oxenholme, with me on Vintora. [His mother, Mrs Kathleen Preston, had been campaigning to reopen Oxenholme loco-sheds as a steam railway museum.] We got there 50 minutes before it was due and, as it was running 45 minutes late, we waited an hour and 35 minutes for it with Ewan perched on a small platform at the top of a derelict semaphore signal post with his camera and me beside the down track 25 yards inside the north portal of Blea Moor tunnel with my tape recorder.

'I had to vacate the tunnel twice for diesel trains to pass along the up line – after the steam special was due – and I was fervently hoping that another up train would not come as the same time as the special. It didn't. I recorded the special coming through the tunnel but it didn't whistle, as it should have done, on approaching the tunnel mouth, even though I was silhouetted in the portal and there were about 100 photographers on the trackside and the railway bank outside the tunnel. The locomotive on the northbound run over the Long Drag was the last survivor of the Britannia class, 70013 *Oliver Cromwell*, and I particularly wanted to record a Britannia chime whistle in the tunnel.

'When the train had passed Dent Head, we mounted Vintora and tried to catch it

A week after the end of regular steam traction, British Railways ran a special commemorative last steam passenger train on 11 August 1968, from Liverpool to Carlisle and back, running each way via Manchester Victoria, Blackburn and 'The Long Drag'. On the return journey two 'Black Fives', Nos 44871 and 44781, are seen here storming up Mallerstang with the 13-coach train. 'Britannia' *Oliver Cromwell*, which pulled the train from Manchester to Carlisle, followed, running light. All the motive power for this trip, including 'Black Five' No 45110 from Liverpool to Manchester, was stabled and prepared at Carnforth shed, which closed the next day.

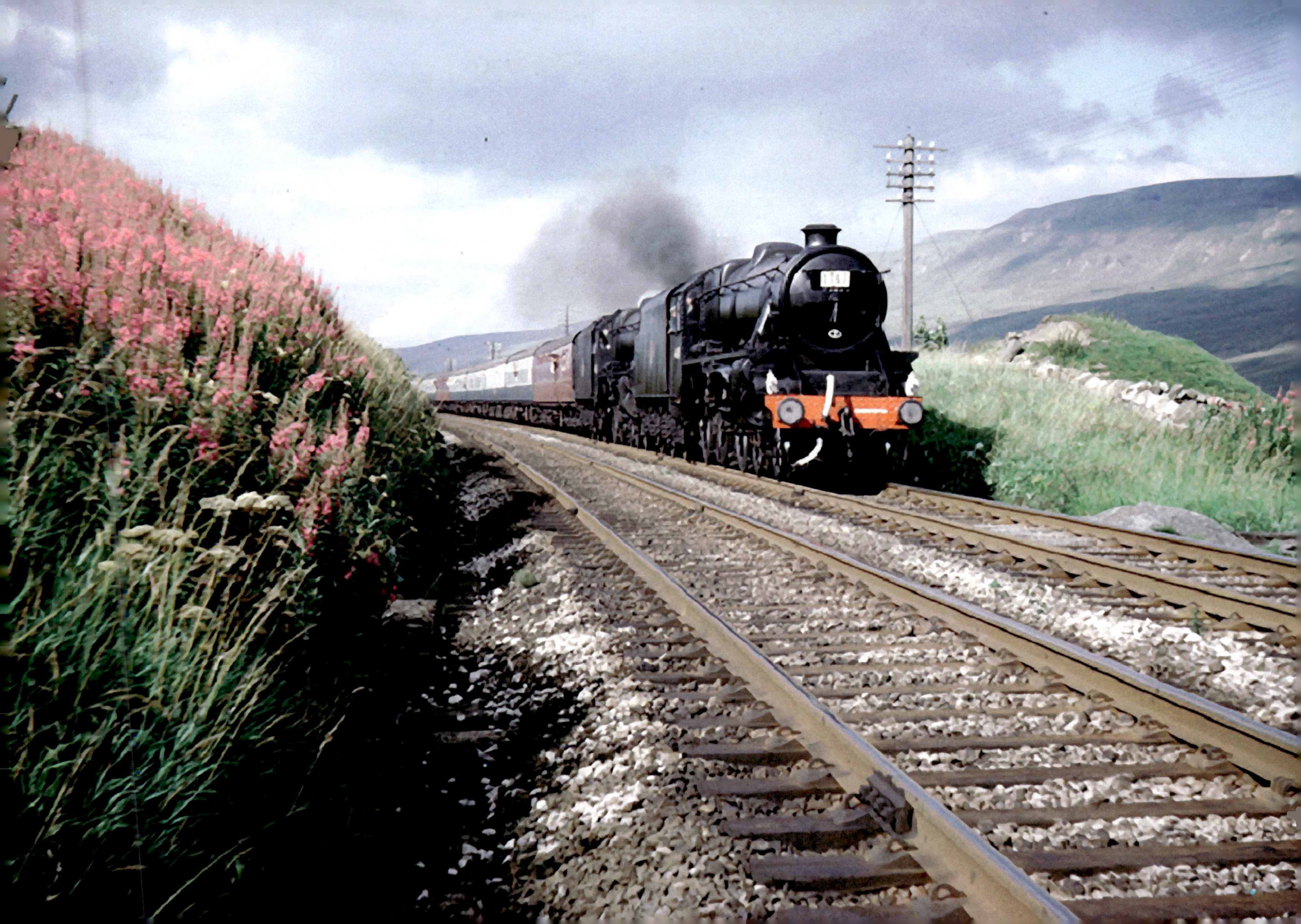

up before it left Ais Gill summit, where it was due to make a 20-minute picture stop. We were thwarted by motorcars – cars that crawled up and down the steep, narrow road to Dent station and prevented us getting the necessary run at the hill, so that Ewan had to dismount and run up – and cars jammed solid three abreast for more than a mile along the B5258 Garsdale-Kirkby Stephen road past Ais Gill railway summit for more than an hour. Bill Sharpe, of Ribblehead, was on duty in Ais Gill signal cabin all that day and later told me there were literally thousands of people milling around the locomotive and on the railway bank when the train stopped there, so we couldn't have got a decent picture anyway.

'I drove on past Ais Gill for Ewan and me to take up positions in Mallerstang for the train's return. There were cameramen about every 50 or 100 yards along the railway bank. The train was double-headed south over the Long Drag by two Black Fives, 44781 and 44871, which came storming up the 1 in 100 gradient faster than I have seen any train climb Mallerstang before. The two locomotives gave a long, mellow whistle for Ais Gill summit and they were gone. Here again, steam went out like a lion.

'On our way home I stopped at Ais Gill cabin to visit Bill Sharpe and give him some duplicate lantern slides I had taken of him on Ribblehead station and in Ribblehead and Ais Gill signal cabins. He said that *Oliver Cromwell* was just about to pass on its return from Carlisle, running light, and I got a photograph and recording of it, which was a very pleasant bonus.'

I learned later that 'Oliver' ran on via Doncaster to Norwich, arriving next day at 1.13pm, to be taken by road to the railway museum at Bressingham Gardens near Diss.

British Railways had announced that no more steam trains were to run on its metals after this event. Little did we think then that we would see many more steam excursions passing over the scenic Settle and Carlisle line and many other main lines in Britain in future years.

There appears to have been little of interest to write about in my diary after the hustle and bustle of the railway steam era. The Mersey steam ferries, Glasgow tramways and British Railways steam – all my main interests – had been replaced by diesel traction in the 1960s and life seemed relatively empty afterwards. Now I had to think about our four-year-old son Earl, who was deaf. He had been boarding at the St John Residential School for the Deaf at Boston Spa near Wetherby, Yorkshire, from 30 April till 18 July 1968, but he was homesick and rebellious while he was there, so we decided to move home to Southport for him to attend as a dayboy at the School for the Partially Hearing in Birkdale, Southport, which was more appropriate for his degree of hearing loss. We eventually found a house in Birkdale and I started work as a news reporter and feature writer for the *Southport Visiter*, a thrice-weekly newspaper, on 28 October 1968. The last entry in my diary was on 3 November.

That was not the end of steam, nor of my tape-recording. I still found other interesting forms of transport to record and, although I had ceased to keep a diary, all that

Part 5 Life after steam, 1968 – 1982

follows was recorded while I was living at Southport.

There was still steam on industrial railways and on the restored narrow gauge railways in Wales. BR still ran steam on the narrow gauge line out of Aberystwyth that it had inherited from the Great Western, and London Transport ran steam work trains till 1971. Steam was being revived by volunteers on preserved standard gauge lines bought from British Railways, such as the Bluebell Railway in Sussex, the Severn Valley Railway in Shropshire and the Worth Valley Railway in Yorkshire. BR had banned steam on its standard gauge metals but a few years later relented and realised the commercial potential of running long-distance steam excursions over its main lines again with locomotives restored by the private-sector preserved railways, and the Settle and Carlisle line became the favourite route for these steam specials.

I was never tempted to record preserved steam railways for tourists because they lacked the urgency and authentic atmosphere of the real thing, nor, for the same reason, did I record any more steam excursions for enthusiasts after my

experience on 'The Zulu' in March 1967, and with the '15-Guinea Special'. I was still only interested in recording steam that provided a necessary, regular service.

One day in May 1969 I went to record the National Coal Board railways at Haig colliery and Whitehaven harbour on the Cumberland coast coalfield by permission of the NCB and the colliery manager. I found 0-4-0 and 0-6-0 saddle tank engines taking trains from the coal screening plant to the weighbridge, to the washing plant at the former Ladysmith colliery (1½ miles away), around the harbour and shunting the trucks along the piers for shipping and into BR exchange sidings. The colliery on the clifftop and the harbour below were linked by a 1 in 5 cable incline with counterbalanced two- or three-truck rakes, and the colliery line from the top of the incline to the washing plant ran along the edge of the clifftop high above the Solway Firth. The following is an extract from a letter to Robin, now back in my archives.

A night in Blea Moor cabin and a day on the Whitehaven coal railways
1 to 6 May 1969

'I set off on a cycle tour straight from the office on the evening of May 1st on my new Claude Butler sports bike, which I named "Norstrom", painted in runic letters on the front mudguard. I rode from Southport up the Ribble valley through Preston, Clitheroe and Settle to Ribblehead and Blea Moor signal cabin. George Horner, the signalman I interviewed in my "Long Drag" programme, was on duty and invited me to sleep the night in his armchair in the cabin rather than stay at the inn. It was warm by the coal stove but sleep was punctuated by the sounds of electric gongs, the crash of levers, diesel freights thundering by and guards coming in for a "brew-up" while their trains were held up in the loop.

'From Ribblehead station I rode over the "Long Drag" in a diesel multiple unit, with a wonderful view through the front cab windows, stopping at Dent, Garsdale and Kirkby Stephen to Appleby, where I alighted. I rode "Norstrom" on via Penrith, round the north side of the Skiddaw massif via Caldbeck to the north end of Bassenthwaite Lake, then via Cockermouth to Whitehaven.

'I got some very interesting and graphic recordings of the 0-4-0 and 0-6-0 saddle-tank engines working the NCB railways at Haig colliery and Whitehaven harbour. The pithead and railway yard is on the top of high cliffs and there is a 1 in 5 incline in the railway from the colliery down to the harbour, on which loaded trucks are lowered by a steel cable. The cable runs round a drum in the engine house and the other end of the cable pulls up empty trucks from the harbour.

'From Whitehaven I rode home round the coast via Ravenglass, Broughton-in-Furness, Lancaster and Preston to Birkdale, arriving home on the evening of May 6th.'

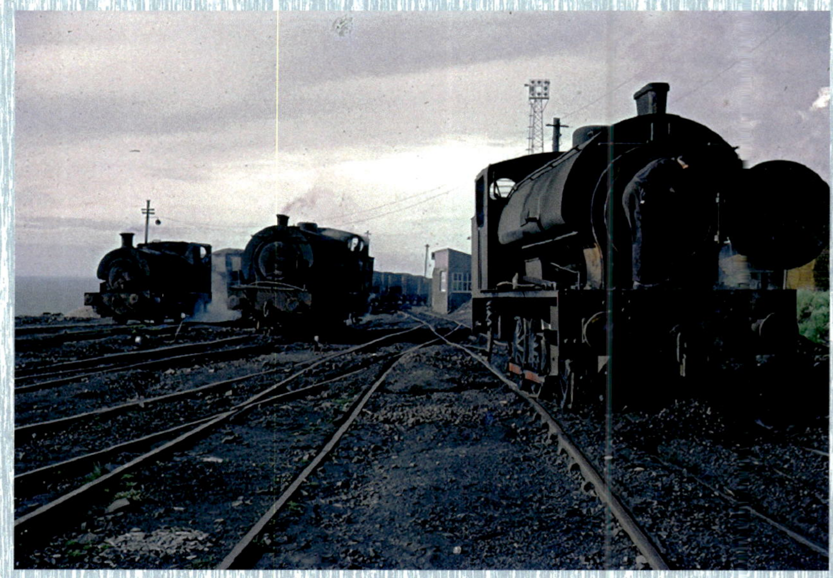

Industrial steam railways at Haig colliery, Whitehaven, in the Cumberland coalfield on 5 May 1969. The fireman of National Coal Board 0-4-0 saddle-tank locomotive *Solway*, built by Hudswell, Clark in 1948, is cleaning his fire grate.

There were more than 70 coalpits around Whitehaven alone at one time, although many of them were small. Some of the galleries extended up to 5 miles under the sea bed. Eight collieries were still at work here in the 1950s, but seven of them closed between 1955 and 1968.

Haig colliery employed about 1,800 men in its heyday in the 1960s. It was the last coal mine in Cumberland and closed in 1986 as a result of a geological fault at the coal face and the national miners' strike of 1984-85. The main building and one of the winding frames in the background survive as the Haig Colliery mining museum, opened in 1997; the rest of the colliery buildings have gone.

Above: Three NCB saddle-tank engines stand in the yard at Haig colliery on 19 June 1969. In the right foreground the fireman of 0-6-0 locomotive *Revenge*, a 1954 Hunslet, is cleaning out his smokebox and burying the track in cinders and soot. Both this engine and the other 0-6-0 on the centre road have the narrow, elongated chimneys of Giesl ejectors, a suction draught system designed by the Austrian engineer Dr Adolph Giesl-Gieslingen to save coal. It was a fairly rare phenomenon in Britain; BR tried it on two locomotives and the Talyllyn on one. On the left is 0-4-0 *Solway*, seen in the previous picture, backing down on to a train of loaded coal wagons from the weighbridge (centre) to take to the washing plant at the former Ladysmith colliery, 1½ miles away.

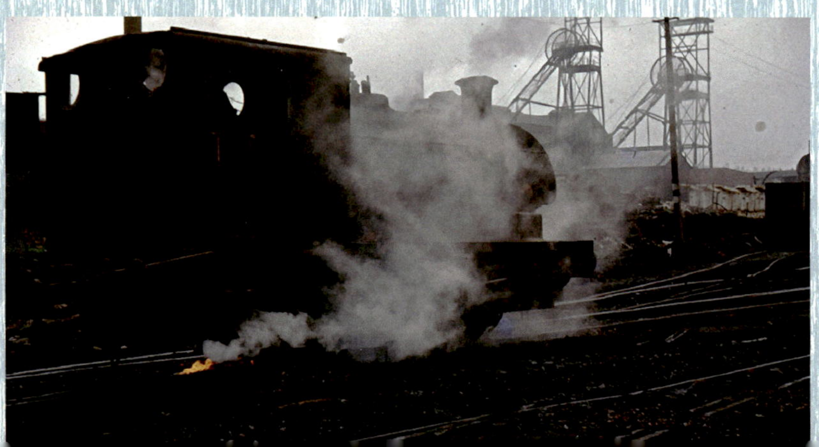

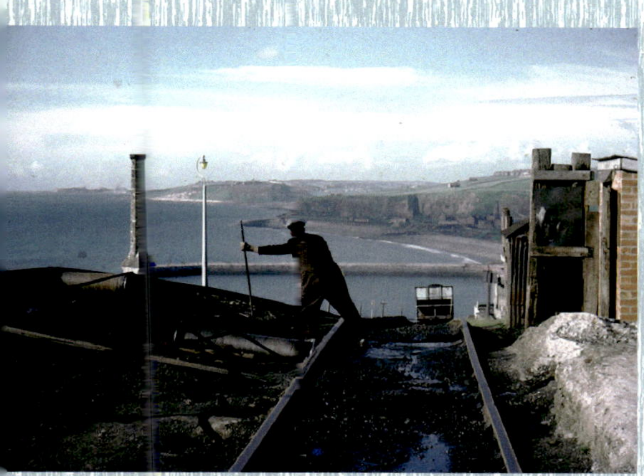

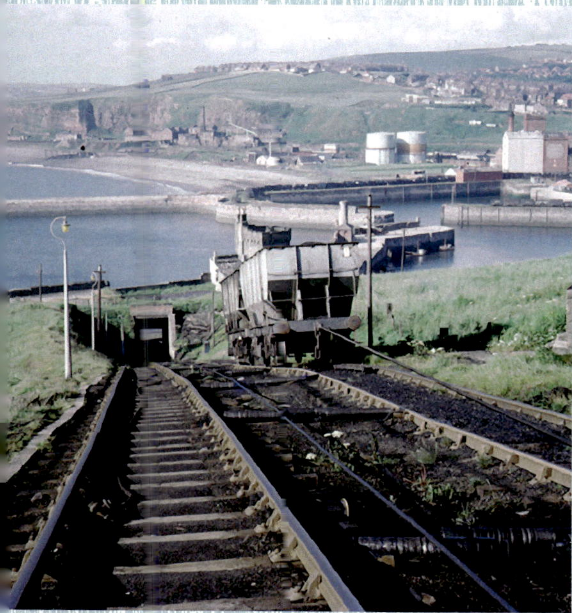

Top left: A man levers the cable on to the rollers as a two-truck rake of coal disappears down the 1 in 5 cable incline from Haig colliery to Whitehaven harbour on 19 June 1969.

Below left: Coal trucks from Haig colliery descended to Whitehaven harbour in two-truck rakes down the Howgill Brake incline. The cable was worked by an electric winding engine at the top of the slope and the empty trucks from the harbour were hooked up to the opposite end of the cable and hauled up on the other track. In this view from the top of the incline on 19 June 1969, the harbour is laid out below with trucks of coal lining the piers, awaiting shipment. We can also see the Quaker Oats mill on the east pier, the gasworks and another colliery, known as William pit, at the foot of the cliffs north of the harbour.

William Pit closed in 1955, the Quaker Oats mill in 1972 and in the same year Howgill Brake stopped working because of a landslip; the coal wagons used Corkickle Brake instead till 1975, when all the coal went by road.

Below: Solway on the Solway. The Haig colliery railway 0-4-0ST locomotive *Solway* runs along the clifftop on the brink of the Solway Firth on 19 June 1969. It is taking a train of empty trucks from the top of the cable incline from the harbour to the washing plant to load more washed coal for the harbour. On the left of the picture is the west pier and lighthouse, built by John Rennie in 1823-38, protecting the harbour entrance. Just to the left of the locomotive we see the top of the chimney of 1840 on the disused Wellington colliery engine house.

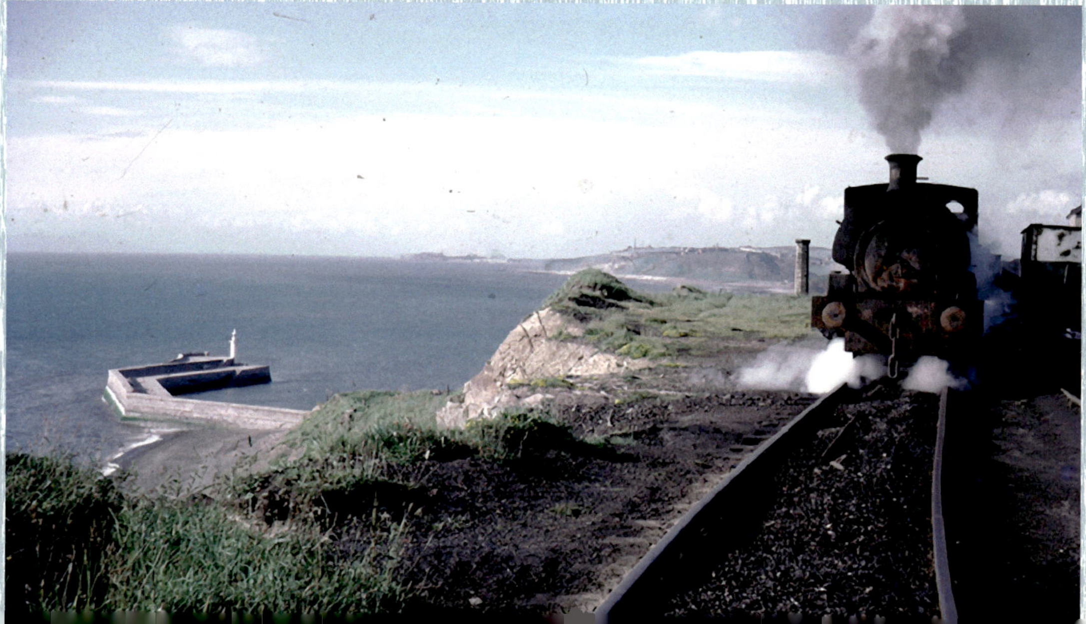

Railway paddle steamers
1974-1981

I discovered a wonderful anachronism on a cycle tour from Lincolnshire to Northumberland in June 1970: British Railways was still operating steam on the Humber ferry with a fleet of three ex-LNER coal-burning paddle steamers, the *Tattersall Castle* and *Wingfield Castle* of 1934 and the *Lincoln Castle* of 1941, plying between floating landing stages at Corporation Pier, Hull, and New Holland Pier on the Lincolnshire bank.

Tattersall Castle was retired in 1973 and I tape-recorded the two remaining paddlers on two later visits, on 19 January 1974 and

Below: NCB 0-4-0 locomotive *Victoria*, a 1942 Peckett, shunts coal wagons on Whitehaven harbour by the Quaker Oats mill (right) on 19 June 1969. The whistles of the harbour railway engines constantly echoed over the town against the surrounding hills and this was the abiding sound of Whitehaven in the industrial age until 1975. The mill closed in 1972.

Below right: The Manchester, Sheffield & Lincolnshire Railway (later the Great Central Railway) opened the line from Grimsby to this windswept, wooden station on New Holland Pier on the Lincolnshire bank of the Humber in 1848 and took over the existing steam ferry service to Hull. The coal trucks on the centre road of this three-track layout were for coaling the ferry steamers.

There were other ferries across the Humber from Roman times but New Holland was the sole Humber crossing from 1930 till the opening of the suspension road bridge in 1981 spelled the closure of the ferry and the pier railway station. This photograph was taken on 16 June 1970.

The quarter-mile-long ferry pier is now owned by New Holland Bulk Services, exporting wheat, barley and rape seed and importing animal feed, aggregates and stone. The wooden station buildings, signal cabin and platforms are still there but the whole space between the platforms is covered by conveyors and pipelines to the pier head.

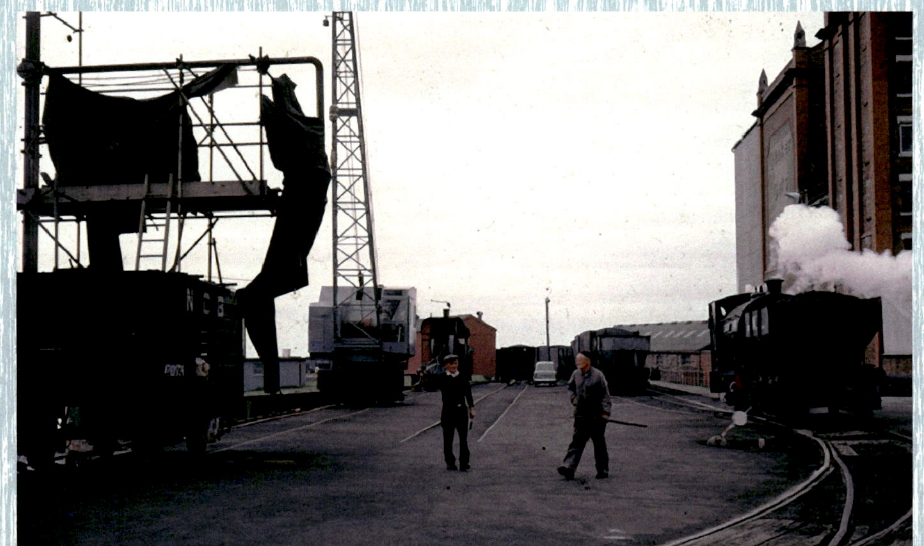

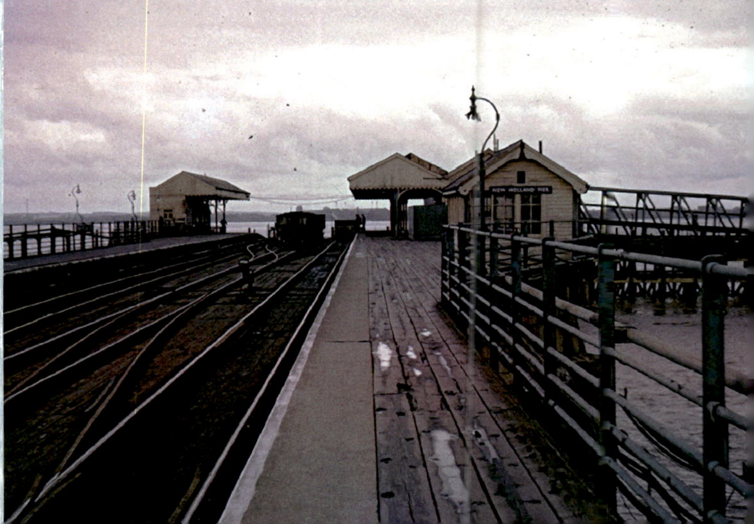

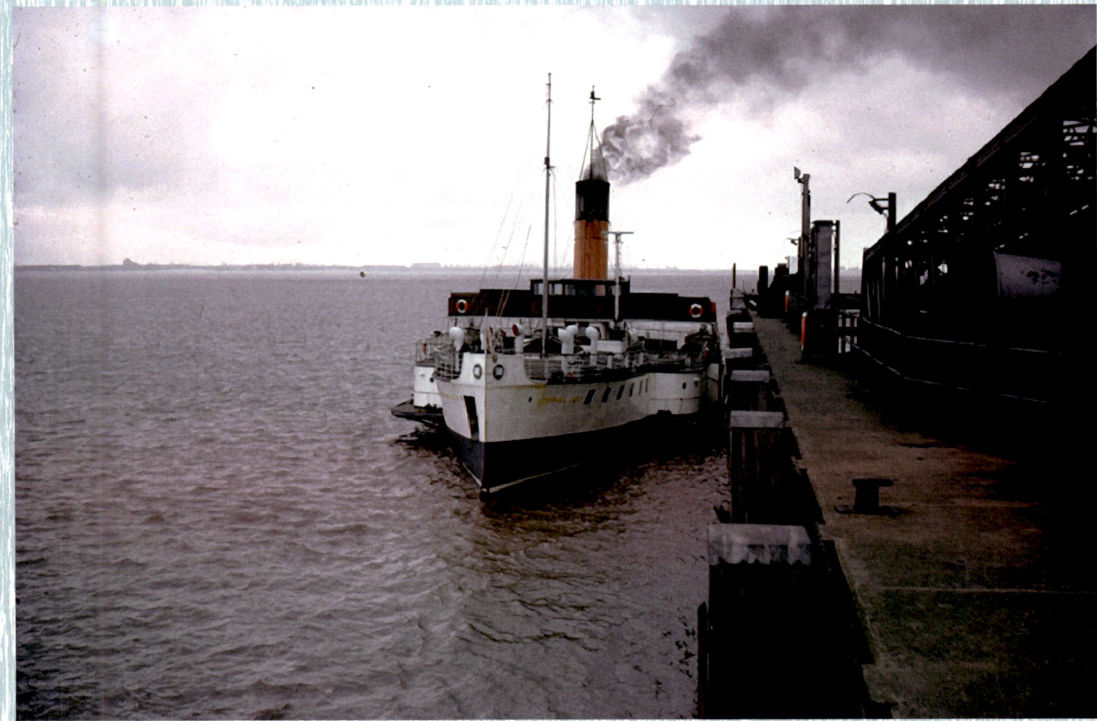

15 January 1975: the fireman feeding the four furnaces in the stokehold, the engine room telegraph bells and thrusting pistons and, up on deck, the therapeutic, steady beat of the threshing paddle wheels and the wind singing through the rigging as we crossed the wide estuary.

The ferry operated from a wooden railway station on bleak New Holland Pier. It was a three-track terminus with coal trucks stationed on the centre tracks for coaling the ferry steamers. By 1975 the two older steamers had been retired and the *Lincoln Castle* was running the service alone; it was the last coal-burning paddle steamer plying in British waters. I stayed overnight at the Lincoln Castle Hotel, New Holland, and in the morning I recorded the interesting manner of coaling the ferry steamer. The coal was trans-shipped from the railway trucks on the pier by small, pneumatic-tyred, four-

British Railways still ran coal-fired paddle steamers across the Humber estuary from New Holland to Hull until 1978. It was a 20-minute passage to the Yorkshire bank, seen on the distant horizon of this picture of PS *Tattersall Castle* loading at New Holland Pier on 15 June 1970, with the BR 'double arrow' insignia on the sides of her red and black funnel.

The Humber ferries were always paddlers because of the shallow draughts required for this wide river with its many sandbanks. The drive-on PS *Tattersall Castle* and its sister ship *Wingfield Castle* were built for the LNER by William Gray at West Hartlepool in 1934 to replace the old vehicular ferries that had to be loaded by crane. They were side-loaders, 200 feet long and 556 gross tons with a draught of 4ft 6in and were augmented by the similar PS *Lincoln Castle* from the Glasgow yard of A. & J. Inglis in 1941.

The *Tattersall Castle* was retired in 1973 and *Wingfield Castle* in 1974, when BR drafted its 1947 diesel-electric paddle ferry *Farringford* from the Solent to the Humber to maintain the two-ship service. The *Lincoln Castle* remained the last coal-fired paddle steamer in British waters till she was withdrawn in 1978 in need of a new boiler. *Farringford* soldiered on alone for the last few years of the ferry service till it was superseded by the new suspension bridge between Barton and Hessle in 1981.

The *Tattersall Castle*, much altered, is berthed as a floating restaurant at Victoria Embankment, Westminster, *Wingfield Castle* is in the maritime museum on the site of the shipyard where she was built at West Hartlepool, and *Lincoln Castle* ended up in Grimsby docks and was scrapped in 2010.

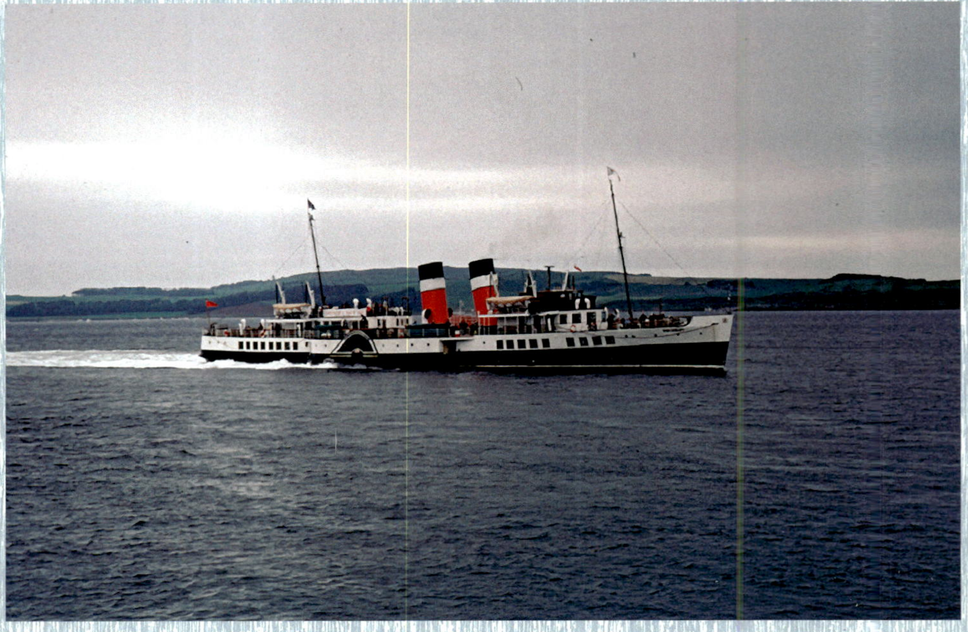

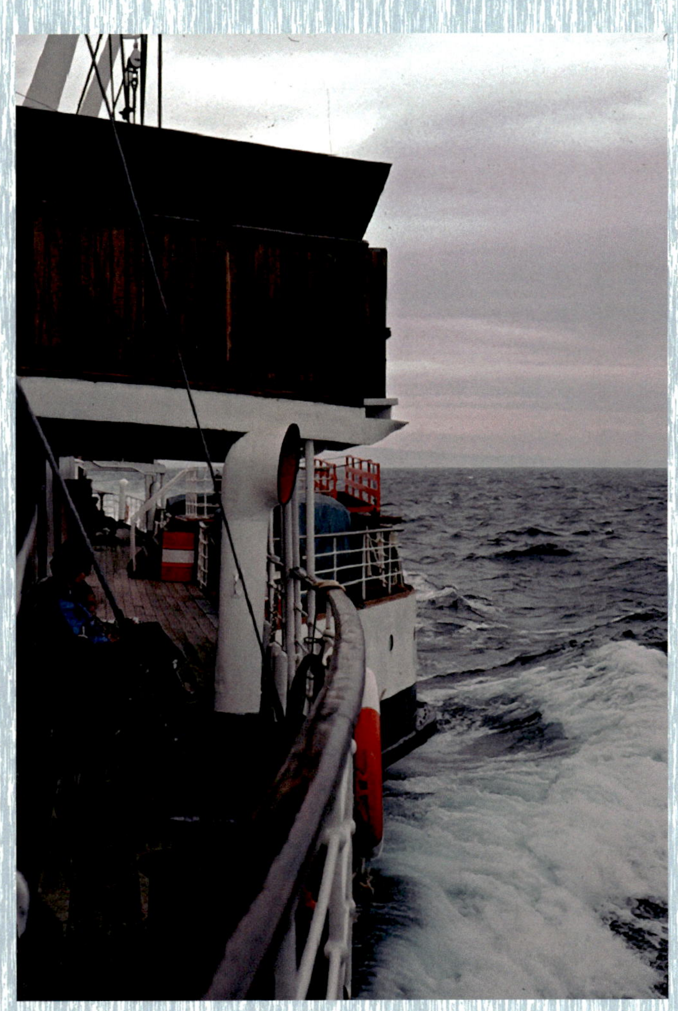

Left. This is the port side of the Firth of Clyde excursion paddle steamer *Waverley* on passage along the Ayrshire coast from Ayr to Millport on 8 July 1981.

Above: The paddle steamer *Waverley* was also of LNER lineage and she has served under five flags. She is seen here leaving Largs, with the island of Great Cumbrae in the background, in the Firth of Clyde on 8 July 1981. She was built by A. & J. Inglis at Glasgow in 1946-47 as a coal-burning ferry and excursion steamer for the LNER, based at Craigendoran. On nationalisation in 1948 she was transferred to the British Transport fleet and in 1951 to the Caledonian Steam Packet Company. She was converted to an oil-burner from 1957 and became part of the Caledonian MacBrayne fleet in 1973. A year later she was sold for £1 to the Paddle Steamer Preservation Society, which formed the Waverley Steam Navigation Company to operate her, as now, on excursions from Glasgow around the Firth of Clyde, the Hebrides, the Bristol Channel, the south coast of England and the Thames estuary. She is said to be the last sea-going paddle steamer in the world.

wheel 'tubs', towed in train up and down the bridge to the landing stage by small, electric tractors and manhandled on deck to the stokehold hatch, which was a hole in the floor in the middle of a passenger walkway. Each truck was hoisted on one end by a chain through a block in the ceiling to tip the coal through the hole into the stokehold bunker while passengers nonchalantly walked by.

The *Lincoln Castle* was retired with a deteriorated boiler in 1978 and was succeeded by the diesel-electric paddler *Farringford* from the Isle of Wight, which I never saw. The ferry closed in 1981, when it was replaced by the Humber suspension bridge.

I recorded another ex-LNER paddle steamer, the Firth of Clyde excursion steamer *Waverley*, built in 1946-47, on a fairly rough passage from Ayr to Millport on 8 July 1981. I enjoyed a lively passage, but my younger son, Ross, then aged 14, who was with me on this trip, did not appreciate it. The *Waverley* was built at the same Clyde shipyard as the *Lincoln Castle*. In 1974 the nationalised railway shipping company Caledonian MacBrayne sold the *Waverley* for £1 to the Paddle Steamer Preservation Society, which formed the Waverley Steam Navigation Company to operate it on its old routes down firth and these excursions now extend around the coast to Oban, the English Channel ports and London River. This is the last sea-going paddle steamer in the world.

Gardner-engined buses with conductors 1982

Buses were my first interest in life, evidently from about the age of three. I liked the buses of the 1930s, the late 1940s and the early 1950s but I began to lose interest in buses when they developed concealed radiators, platform doors and rear engines. In my 'winter of discontent' with little of interest to tape-record and photograph after the end of steam I decided to record the last dinosaurs of the old bus age, the Gardner-engined Guy Arabs and Bristol Lodekkas with their 'half cabs', crash gearboxes and – with the entrances behind the front bulkheads – conductors collecting the fares.

Chester City Transport still operated Massey- and Northern Counties-bodied Guys of 1965-69 on services from the front of the Town Hall to Blacon in 1982, when

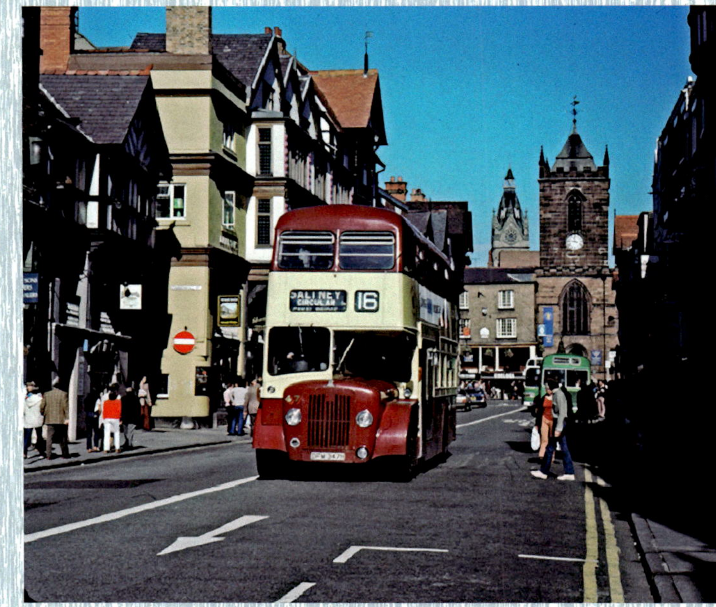

Chester City Transport was one of the last operators to use buses with chassis built by Guy Motors of Wolverhampton. The Guy Arab chassis, powered by a Gardner diesel engine, was built from 1934 to 1970. Chester's No 47, with a Northern Counties body, was the last Guy bus built for Britain, in 1969; the rest went to Hong Kong. Chester's last Guy bus in service – and the last bus with a conductor collecting the fares – ran in 1982.

This bus was pictured in Bridge Street on 22 September 1979, wearing the later style of livery for the fleet of modern, rear-engined buses, but for most of its time it had maroon panels on the upper deck with a cream band under the windows. In the background are two NBC Crosville single-deckers on country services, and the towers of St Peter's Church and the Town Hall. This part of Bridge Street is now a pedestrian precinct.

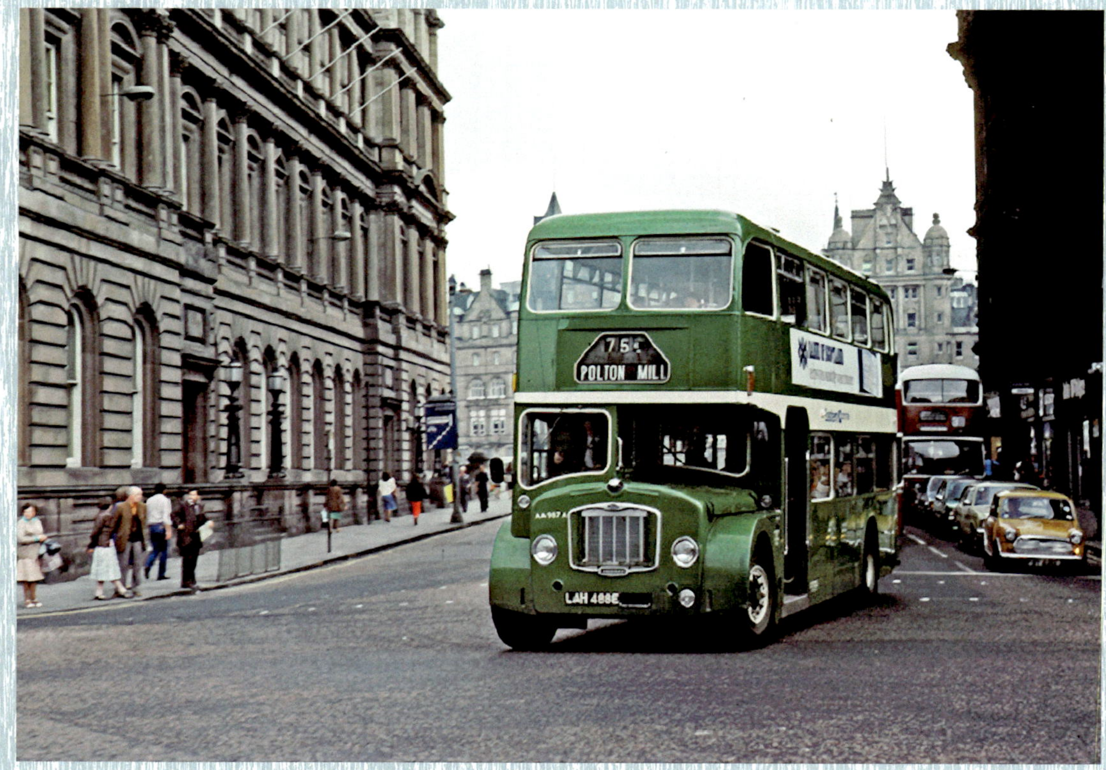

I recorded one starting up from cold in the garage early one winter's morning, going out into service and the conductor collecting the fares; I also put the microphone in the cab to capture in high fidelity the resonant, low-pitched whine of the Gardner engine as a bus climbed through the narrows of Whipcord Lane and Canal Street into the city.

In the same year I went to Edinburgh to record the Bristol Lodekkas of the Eastern Scottish Motor Traction Company. The Lodekka chassis and transmission permitted normal seating and headroom within the low-bridge height of 13ft 4in and the entire production run from 1953 to 1967 carried Eastern Coachwork from Lowestoft, at first 27ft 6in long with back doors then, from the early 1960s, 30 feet long with the doors aft of the front bulkhead, so the Lodekka was still a bus with a conductor. It was eclipsed by rear-engined buses with direct drive to the back axle, which allowed not only for

The Eastern Scottish Motor Traction Company was still operating Bristol Lodekka buses with conductors on its country services out of Edinburgh while the city's Corporation buses were all one-man-operated, which was the reverse of the situation elsewhere. Here again, the entrance was behind the front bulkhead so the Lodekka was necessarily a bus with a conductor. This 1967 Bristol Lodekka is turning from North Bridge into Leith Street, Edinburgh, on

27 May 1980. From this junction it worked around a one-way loop via York Place and St Andrew's Square bus station and the destination blind has already been turned for the return run to Polton, 7 miles south. A 1969 Alexander-bodied Leyland Atlantean city bus can be seen on the right.

In the exchange of new for old buses with England and Wales, the Eastern SMT had second-hand Lodekkas from the Eastern Counties Omnibus

Company, like this one, and from the Brighton, Hove & District Omnibus Company. These buses, with Norfolk and East Sussex registrations, worked in Midlothian on services into the coal-mining towns of the Pentland Hills along with indigenous Edinburgh-registered Lodekkas. In earlier days Lodekkas looked smarter with black mudguards offsetting the main body colours, both in England and Wales and in Scotland.

low-slung bodies but also one-man operation with the entrance beside the driver.

The Bristol Lodekka, however, was a long time a-dying. They were happiest on the long country hauls of Eastern Counties and Hants & Dorset and the hill-climbing routes of Western National and Crosville, but their need for crew operation with conductors found them making their last stand on town services at Norwich, Poole, Bath, Bristol and York. At Edinburgh, conversely, they were still running country services up to the mining towns in the Pentland Hills with conductors while the city's Corporation buses were all one-manned.

The Scottish Bus Group preferred the reliability of the front-engined, two-man Bristol Lodekka to the economy of the later, one-man, rear-engined buses, and in 1973 exchanged its newer Eastern-bodied Bristol VRTs for 91 older Bristol FLF Lodekkas with the National Bus Company in England and Wales, and these saw service in the Eastern, Western, Central, Midland and Northern SMT fleets.

On 26 May 1982 I recorded an ex-Brighton, Hove & District Bristol Lodekka of 1966 on the 13-mile route from Edinburgh to Dalkeith and Birkenside, singing and slogging along the open country road and hammering up the long climb from Dalkeith at 200 feet to Birkenside at 500 feet. I still have these Lodekka recordings on tape but they have not been transcribed on to disc.

Apart from these interludes, after the steam era I ended my recording days on the iron road in pursuit of pre-war electric traction on the Southern Electric and other London suburban lines, on the Manchester South Junction & Altrincham line, the Liverpool suburban lines, Blackpool tramways, the Glasgow subway and on the Chicago, South Shore & South Bend Railroad, the last interurban in North America.

A 1966 Eastern SMT Bristol Lodekka climbs North Bridge, Edinburgh, on route 86 to Dalkeith and Birkenside on 31 May 1980, with two city buses in the background. This bus was indigenous to the Eastern SMT.

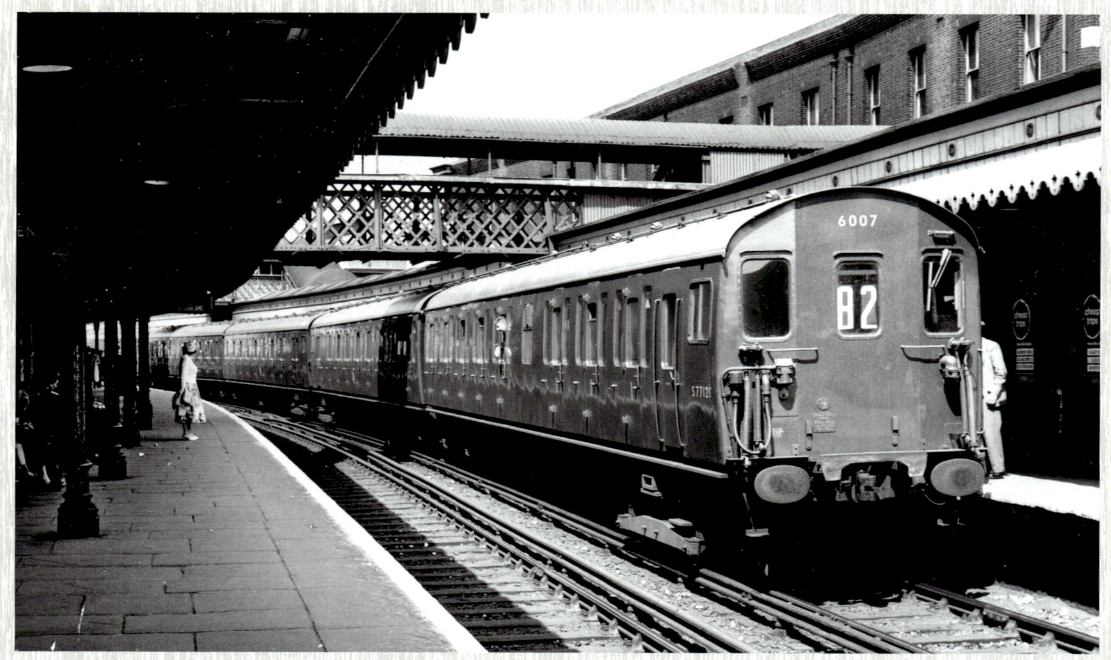

In those days when steam trains and tramcars were almost extinct in Great Britain, when traffic on British Railways was declining, the system was being pruned and thinned and diesel noise and smell prevailed, it was refreshing to find such a thriving and developing part of the system as the Southern Electric. In 1968 British Railways' Southern Region operated the biggest and busiest electric railway system in the world with 1,003 miles of third-rail electric route (no overhead wires) in a maze of lines radiating from seven London terminals, worked by four-, six-, eight- and 12-car electric multiple unit trains on fast and frequent local and limited-stop services. It was south London's local railway and the main line to the sea – to all ports

Southern Electric: looking at this picture, one can almost hear the electro-pneumatic brake pump ticking over quietly as this eight-car train, made up of four 2-HAP electric multiple units, slides into platform 2 at London Bridge (high-level) station in Bermondsey. The pick-up shoe beams on the third rail mark the traction bogies under both ends of each two-car set. This train is on a semi-fast run from Charing Cross via Woolwich to Gillingham on 11 May 1958.

These units, geared to run up to 90mph, were built from 1956 to 1963 for the Kent coast electrification. This leading set dates from 1956. On 9 June 1959 the route of headcode 82 was extended from Gillingham to Margate and Ramsgate with only shortworkings terminating at Gillingham. The 2-HAP units were said to be classified as 2-car, HAlf saloon/compartment sets with Pneumatic brakes. They were withdrawn from service in 1982.

London Bridge (high-level) was the terminus of the London & Greenwich Railway, the first railway in London, opened to Deptford in 1837. The building in the background is the former headquarters of the South Eastern Railway fronting Tooley Street and it was still used as railway offices until recent redevelopments. From the elevated terminal and river bridges tracks run atop brick arched viaducts over the roofs of south London to maintain height for the climb through the encircling hills of Kent and Surrey. *J. H. Aston, Burgess Hill* and resorts from Ramsgate in the east to Bournemouth in the west.

The green trains brought a touch of the country into London and took the Londoner into the country with 'Trains every few minutes to the leafy suburbs, the North Downs the Weald, the South Downs and the sea. Southern Electric was synonymous with the sight of these long, green trains snaking and rocking through

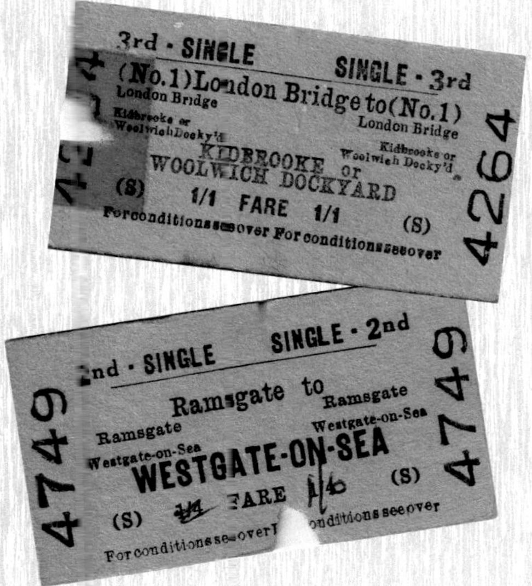

A tickets from London Bridge to Kidbrooke or Woolwich Dockyard on 17 September 1955, fare 1s 1d, and one from Ramsgate to Westgate-on-Sea on 11 December 1960, fare 1s 6d.

the complex of tracks at the approaches to the London terminals, streaking along the viaducts over south London, converging, diverging, ever energetically surging objectively onward, making short work of long distances, trailing sparks as they went and lighting up the night sky with their arc flashes. The aural experience of the Southern Electric was the sound of slamming doors, pulsating electric brake pumps, shrieking guards' whistles, humming traction motors, jangling bogies over junctions, the rumble and thunder of trains over Southwark's iron viaducts, the echoes of Cockney station announcements and the cacophony of 16-, 24-, 32- and 48-axle trains clattering past your window on other tracks.

In those days you could stick your head out of the window behind the motorman's cab of an electric multiple-unit train leaving a city terminus at night and catch the excitement and fascination of electric traction. The train jerked to life as the motors lunged in on first notch. It glided over the complex of tracks and switches outside the station. You could feed the surge of power and hear the growling whine of the electric traction motors as the train accelerated rapidly and raced and rocked along the steel ribbons curving ahead, the wheels of its heavy traction bogies stunning the rail joints and the pick-up shoes on the

third rail trailing fireworks. The fresh air, unpolluted by coal smoke or diesel fumes, was tinged with warm ozone rising from the motors. The dim lights of a station loomed up ahead and you felt the train was going too fast to stop. It crashed through the points at the approaches to the station, arrested its onward proclivity with the same mysterious power as in acceleration and ground to a halt within the length of the platform.

Alas, the Southern Electric is not like this today. As the trains were repainted BR blue with yellow faces, the name Southern Electric was dropped, the green signs with their yellow flashes of lightning disappeared and it seemed as if the Health & Safety Executive progressively exerted its influence over the running of trains and the spirit and excitement was drained out of the operations. Today the system is operated by three companies whose lines correspond with those of the three constituent pre-Grouping companies and are worked with sleek, plush trains with sliding doors, ever-changing liveries and a traction sound that is a mild, high-pitched, monotone whine because the technology has changed. The station announcements are recordings by women with polished diction, which sound cold, and all the sights and sounds of the old Southern Electric have gone forever.

Electrification of the south London suburban lines was completed between 1909 and 1930 to compete with electric tramcars, which were taking passengers from the suburban steam trains. It was a case of using electric rail traction to compete with electric rail traction – of out-tramming the tramcar with a higher degree of development. Most of the main-line electric system as we know it today was completed between 1932 and 1939, to the whole Sussex coast, Portsmouth, Alton, Reading, Sevenoaks, Gillingham and Maidstone, all on the 660-volt third rail and featuring, notably,

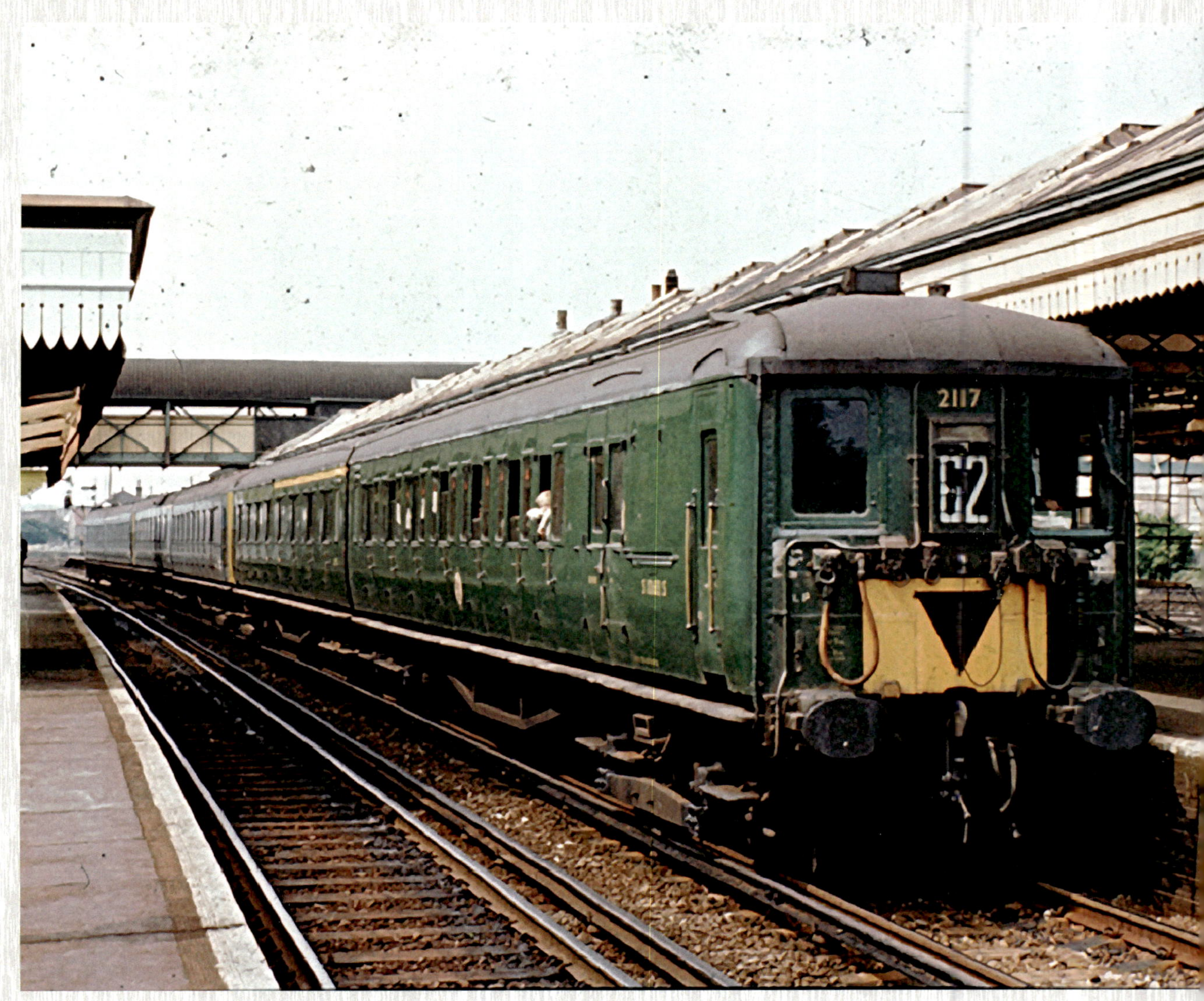

A south coast local stops at Hove on its way from Portsmouth Harbour to Brighton on 7 April 1970. This was the end of the Southern Region green era; the last four cars of this six-car train of 2-BIL stock were repainted blue with fellow cab fronts. The black triangle on the yellow warning panel indicates the traction car with the power and air couplings and the mail and luggage compartment.

the 'Brighton Belle', the only all-Pullman electric multiple unit train in the world. The post-war extensions to the Kent coast were completed in 1959–62, and to Basingstoke, Southampton and Bournemouth in 1967, all at 750 volts.

The labyrinth of lines criss-crossing south London provided dense suburban coverage while north of the Thames the main-line railway companies provided suburban services merely as local short-workings of the trunk lines, which is why so much of London Transport's electric railway system (the 'Underground') lies north of the river and has relatively little penetration south of the river.

The name of this electric railway system, Southern Electric, smacked of North American interurban names like Texas Electric and Pacific Electric and our own British interurban, the Manx Electric. The Southern Electric was more like a tramway system than any other electric railway because of its intensive network with an intensive service of trains, the multiplicity of junctions, the short hops between stops on local services and the display of route numbers, called headcodes, in white-on-black stencils and roller blinds on the front of the trains, a feature not used on any other British railway system to my knowledge.

I found that the best position for recording on board Southern Electric trains was the guard's, mail and luggage compartment behind the motorman's cab, to be found at each end of every four-car set. This was the compartment where a passenger could put a bicycle or a pram, a facility no longer available today. I recorded at the front end of the train as the guard was at the back. The motormen, who had to walk through the luggage compartment at the front of the train to get to the cab, were very friendly and often invited me into the cab, even in and out of the large terminals. I rode with them a few times but when I was recording I usually declined the invitation because the traction bogies were right under the floor of the luggage compartment. Here I was able to open the windows on both sides of the train to record the echoes and had the freedom of movement from one side to the other without disturbing the passengers or the motorman, who probably wouldn't like the windows open anyway. I could also hear the starting bell in the motorman's cab and the sound of his controller notching up and down.

In all my recording quests I rarely got the sounds I wanted first time because they weren't graphic enough. I was a perfectionist and I nearly always had to go back to retake them until I got just what I wanted. I persisted with the London recordings several times over the same itinerary north and south of the river until I got them 'in the can' in 1969, a year after I finished all my steam recordings. Here are a few extracts from my diary entries of that endeavour. You will see from the dates of these extracts that I not only ended my railway recordings this way but I began recording electric traction before steam.

**The electric railways of London
19 December 1966**

'The ride in the motorman's cab from Victoria to Clapham Junction was a fascinating experience. I liked the sturdy, hefty controls in brass and black iron, to feel the smooth gliding over the rails, the surge of power as the motorman notched-up and the way we rocked over the converging and diverging rails, which glinted in the darkness from the lights of the city reflected on the underside of the low cloud.

'Clapham Junction is the largest and busiest station in Britain, covering 28 acres and handling up to 1,500 trains a day. I spent some time here during the afternoon peak period recording the trains, some stopping, others rushing through. Clapham Junction was a wonderful place with long trains racing and clattering through almost continuously, their lines of light snaking into and out of the darkness. I even caught the sound of a steam train coming in off the west London belt line.'

19 June 1968

While on a visit with Ruth to her mother at Folkestone: 'I left Folkestone on an early train from Central station to Waterloo East, then caught another train to London Bridge, where I recorded the verbal introduction to my programme "The Electric Railways of London" [eventually called 'Vintage Voltage'] against the background sounds of a pre-war Southern Electric train (a 4-LAV or 2-BIL) groaning westbound out of London Bridge (high-level) station.

'Then I rode to New Cross and changed to the London Transport sub-surface East London Line to record on board a vintage, clerestory-roofed traction car of District Railway ancestry on a four-car Q-stock train from Rotherhithe through the oldest tunnel under the river, to Wapping and Shadwell.'

London Transport appeared to relegate its oldest stock to this branch-line backwater between Shoreditch and New Cross. The Q stock was an LT designation for the mixture of District Railway stock of

1927 and 1931 and LT stock of 1935, all identical, rectangular cars with clerestory roofs and segmental arched cab windows, combined with the more modern-style LT stock of 1938 with flared sides, and there were two traction cars and two trailer cars in each four-car set. I always rode the line in one of the clerestory-roofed traction cars. The electric air brake pump ticked over quietly in the station, the pneumatic sliding doors clunked shut, a tramcar-type starting bell tinkled behind the bulkhead of the motorman's cab, the train started with a jerk and accelerated with violent tugging every time the motorman notched up, accompanied by the rising pitch of the deep, growling drone from the traction motors resounding against the tunnel walls. The jerky starts and stops were reminiscent of the Liverpool Overhead Railway.

'At Shadwell I changed to the old London, Tilbury & Southend Railway to record Eastern Region overhead-electric multiple units from the traction car in the middle of the train from Stepney East to Fenchurch Street and from Bethnal Green to Liverpool Street. Then I went back south of the river to record a run on the Southern from Charing Cross to St John's.

An eclectic mixture of old stock built between 1923 and 1938 was to be found operating London Transport's Metropolitan (East London) Line between New Cross and Shoreditch in the 1960s. This train in Rotherhithe station on 19 June 1968 is headed and tailed by two ex-District Railway clerestory-roofed traction cars of 1927, sandwiching two LT flared-side trailer cars of 1938. In the background is the mouth of the oldest under-river tunnel in the world, built by Marc and Isambard Brunel and opened as a foot tunnel in 1843 and for the East London Railway in 1869.

This 4-mile branch of the LT system was originally an important cross-London link between the London, Brighton & South Coast Railway, the South Eastern Railway and the Great Eastern Railway with steam goods and passenger trains south of the river to Croydon, Brighton, Peckham Rye, Crystal Palace and Addiscombe Road and north of the river to Liverpool Street and Hammersmith. After electrification of the East London Line on the four-rail system in 1913 the District and Metropolitan companies ran through from Hammersmith to New Cross via a junction at Whitechapel.

LT took over passenger operations from 1933 and split the services at Whitechapel in 1941 when the line was badly bombed in the air raids on London docks and closed for three months. From 1941 till 2006 the East London Line was a detached branch of the LT system with passengers changing at Whitechapel although steam freights still worked through the tunnel between New Cross and Bishopsgate till 1962 and parcels trains till 1966.

The old stock in this picture was scrapped in 1971 and the line closed from 2006 to 2010 for a complete rehabilitation and revival of its connections north and south of the river. It is now part of London's orbital 'Overground' third-rail electric system and the stations have been transformed with white wall panels, strip lighting and false ceilings.

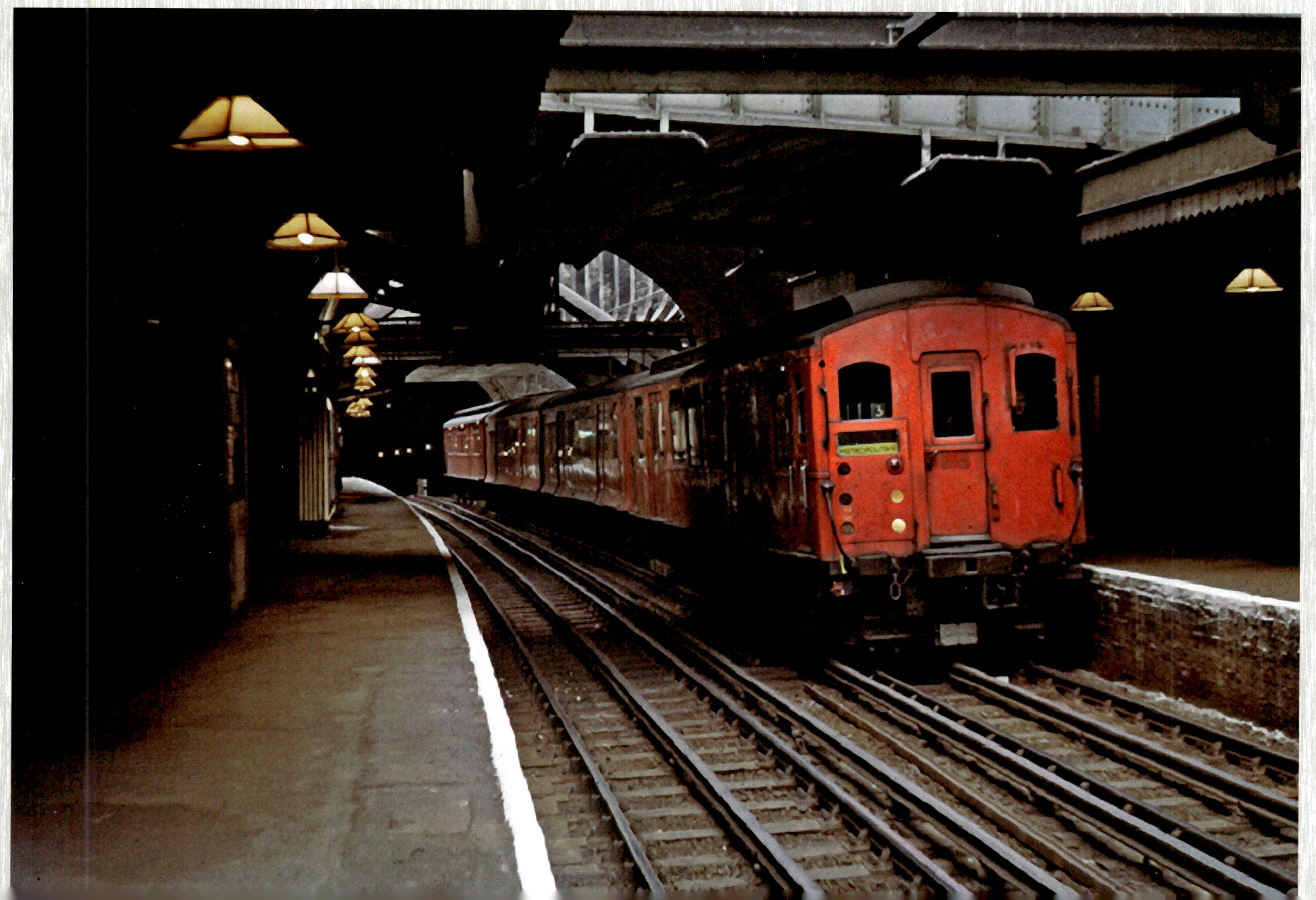

'I recorded the introduction to a new tape programme, "Southern Electric", at London Bridge (Central Division) terminus followed by a ride in the motorman's cab on the semi-circular belt line around south London from London Bridge to Victoria via Denmark Hill.'

20 June 1968

I stayed the night with my old RAF friend Robin Hogg and his wife Hazel at St Albans, and next day: 'I travelled with Robin to St Pancras as he went to work in London and I continued my recordings, mostly of post-war EPBs, on the Southern Electric. I re-recorded the introduction to my "Southern Electric" tape at London Bridge (Central Division) and the ride around the South London line from London Bridge to Victoria. Then I went on a Western Division train from Waterloo to Shepperton, recording from Hampton to the terminus. I returned to Waterloo and travelled on the Waterloo & City Line for the first time to the Bank. This small-scale extension of the old London & South Western Railway into the city is the only main-line railway company's version of a tube railway, with rather strange Southern Railway rolling stock, built in 1940. It is the kind of tube train one might ride in a dream: the coaches are small and rounded – almost tubular – with matching small, rounded windows and a claustrophobic feeling inside.

'Next I recorded trains on the Eastern Division of the Southern Electric, first with a ride in the motorman's cab from Holborn Viaduct station to Herne Hill. The motorman, a Scotsman, was a former Glasgow tram driver, who stayed faithful to electric traction after the tramways closed and he joined BR. He told me he refused to drive diesel trains because the fumes gave him dermatitis. The controls in the cab were almost identical to those of a tramcar but everything was a bit heftier and he had no motor traffic to contend with.

'Then I made two recorded runs from Charing Cross to Hither Green, the first in the motorman's cab for my "Southern Electric" programme, the second in the leading luggage compartment for the "Electric Railways of London", having found this to be the better recording position. From this position I then recorded a short run from Victoria to Clapham Junction, calling at Battersea, and re-recorded part of the afternoon peak period at Clapham Junction.

'At the end of the day I returned to Victoria to board a Ramsgate/Dover train and recorded from the luggage compartment as we traversed the bridges, stations and tunnels of the Medway towns from Strood to Gillingham and the last stage of the journey from Kearsney through Buckland Junction and the tunnels into Dover Priory terminus. I returned to Folkestone in a train along the foot of the cliffs in the twilight.'

23 June 1968

'I took all my luggage as I was now on my way home to Kendal and thumbed a lift in a car from London Road, Folkestone, to Cheapside, London. I left my luggage at Liverpool Street station and continued recording my tape programme "The Electric Railways of London" with a ride on the Great Eastern Line from Liverpool Street to Bethnal Green to replace the recording I made on June 19th in the opposite direction – upgrade instead of downgrade to hear the electric traction motors working harder. I went on to do the North London Line from Broad Street to Dalston Junction. I had recorded this previously but from the lead car, which proved to be a trailer. This time I recorded from the traction car, which was the last car of the train. I finished the north of the river side of the tape with frequent electric trains stopping at Willesden Junction low-level with the male voice of the station announcer.'

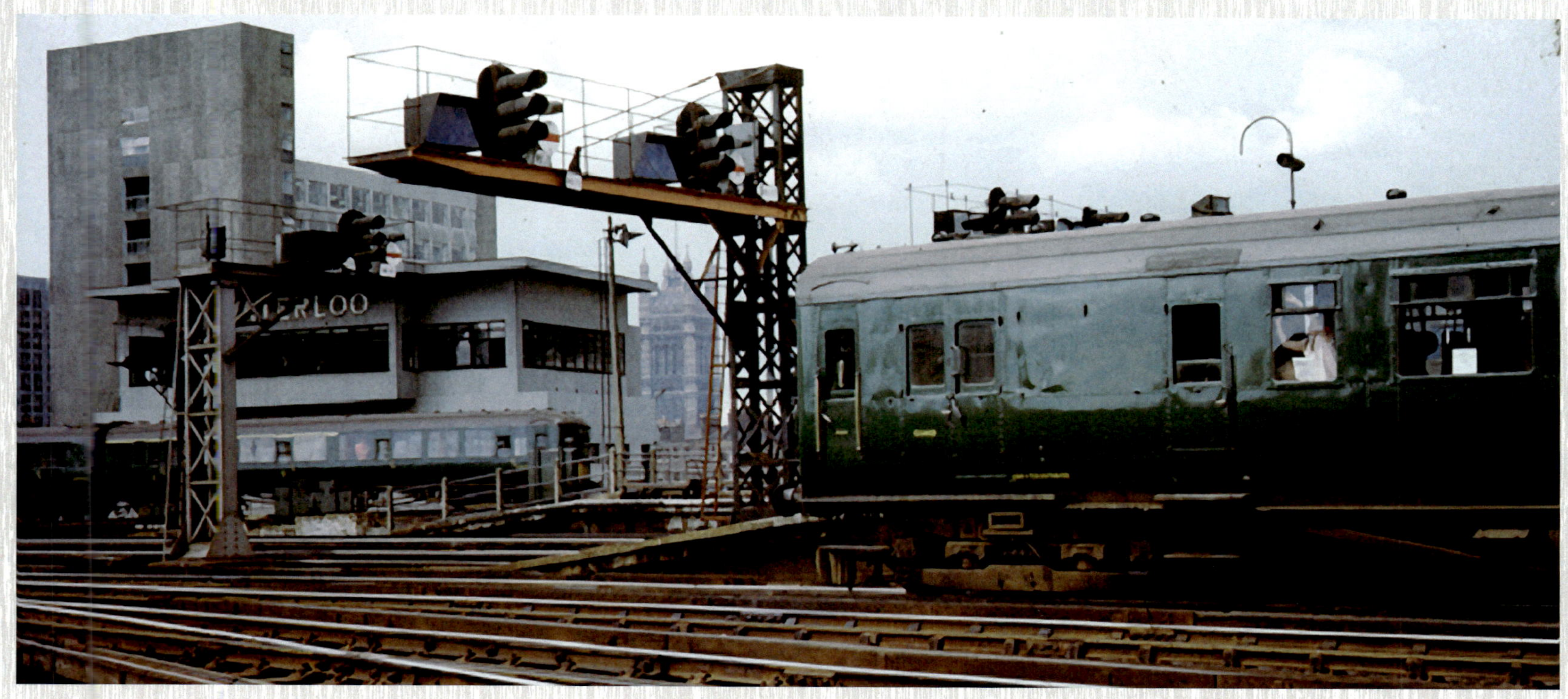

Southern Electric 2-BIL electric multiple units enter and leave Waterloo terminus in Lambeth on 20 June 1968. The last steam train left here on 9 July 1967. The Victoria Tower of the Houses of Parliament, across the river in Westminster, is framed by the modern-looking 1936 signal cabin and the signal gantry.

The 2-BIL was classified as a 2-car, BI-Lavatory unit (one lavatory in each car) with two English Electric traction motors. A total of 150 units were built between 1935 and 1938 for semi-fast services from London to Brighton, Portsmouth, Alton and Reading and along the Sussex coast. They remained in service till withdrawal between 1968 and 1972. They usually ran in four-, six-, eight- and 12-car multiple unit trains, a 12-car train mustering 1,650hp. Observe the hefty timber shoebeam on the traction bogie to pick up the current from the live third rail. The guard's and luggage compartment above the bogie, between the motorman's cab and the passenger saloon at each end of a two-car unit, was the ideal position for tape-recording.

Waterloo station was the London terminus of the London & South Western Railway. It was rebuilt between 1900 and 1921 with a concourse and 21 platforms covering 2¼ acres, a spacious station on a curve and the largest railway terminus in Britain. At the time of this picture it was served by 1,200 trains a day. It took 21 years to rebuild the station because the LSWR found the money from annual revenue instead of borrowing it – a lesson that could be learned for today. The First World War also intervened in the construction.

Despite orbiting London's suburban lines at least twice to get better recordings and despite all the miles I travelled by Southern Electric, my intended programmes 'The Electric Railways of London' and 'Southern Electric' were sacrificed to a more selective programme of pre-war electric traction in and around London, Manchester, Merseyside and Glasgow on the CD 'Vintage Voltage'. I used only two London sequences – the introduction at London Bridge high-level and the journey on the East London Line – in the final CD programme. The other London recordings did not seem as graphic or interesting as those further north but now that those sounds are no longer with us I should like to compile those programmes from my existing tapes if I could find the equipment to do so.

Manchester South Junction & Altrincham Railway
9 April 1969

The original LNER/LMS 1931 non-corridor compartment stock was still working this former joint line south-west of the city into the Cheshire suburbs. It was electrified with 1,500 volts d.c. overhead wire and pantograph collection. Trains had been curtailed at Manchester Oxford Road in 1965 when BR re-electrified the half mile

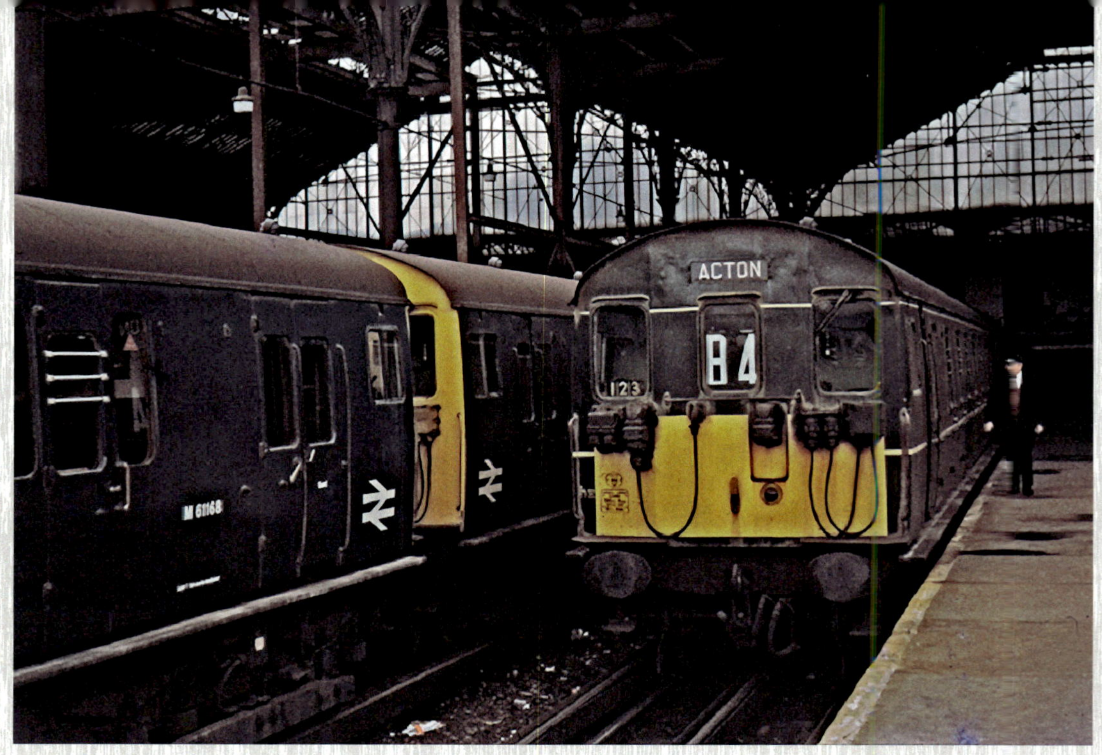

Broad Street was the city terminus of the BR (Midland) North London Line, next door to Liverpool Street station. Pictured on 24 June 1968, these BR standard third-rail electric multiple units for the London district ran from here to Richmond via Hampstead and to Watford via Kilburn, the two lines crossing at Willesden Junction. This two-car unit is on a short-working to Acton on the Richmond line.

This was the third busiest railway terminus in London after Liverpool Street and Victoria in Edwardian times with trains arriving and departing every minute in peak periods and the line was electrified in 1916 to cope with the traffic. As passengers found other routes, their numbers declined from 27 million in 1902 to 312,000 in 1985. The station was damaged in both world wars, the outer end of the trainshed roof was removed in 1947 and in 1969 four of the nine passenger platforms were abandoned and the goods yard closed.

Broad Street station and the line to Dalston Junction closed in 1986 and the North London Line was diverted from Dalston to Shoreditch to link up with the East London Line and its extensions south of the river as part of the London Overground system. The two-storey station building, with Romanesque arcading and windows and a convex, French baroque roof, was demolished and the site of Broad Street station is now occupied by a modern block of offices and shops called Broadgate.

from South Junction with 25,000 volts a.c. preparatory to rewiring the whole line. On 9 April 1969 I made a continuous recording of a journey in the leading compartment of a train along the remaining 8 miles from Oxford Road to Altrincham.

Here was the traditional heavy-sounding groan and drone of electric traction motors together with the chug of the pneumatic air brake pump and slamming doors in the nine intermediate stations, only three-quarters of a mile apart on average, and the starting bell and deep-toned air whistle before departure. The sound track was coloured by

cheerful chatter in the local accent among the women passengers in the compartment, which in no way detracted from the potent sounds of the train.

My trip on the Altrincham line was a by-product of a visit to Manchester for the *Southport Visiter* to interview businessmen from Southport, commuting on the morning and evening trains, about their dissatisfaction with the diesel multiple

unit service and to get a response from the railway management in Manchester. As the Southport-Manchester line was half in Liverpool division and half in Manchester division, the head public relations officer in Manchester spent nearly an hour on the phone to the Liverpool office discussing whether Liverpool or Manchester should reply to the complaints. In the end I suggested that I sent copies of the paper

An LNER and LMS joint stock electric multiple unit on the Manchester South Junction & Altrincham Railway is seen at Manchester Oxford Road station on 9 April 1969. This 8½-mile line was the first railway to be electrified at 1,500 volts d.c. and these original three-car sets of compartment stock were built in 1931 by the Metropolitan, Cammell Carriage & Wagon Company, Birmingham. This stock was almost identical in appearance to the LMS electric stock on its Watford and Ormskirk lines. The train is standing in the bay spur at Oxford Road after the half-mile from South Junction was closed for the first stage of re-electrification to high voltage a.c.

The Altrincham line out of Manchester was the suburban section of the route to Northwich and Chester, built by the Cheshire Lines, a joint committee of the Great Northern, Great Central and Midland railways. In 1923 the GN and the GC were absorbed into the LNER and the Midland became part of the LMS, hence the LNER and LMS joint ownership of this line and its stock.

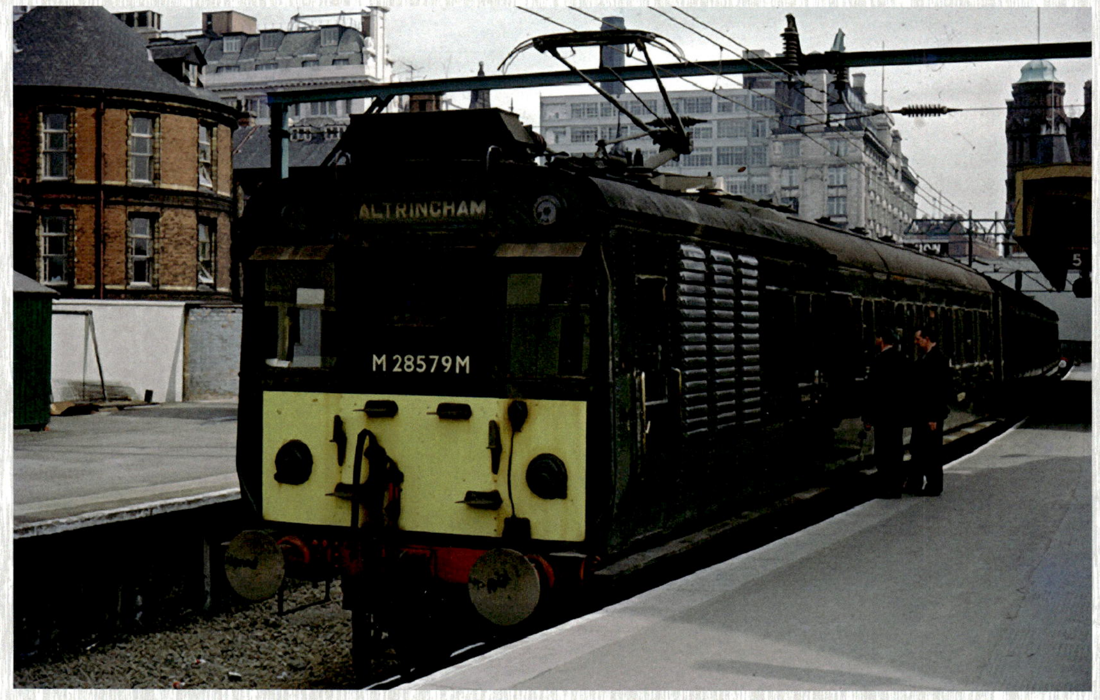

with my report to both the Manchester and the Liverpool offices and they put their heads together to draft a reply. They agreed. All we got in the end was a very brief, nebulous reply from Liverpool to say, in effect, that, as the service was subsidised by a grant, the commuters would have to put up with the stock and the service and be grateful for that – and what a marvellous electric train service there was between Liverpool/Manchester and London! Anyway, the report and

the reply elicited a lot of interesting letters to the editor about diesel multiple units and how to run a railway.

I took that opportunity to take my tape recorder to Manchester to record the old electric trains on the Altrincham line before returning on the evening commuter train to Southport, and it was fortunate that I did so shortly before the re-electrification for modern a.c. trains. The Altrincham line has since been electrified a third time as part of the Manchester tramway system, Metrolink.

Mersey Railway
June 1969

The cavernous underground station at Hamilton Square, Birkenhead, was the sounding board for the arrival and departure of seven electric trains in 11½ minutes of recording there during the peak period one afternoon in June 1969. The double-track station, lined with glazed brick walls and a cement rendered, arched ceiling, had a span of 56ft 6in and a height of 32 feet. The Mersey Railway, originally worked by steam, was relaid and electrified on the four-rail system in 1903 by Westinghouse without any disruption of services – a remarkable achievement in contrast to today's practice of total possession. The original, wooden, clerestory-roofed electric multiple units of 1903 remained in service till 1956 and

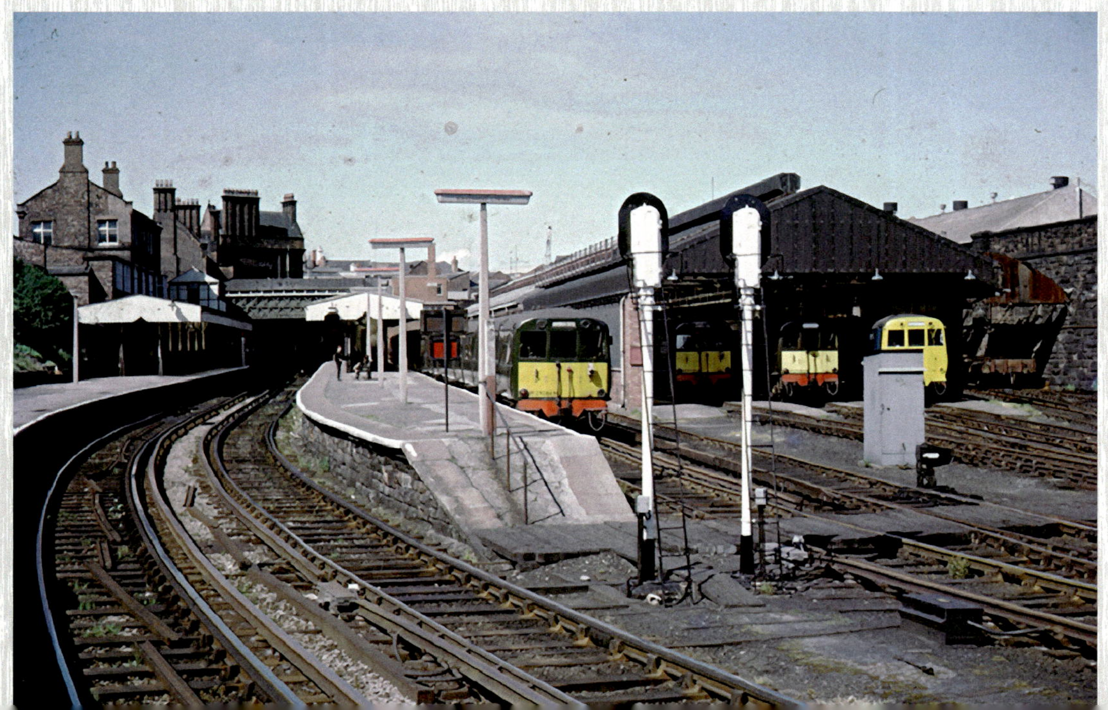

Birkenhead Central station (left) and car shed (right) on 6 June 1968. The station offices housed the headquarters of the Mersey Railway, which remained independent until it was nationalised under BR in 1948, although the LMS also ran its north Wirral electric trains through the tunnel to Liverpool from 1938. The picture shows both the ex-LMS Wirral Line stock of 1938 and the similar BR stock of 1956 that replaced the original MR wooden stock of 1903. The livery, originally MR dark Indian red then BR(M) crimson, was again in transition at this time with three trains in BR dark green with yellow dash panels and one in blue with a yellow front.

the line was shared with LMS electrics on Wirral Line services from 1938.

In this recording I got both LMS stock and the identical BR Mersey Line replacement stock of 1956, stopping on their way to and from Liverpool Central and the outer terminals at Rock Ferry, New Brighton and West Kirby. The six-car trains came crashing heavy-footedly into the station with squealing brakes, and motors groaned as they climbed laboriously up the 1 in 30 grade south. Workmen whistled cheerful tunes as they waited on the platform, as people did habitually in those days, and I persuaded one motorman to blast his air horn before leaving downgrade through the under-river tunnel to Liverpool.

Liverpool-Southport line
September 1969 to April 1977

I worked for the *Southport Visiter* newspaper and lived in Birkdale from 1968 till 1989 and for the last 13 years I lived in a house on Sunnyside fronting on to the electric railway to Liverpool with electric multiple units passing every 15 minutes each way. The ex-LMS stock of 1939 was still in service till 1978 and I have a nice recording from the front garden with birdsong one still spring morning, 28 April 1977, of a southbound train lifting out of Birkdale

station upgrade to Hillside. It was so quiet as it pulled out of the nearby station that the first sound of its approach was of the pick-up shoes twanging the live rail. The six-car train thudded past and whistled for the next crossing as it headed south to Liverpool and the air was so still that the train could be heard for 1½ minutes into the distance.

The Liverpool-Southport line was another pioneer of electric traction, having been electrified in 1904 by the Lancashire & Yorkshire Railway with a third rail at 630 volts d.c., supplied by its own power station at Formby. The 1904 electrification extended beyond Southport Chapel Street terminus to Meols Cop and Crossens on the line to Preston so that the whole borough of Southport was served by electric trains with a total of nine stations from Ainsdale to Crossens. The Crossens service ended with the closure of the Preston line under Beeching in 1964 but the third rail still ran to Meols Cop electric car repair workshops until they shut down in September 1970.

All the electric multiple unit trains that worked the Liverpool, Southport and Ormskirk lines went to Meols Cop for maintenance and overhaul of electrical and mechanical equipment. In September 1969 I made recordings inside the main shed and found three gauges there: the standard

gauge for the electric cars, a 1ft 6in-gauge workshop line, which was operated manually to carry components of the running gear, and a 90-foot-gauge electric travelling crane spanning and running the length of the shed. The crane, which was operated by a small tramcar-type controller, droned like an ancient Glasgow tram and was the very epitome of the electric traction sounds I was seeking. I also recorded the stationary air compressor, which came off an Ormskirk line train of 1922 and was used to power some of the machines in the workshop. Both the compressor and the crane took their current from the 650-volt third rail outside. After the workshops closed the Southport and Ormskirk electric trains had to go to Birkenhead North workshops for repair.

Liverpool Exchange terminus closed on 28 April 1977, so on the 21st I recorded sounds in the great trainshed of the station, continuing with a ride on a train through Liverpool's north dockland to Sandhills, Bank Hall and Bootle. I recorded this sequence from the trailing motorman's cab in the middle of a six-car train in company with my younger son, Ross, who was then 10 years old and, having missed the steam era, was as keen on electric multiple units as his elder brother, Karl, was on steam trains. The advantage of the cab location was that I could drop the side windows wide open and hear the starting bell.

My last recording on this line was made in Birkdale signal cabin on a wet night, 1 May 1977, with the wheel-operated crossing gates and the signal levers being pulled and thrown as two six-car trains met: an up train stopping in the station and a down empty stock train passing through.

I have always felt that, if Cheshire and Lancashire had been on the Southern Railway, all the lines between Chester and Carnforth, the Pennines and the Irish Sea would have been electrified by 1939. Commuters between Manchester and Southport and on other lines still suffer nodding, four-wheel diesel railbuses.

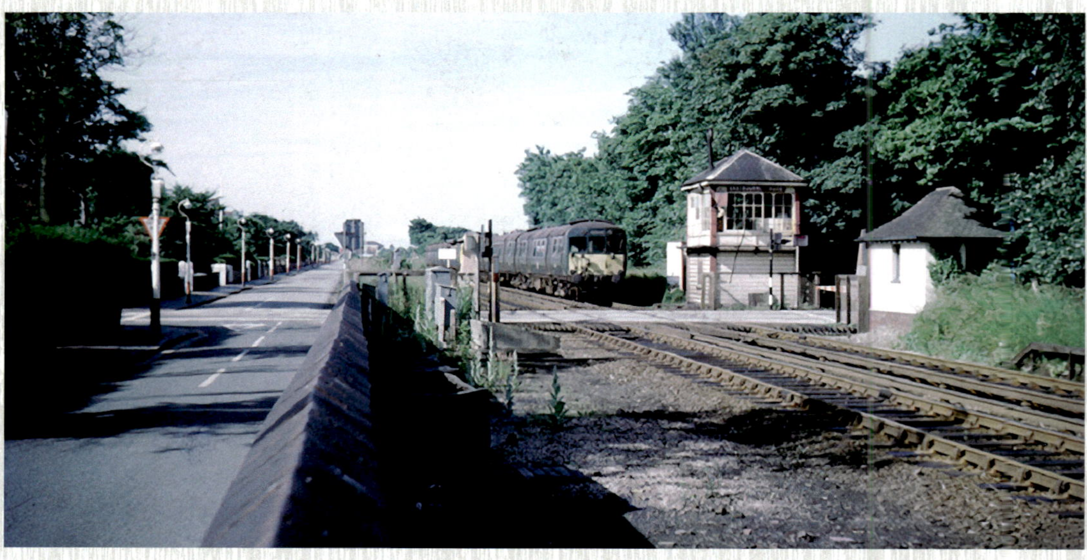

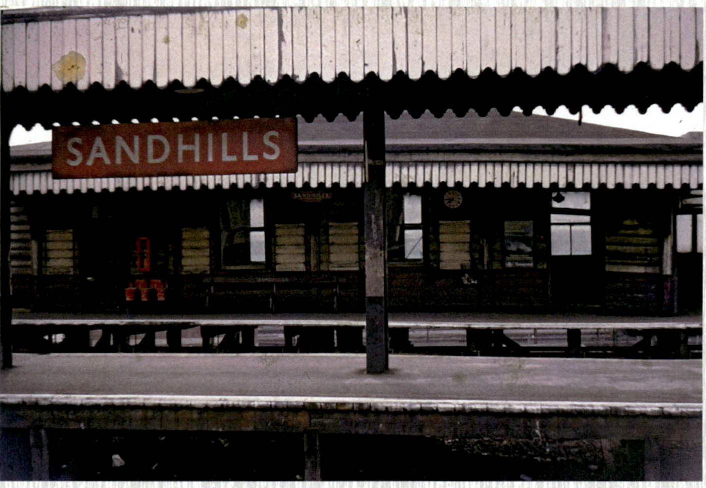

Left: A cross-section of the tumbledown shanty station at Sandhills, first stop out of Liverpool Exchange on the electric lines to Southport and Ormskirk, on 8 July 1969, shortly before demolition and modernisation. The platforms were built on timber trestles. The name Sandhills seems incongruous in Liverpool's industrial north dockland but in the early 19th century the sandy shore north of Liverpool was described as 'a wilderness of sandhills' and the bathing was 'unusually safe and good'.

Above: Roads, houses and gardens front on to the railway on the last 3½ miles of the line from Liverpool into Southport, giving the railway approach to the 'Garden city by the sea' a spacious and more pleasant approach than the backyard view the railways have of most towns and cities. Southport's visionary town planners laid out roads immediately flanking both sides of the line, although that tradition was forgotten in the late-20th-century housing developments at the south end of Ainsdale. In this view from Dover Road, Birkdale, one morning in July 1969, a six-car LMS electric multiple unit of 1939 from Liverpool is passing Eastbourne Road signal cabin between Hillside and Birkdale stations. The cabin guarded the level crossing of Crescent Road (left) and Grosvenor Road (right); the last quarter of a mile of Eastbourne Road had been renamed Crescent Road.

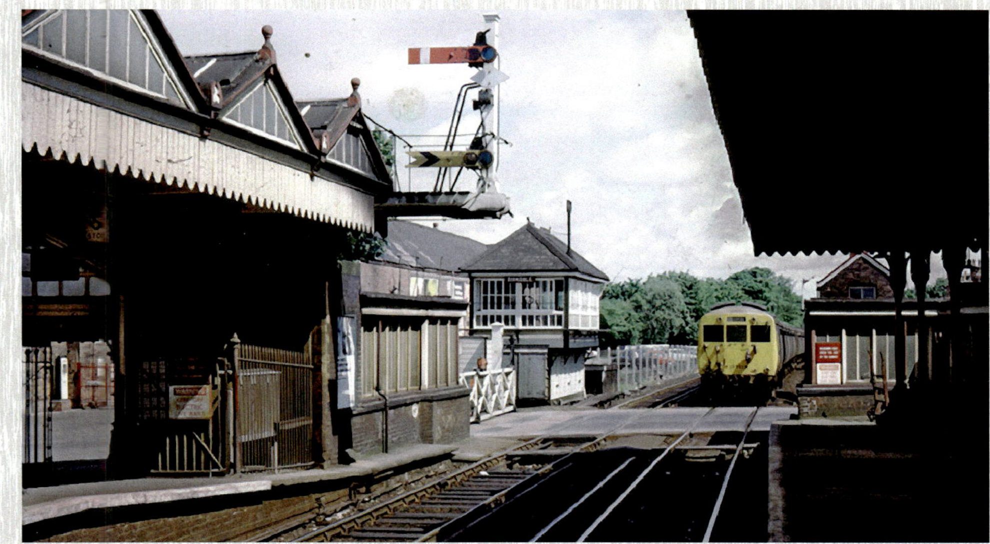

A Southport to Liverpool six-car electric multiple unit, built by the LMS at Derby in 1939, passes Birkdale signal cabin and crosses Weld Road as it enters Birkdale station one morning in July 1969. The station dates from 1851, the line was electrified in 1904 and the signal cabin, dating from 1905, was saved as part of Birkdale conservation area, and is now also a listed building. Thus it is the only surviving signal cabin on the Liverpool-Southport line since signalling was centralised in an automatic control panel cabin at Sandhills.

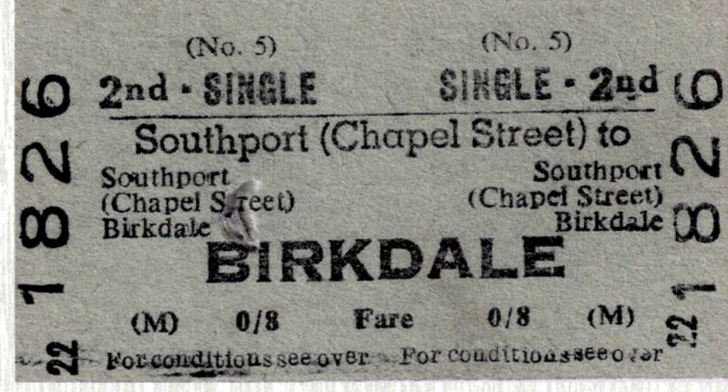

A ticket from Southport Chapel Street to Birkdale on 17 May 1969, fare 8d.

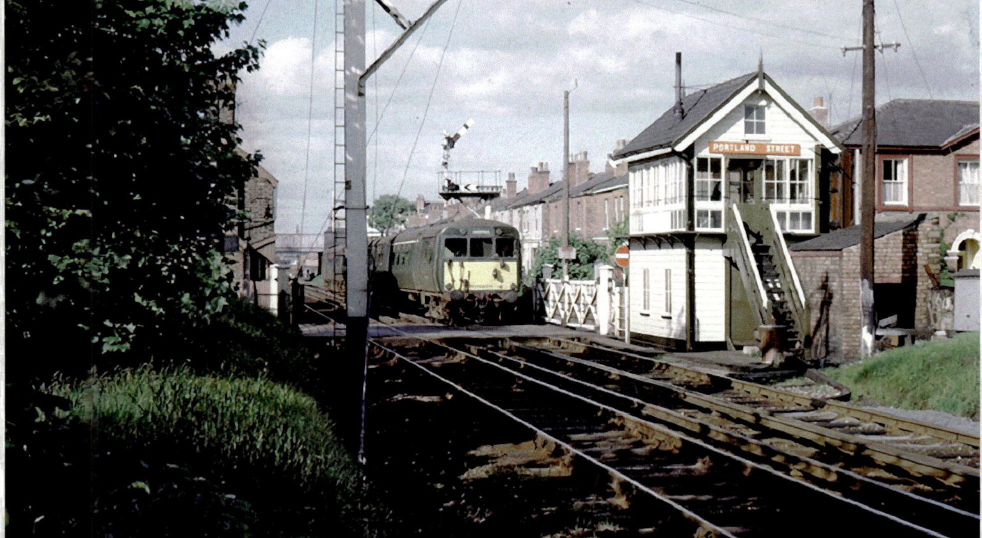

Leaving Southport for Liverpool, an ex-LMS six-car electric multiple unit of 1939 crosses Portland Street as it picks up speed on the first leg of its run to Birkdale in June 1969. Portland Street was the original terminus of the Liverpool, Crosby & Southport Railway in 1848 and the original station house, now a listed building, is extant on the left, its front door only 4ft 6in from the passing trains. The line was extended to Chapel Street in 1850 and the Lancashire & Yorkshire Railway, which took over in 1855, electrified the line in 1904. Portland Street signal cabin was built by the LYR in 1920. The train and the cabin are in matching dark green. Railway Street runs alongside the line behind the cabin.

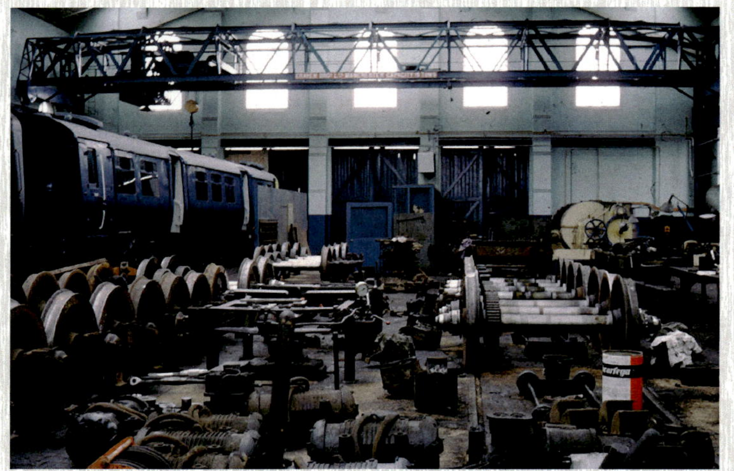

Inside Meols Cop electric car repair shop at Southport the electric, travelling, gantry crane spans the main shed on its 90-foot-gauge track. Electrical and mechanical maintenance was carried out here on all stock working the Liverpool to Southport and Ormskirk lines, the bodies being towed on accommodation bogies to Horwich Works for repair.

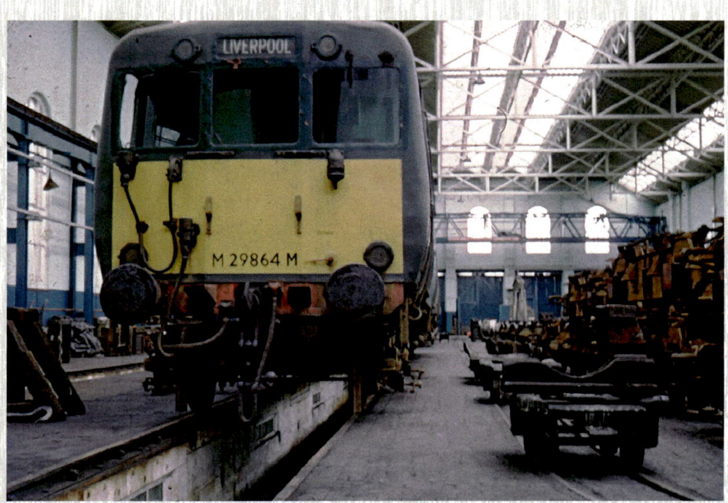

Two gauges can be seen inside Meols Cop electric car repair shop at Southport. A 1ft 6in-gauge workshop line runs alongside a disabled 1939 LMS traction car on the standard gauge over the inspection pit. The narrow-gauge bogies were pushed manually, conveying bogie frames and other components around the premises and taking them outside for blasting. These two photographs of the works were taken on 4 September 1969, 12 months before closure. Cars then had to be taken on a circuitous route to Birkenhead North works.

Blackpool tramways
August to October 1976

The Liverpool-Southport line and the Starr Gate-Fleetwood line of Blackpool tramways delineated a total of 30 miles of the Lancashire coast. Blackpool Corporation closed its last three street tramways – Lytham Road, Marton and Dickson Road – in 1961, '62 and '63 respectively, leaving only the coast line from Starr Gate to Fleetwood. The Blackpool section, from Starr Gate to Bispham, is on paved roadside reservation between the promenade and the sea with a short street section passing inland of the Metropole Hotel on the sea wall.

Blackpool Promenade still sounded like a city of the 1920s or '30s when I recorded it at Manchester Square on 15 August 1976, with frequent horse-drawn landaus and electric tramcars passing by on what was the first and last electric tramway in Great Britain. The tramcars slid by almost inaudibly against the sound of the horses and motor traffic.

There is also a short section of street tramway along the old Lytham Road line for access to Rigby Road depot and workshops. With my recorder on, I jumped aboard streamlined, 94-seat, double-deck car 708 as it turned out of the tramsheds, clumped through the trackfan in the forecourt stopped for the conductor to reverse the trolley pole, then moved out along Lytham Road, waited at the signals in Manchester Square and accelerated with characteristic tramcar whine as it went into service on the Promenade.

North of Bispham the trams run on sleeper track roadside and cross-country reservation to Fleetwood then roll through the main street of the fishing port for 1 mile to the ferry. On 29 September 1976 I recorded a ride on board single-deck car 9, rebuilt in 1974 for one-man operation on 1934 trucks, picking up passengers at a stop on the main street and running out along the sleeper track to Rossall. The car grinded along the street track, which was badly worn and due for renewal, stopped at Ash Street then sped quietly and smoothly along the sleeper track reservation to Broadwater and Rossall.

I closed my Blackpool programme back at Manchester Square with double-deck car 708 again, going off service to the depot on a wet night in October 1976. Two single-deckers rolled by, followed by 708 which pulled up with a hiss of brakes. Another single-decker passed on the northbound track as the conductor set the points for the left-hand turnout with a

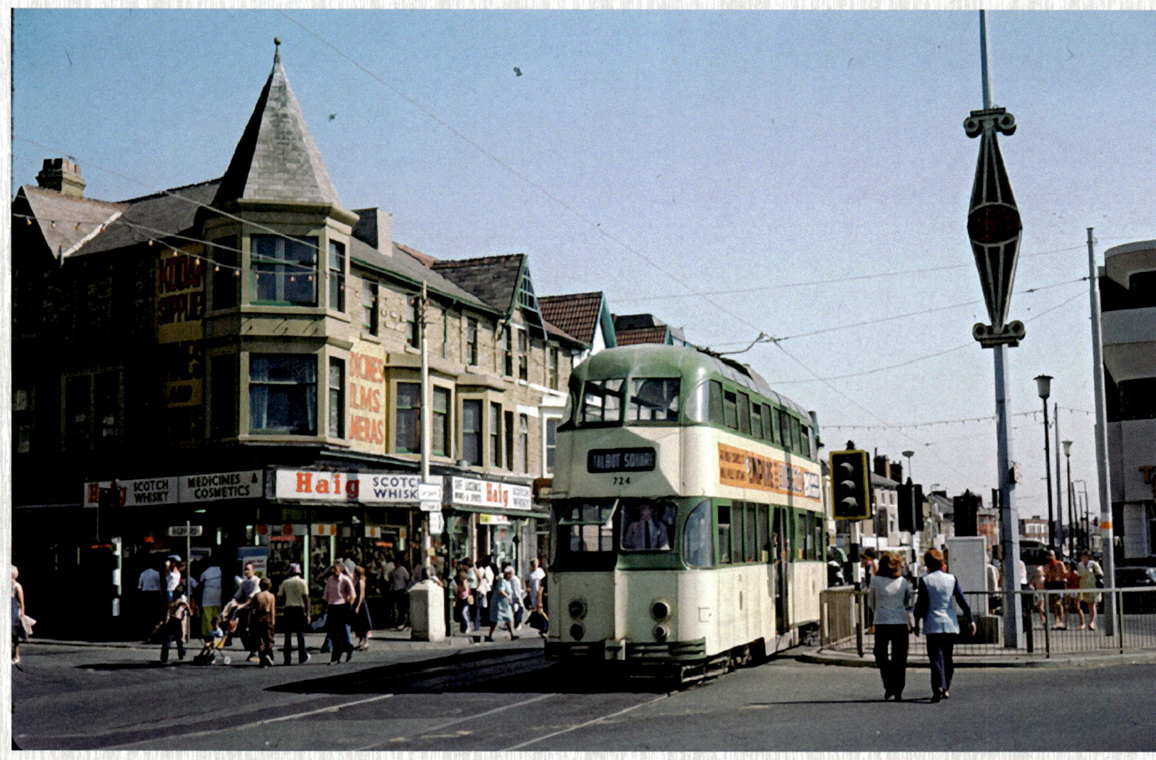

'clunk', using the crowbar, or 'switch iron', that hung on a post at the trackside. The car moved by and the conductor reset the points. The car waited for the green signal then moved across the square into Lytham Road bound for the depot.

Blackpool Corporation's former Lytham Road tram line to Squire's Gate, closed in 1961, is still in use for a few hundred yards from the Promenade for access to Rigby Road depot. A 1935 English Electric 100-seater tramcar is seen leaving Lytham Road at Manchester Square as it goes into service on the Promenade on 15 August 1976. It is destined for Talbot Square (alias North Pier), where it would reverse to head south to the Pleasure Beach or Starr Gate.

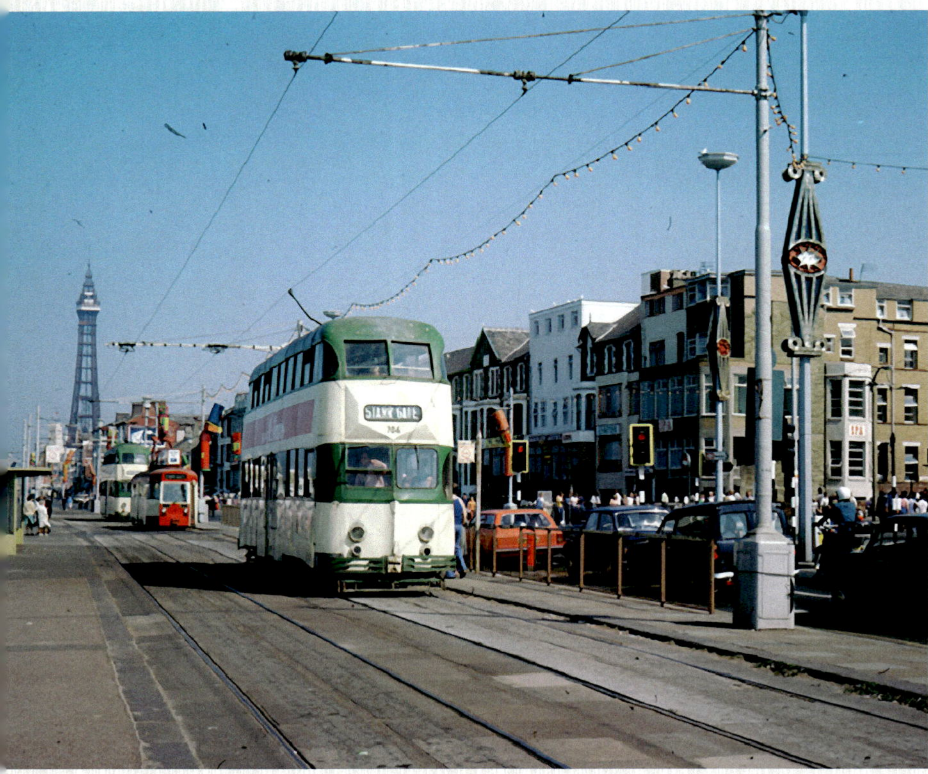

Above: Blackpool Corporation tramcars on the Promenade on 15 August 1976: two 100-seat English Electric double-deckers of 1934-35, in traditional green and cream livery, and a 48-seat single-decker of 1975, one of 13 pre-war cars rebuilt by the Corporation in 1972-75 for one-man operation and distinguished by the pre-1934 red and cream livery for passengers to pay the motorman. These were the two types of car featured in the recordings that year.

Below: Slow loading as passengers pay the motorman on boarding a Blackpool-bound one-man-operated car of 1975 at Fleetwood Ash Street stop on 26 February 1977. The railway-style nameboard and the concrete pale fencing were features of the 1920s upgrading of the light railway after Blackpool Corporation took over the Blackpool & Fleetwood Tramroad in 1919. Also dating from that period, the former tram stop here was a large brick and pitched-roofed waiting room with a canopy and clock turret in the middle of the road junction; it had only recently been removed before this photograph. The NBC Ribble bus on the left is a Leyland National in National Bus red livery, coincidentally matching the pre-1934 Blackpool red livery used to mark the one-man-operated tramcar.

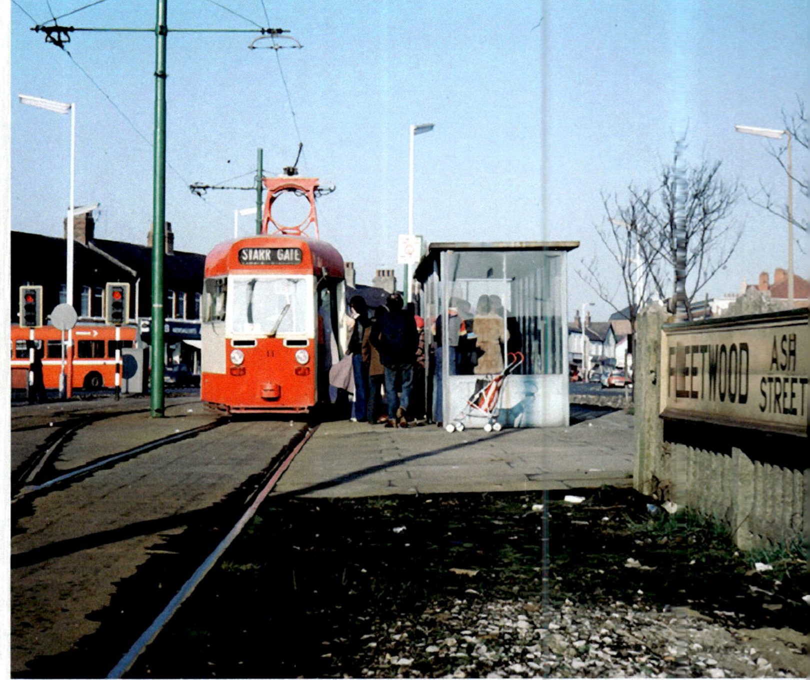

A tramcar passes the lighthouse in Pharos Street, Fleetwood, on 26 February 1977, on the single-line terminal loop serving Fleetwood ferry. The 1975 one-man-operated single-decker is seen swinging into North Albert Street on its return run to Blackpool and Starr Gate, 11 miles south. The lighthouse, dating from 1840, had recently been stripped of its Regency stucco sheathing to reveal its red sandstone construction.

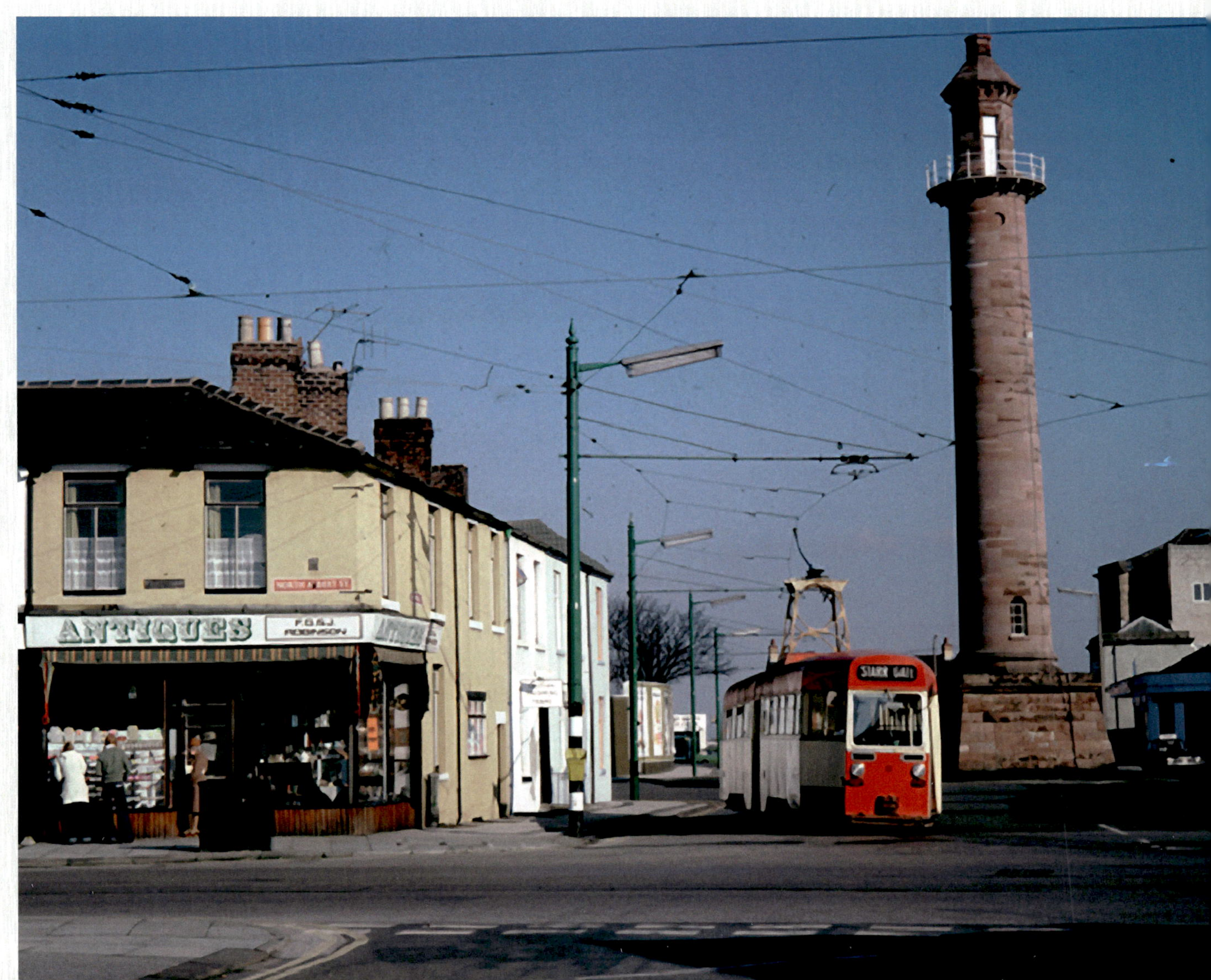

Glasgow subway
20 August 1975

The final recording of my 'Vintage Voltage' CD programme was of a ride on one of the 78-year-old trains of the Glasgow subway from Kelvin Bridge to St George's Cross and Cowcaddens on 20 August 1975. This was on a four-day visit to south-west Scotland with Ruth and the two boys, staying at Ayr youth hostel, and we also went on a day excursion on the PS *Waverley* around Arran and Bute.

The Glasgow subway is a gnome-scale underground railway with a 4-foot gauge double track that runs in a circle, like a boy's train set, for 6½ miles between the city centre and the west end. The city centre station on the subway at St Enoch was an ostentatious fantasy of ornate, Victorian, Scottish baronial architecture in red sandstone in the middle of St Enoch Square outside St Enoch main-line station. Other stations around the circuit had modest, hole-in-the-wall entrances from the street with steps leading down to narrow island platforms between the tracks in stations only long enough for two-car

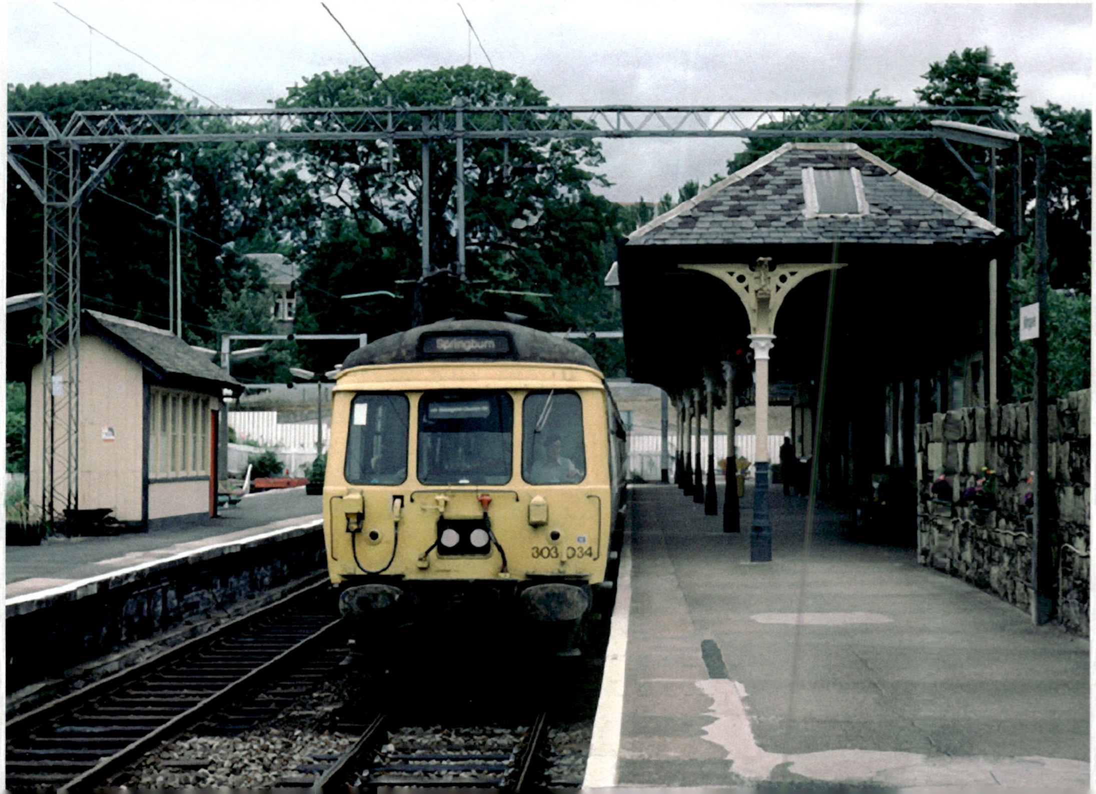

British Railways electrified its suburban lines around Glasgow from 1960 to replace the city's extensive tramway system, which closed down in 1957-62. In 1980 BR reopened the old Caledonian Railway tunnel that runs for 3 miles under the city centre from Finnieston to Dalmarnock to link its suburban lines north and south of the Clyde and bring the total route mileage – electrified in 20 years – to 162 miles! Here is one of the original Clydeside 'blue trains', since modified and repainted, at the Milngavie terminus of the former North British Railway route to Queen Street and Springburn on 4 August 1984.

Single ticket on the Glasgow Corporation subway, dated 3 June 1962.

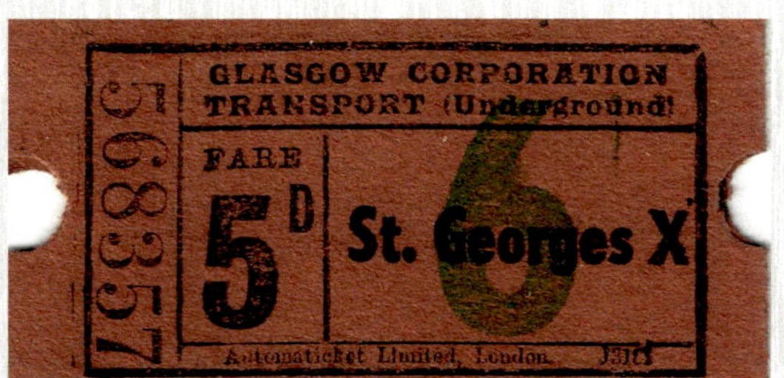

trains. The 4-foot-gauge cars were smaller in cross-section than London tube trains, with lattice iron gates on the vestibules and longitudinal seating as in old tramcars. It was a real period piece like something in a museum and the staff had an old-fashioned courtesy and a friendliness not found on other subway systems. One motorman invited Ross, Karl and me, singly, to ride with him in the cramped motorman's cab on consecutive sections of the route and when I made my recording on another train the motorman obliged me by sounding his whistle before leaving the station and disappearing into the tunnel.

The Glasgow District Subway Company built the twin-bore subway in 1896 and the trains were cable-hauled. Glasgow Corporation bought the subway in 1922 and electrified the line in 1935 but continued to use the cable-hauled rolling stock dating from 1896 and 1898, fitted with pick-up shoes for the 600-volt third rail supply from the tramway power station at Pinkston. Twin wires along the tunnel walls supplied lighting to the cars via short side trolleys and powered the colour-light signalling. In 1977 the 80-year-old trains were withdrawn from service and the subway was closed, completely modernised and reopened in 1980 with new station entrances. The old subway station building in St Enoch Square is extant as a tourist information centre and shops.

Clydeside electric
8 July 1981

Also in 1980 British Railways reopened the old Caledonian Railway tunnel that runs for 3 miles under the streets of Glasgow from Finnieston to Dalmarnock with electric multiple unit trains to link its suburban electric lines north and south of the Clyde. I revisited Glasgow in 1981, not to see the new subway – I preferred to remember it as it was – but to record something of the growing Clydeside suburban railway system, electrified only since 1960 at 25,000 volts a.c. and now covering 162 miles of the former Caledonian Railway extending as far as Lanark, Neilston, Gourock and Wemyss Bay and the former North British Railway to Airdrie, Springburn, Milngavie, Balloch and Helensburgh – far more adventurous than the Merseyside and Tyneside electric systems dating from 1903 and 1904. Much of the system was in tunnel under the city centre, which was suffocating in steam days and not suitable for dieselisation. My younger son Ross came with me to explore independently as much as possible of the system, which he had not seen before, while I took recordings and photographs.

I recorded a ride on the North British line from Glasgow Queen Street (low level) in tunnel to High Street and on the surface to Bellgrove and Duke Street. Characteristic sounds were the resonant Scottish male voice of the station announcer at Queen Street, the thumping air brake pump, the shrill guard's whistle and the clear bells and buzzers of the automatic warning system from the motorman's cab, telling of green and yellow light signals ahead. This was one of many recordings, like most of those of London, that has never been transcribed on to a compact disc programme.

Both my sons, who were born in Kendal, share my interests to some extent and sought careers in transport. My younger son, Ross, whom I have mentioned in my latter-day electric traction expeditions, worked for the railways for 21 years after leaving school and a business studies course at technical college. He worked in the travel centres at Liverpool Lime Street, Hastings and London Waterloo, then in train planning for special trains, engineering works and freight, based in London and Crewe. When commuting from Southport to Liverpool and from Hastings to London he usually travelled with the motorman or the guard on the electric multiple units, often deputising 'on the handles' at the front or acting guard at the back while the guard read the newspaper. In 2006 he embarked on a peripatetic teaching career in south-east Asia, where he is busy now. His elder brother, Karl, has been limited by deafness in his work prospects but, as a qualified carpenter, he found happiness employed as a full-time joiner and painter at Exeter Maritime Museum … for two years till it closed down for lack of visitors and the collection was dispersed. He is still in employment but opportunities in transport elude the deaf. He is also active in the Exeter Model Railway Club.

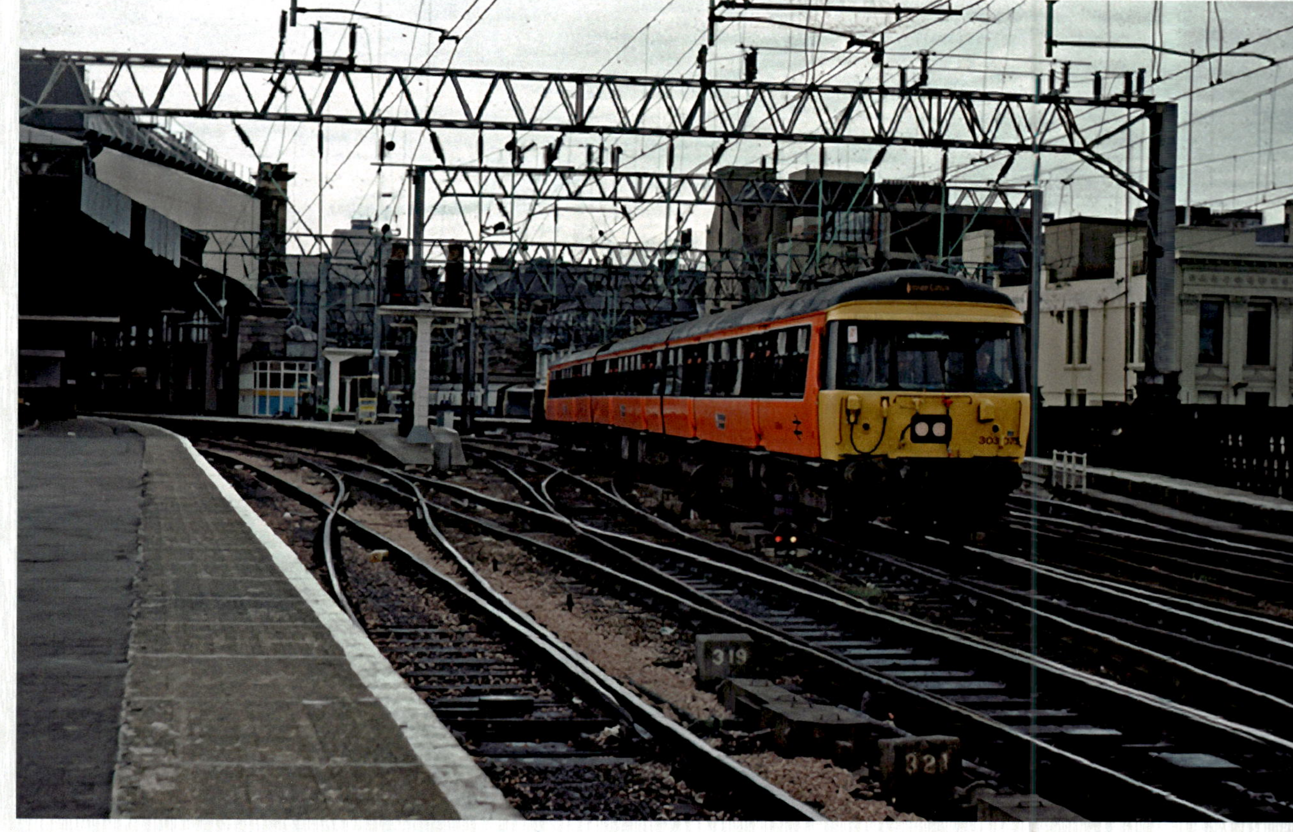

One of the first Clydeside electric trains to sport the attractive new Strathclyde Passenger Transport livery of orange and black leaves Glasgow Central station for the Cathcart Circle line on 4 August 1984. This livery was being applied to all suburban trains and former Corporation buses controlled by Strathclyde Passenger Transport Authority in and around Glasgow, although the 'high visibility' yellow cab ends of the trains detracted from the aesthetic effect.

British Railways launched the Clydeside electric system in 1960 with these trains in an overall Caledonian Railway blue livery, hence the old name 'blue trains', but they later appeared in BR standard blue and off-white with yellow ends. Operators and liveries have come in quick succession since the mid-1970s with control passing to Trans-Clyde PTA, Strathclyde PTA and now Strathclyde Partnership for Transport, while the Strathclyde PTA orange and black was succeeded by crimson and cream and now by 'Scotland blue', making them 'blue trains' once more.

Chicago, South Shore & South Bend Railroad
4 and 5 August 1972

The 'South Shore Line' is the last surviving passenger operation of the lost empire of the 'interurban' electric railways that were common across North America in the first half of the 20th century, although freight is the mainstay of South Shore revenue and diesel freight remnants of former interurban lines still operate here and there and one electric trolley freight system at Mason City, Iowa.

The interurban was a phenomenon never seen in Britain and is now unknown to most living Americans. It was a cross between a tramway and a railway but was actually an overgrown tramway. A few interurbans were electrified

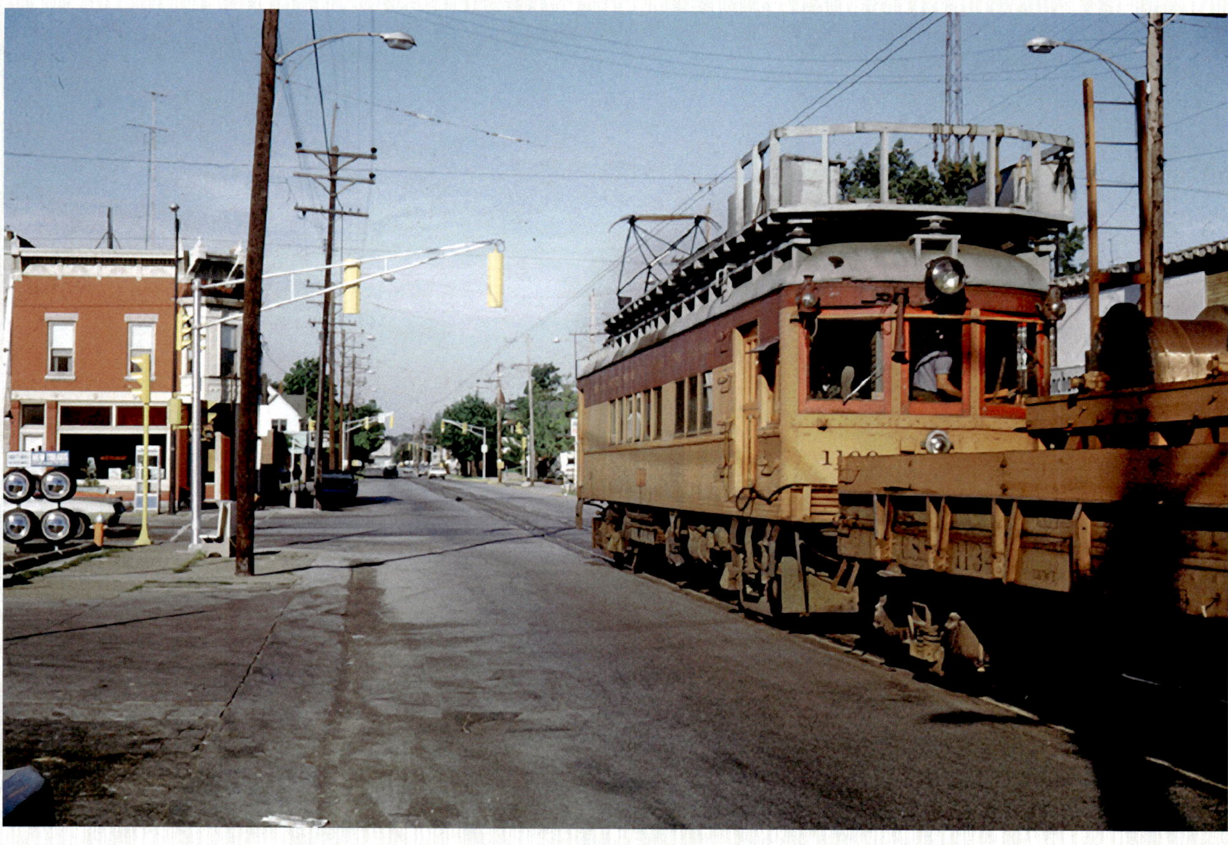

In its third incarnation on three Indiana interurban electric railways, line car 1100, fitted with a elevating wooden platform on the roof, tows a cable-drum flatcar and a diesel switcher westbound through Michigan City, Indiana, to work on the overhead wires on the Chicago, South Shore & South Bend Railroad.

This car was built in 1926 as a steel combination passenger and baggage car for the Indiana Service Corporation. It was amalgamated into the Indiana Railroad system in 1930 and converted to a railway post office car with a sorting office and a shorter passenger saloon. It was sold again in 1941 to the South Shore Line, being converted to a line car, and was retired in 2003 to the Illinois Railway Museum at Union after 77 years in service. All these pictures of the South Shore Line were taken on 11th Street, Michigan City, on 5 August 1972.

steam lines but most of them grew historically out of the development and extension of street tramways from one town to the next. They carried passengers, mail and freight on roadside and cross-country lines between towns and on street tracks through the towns on the way. In Britain today we would call them 'light railways' as they operated on light railway principles, often with single cars, tight curves, steep gradients and not necessarily any stations or signals, but there was nothing much 'light' about American interurbans, except the infrastructure.

The cars, first of wood, then of steel, grew to grandiose proportions the size of railway coaches with arched windows, big headlamps and cowcatchers. The standard interurban car could be said to be in the

The 8am two-car passenger train from Chicago has unloaded the morning newspapers on to a veteran, iron-tyred, luggage trolley at Michigan City station and prepares to leave at 9.25 for the company workshops and yard at the east end of town, where most eastbound trains terminate. Both the Pullman-built steel cars and the station building, with its classical, terracotta façade, dated from 1927, when the whole line was upgraded under the new management of Sam Insull's utilities empire.

The station housed a large waiting room, ticket and parcels office, a ladies' room, a men's smoking room and a baggage room. Upstairs were offices and a staff function hall. There was a bus station at the back with platforms for the subsidiary Shore Line Motor Coach Company and several independent coach lines operating feeder services to the interurban.

After the closure of Insull's Chicago, North Shore & Milwaukee Railroad in 1963, the South Shore Line became America's last 'interurban'. The passenger cars were replaced in 1982-83 by similar new stock built in Japan, the line is now operated by the Northern Indiana Commuter Transportation District, and Michigan City station building has closed.

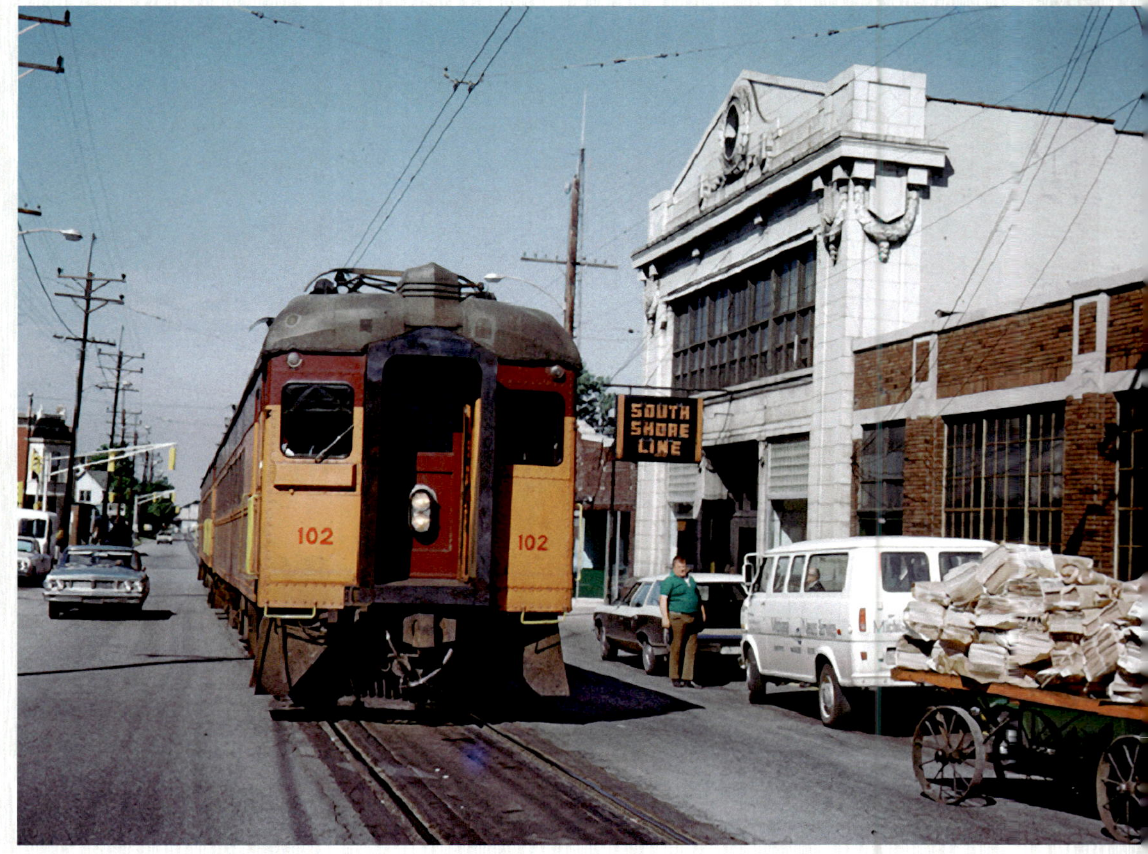

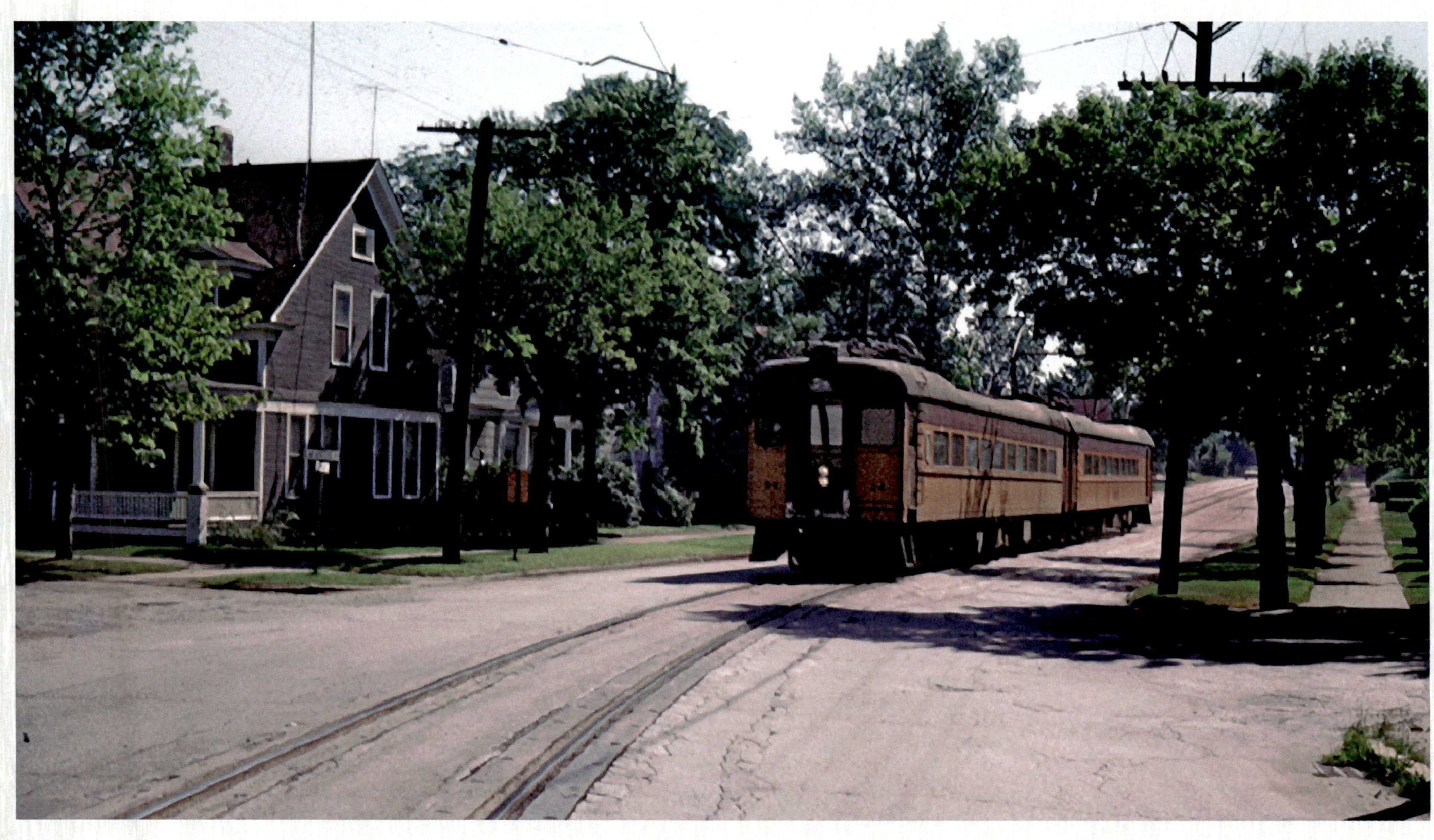

The bosky ne ghbourhood of wooden villas trembles as the 140-ton, two-car interurban rolls down 11th Street East in Michigan City, westbound for Chicago. Long, heavy, freight trains still work through 10th and 11th Streets, traction switching from electric to diesel in 1982. In this picture the rails are flanked by longitudinal baulks of timber to absorb the vibration but the paving is still crazed.

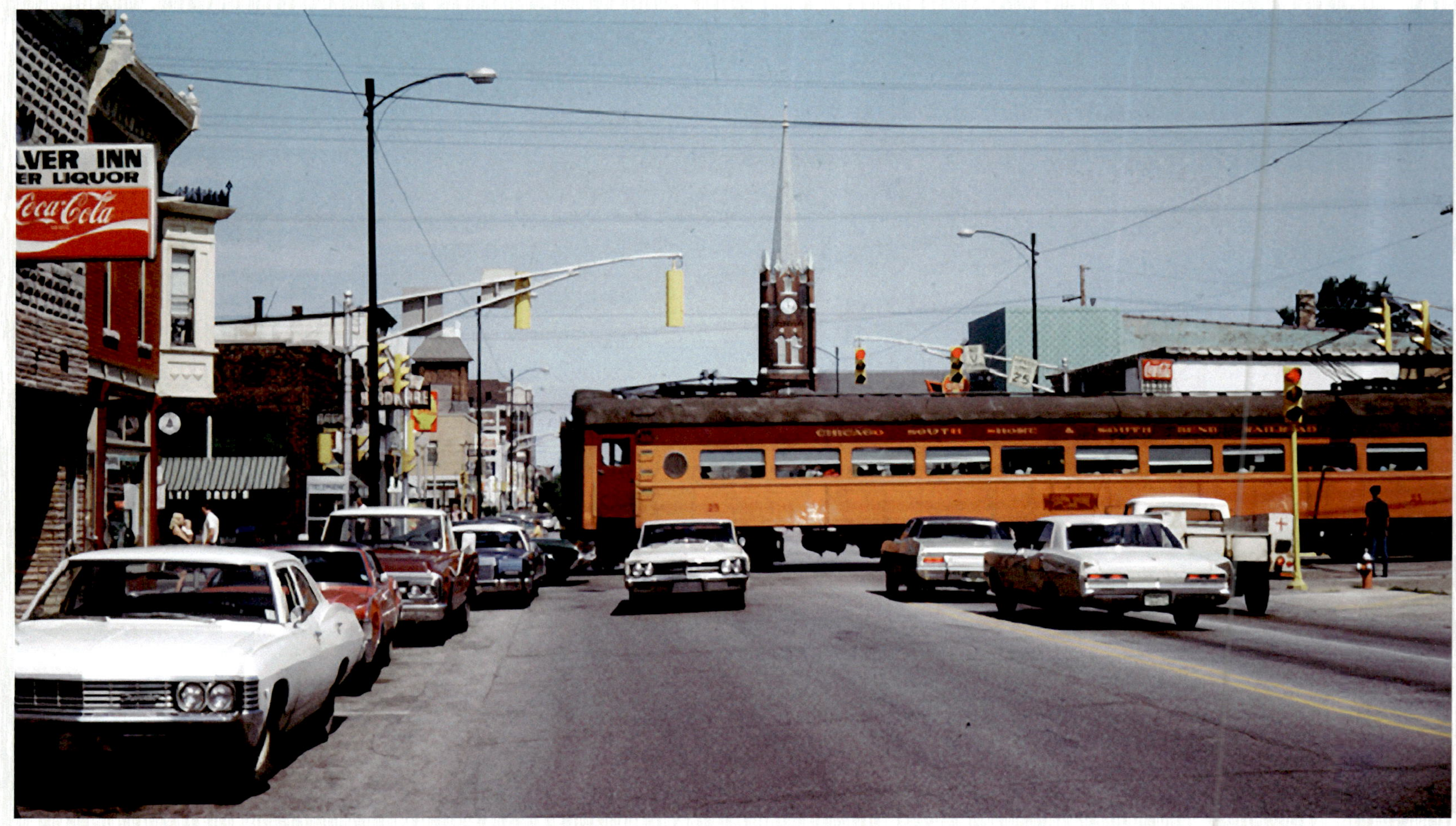

Seventy-eight feet and 70 tons of interurban car launches itself across Franklin Street, Michigan City, as it heads the 11.10am two-car train west along 11th Street towards Chicago. The passenger and freight trains were regulated by the normal highway signals. The company name is painted in full along the letterboard above the windows in traditional American railroad style. In the background is the steeple of St Paul's Lutheran Church.

range of 50 to 70 in feet, tons and maximum speed. Most of them still used overhead trolley pick-up from single overhead wires. Some high-speed, long-distance lines used pantographs under catenary but the fastest lines, the Pacific Electric and the Chicago, North Shore & Milwaukee, stuck to trolleys on single wire as well as catenary.

The interurban empire was the whole of civilised North America; they were thin on the ground in the south-eastern and the mountain states. By the peak of mileage and patronage in 1916-19 there were well over 15,000 miles of passenger lines shared with freight – and up to 3,000 miles of lines for trolley freight only – lacing up almost every state of the Union. Almost half of the mileage was in the neighbouring states of Ohio, Indiana, Michigan, Illinois and Wisconsin, south and west of the Great Lakes.

Construction continued till 1927 but the network was already in decline. Paved roads, private cars, buses and lorries made inroads into interurban traffic and revenue. The great Depression of 1929-32 saw the rundown of the interurban network within a decade The war of 1942 to 1945 was a boom time for the surviving lines, mainly those providing commuter service to the big cities, like Montreal, Vancouver, Chicago and Los Angeles, and those with freight as the staple

source of revenue. The last new passenger stock was built for two Illinois systems in 1941 and 1949. Most of the surviving lines closed during the 1950s contemporarily with the last British tramway systems. The Chicago, North Shore & Milwaukee Railroad closed out the era in 1963, leaving only its sister line, the Chicago, South Shore & South Bend, to soldier on alone ever since. Interurbans also survive in Cuba, Italy, Austria, Switzerland, Germany, Belgium – and the Isle of Man.

The South Shore Line began as a 3½-mile streetcar line between East Chicago and Indiana Harbor and now extends 88 miles around the south shore of Lake Michigan. It was one of the three big interurbans that once radiated from Chicago under the common ownership of Sam Insull's utilities empire in the Midwest. It has lost much of its classical 'interurban' character since 1926 as it was developed to a heavy freight and commuter line, but it retains an interurban character where the big cars and freight trains still run 2 miles through the streets of Michigan City, Indiana, like a classic scene from the past.

The line originally ran through the streets of East Chicago and South Bend too but the line through East Chicago was diverted to the side of the bypass in 1956 and street running into South Bend was cut

back to the west side of town in 1970.

The 59 standard South Shore passenger cars at the time of my visit in 1972 dated from 1926-29 – all appreciably older than the steam locomotives that saw out the steam era on British Railways in 1968. Each car was 78 feet long, 10 feet wide and stood 13ft 4½in above the road and weighed nearly 70 tons, larger than British railway carriages, built of steel and bristling with rivets. They ran as single cars or in multiple unit trains of anything up to eight cars. The livery was traditional 'traction orange' with a maroon letterboard above the windows with the full name of the railway company written in extended Roman capitals in traditional railroad style. Pantographs picked up the 1,500-volt d.c. current from overhead catenary. The rails through the street were flanked by timber baulks but still the tarmac paving was crazed around them and the ground trembled as the trains drifted slowly through town.

On Friday 4 August 1972 I arrived at South Bend by Greyhound coach from Detroit in the early afternoon to ride the South Shore Line to Michigan City. I found that the South Shore service had been cut back 2 miles to the west side of town near the Bendix industrial site, unbeknown to me, two years before my visit, and the last train of the day had left town 6 hours ago.

The regular service was over the 56 miles between Michigan City and Chicago and the passenger operations only extended over the remaining 32 miles to South Bend for commuter runs west in the morning and east in the evening, although at weekends and holiday time there were four trains each way serving the lakes between South Bend and Michigan City.

I thumbed a lift on the road west for Michigan City and was almost immediately picked up by a young man in a car. When he learned I had come to see the South Shore Line he voluntarily turned the car round to show me the former terminal storage yard in the town centre. Then we followed the abandoned single line – still with overhead wire – along a dirt road through the residential western outskirts to the cut-back terminus. We continued on our way west and he dropped me at a motel on the interstate turnpike on the southern perimeter of Michigan City.

In the evening I walked into town past the bosky, wooden villas along Franklin Street to the intersection with 11th Street, where the South Shore trains, including the long freights, have to conform to the highway signals. Michigan City is at the south end of Lake Michigan just inland of the big sand dunes along the Indiana shore. It was a quiet town; I had no problem with motor traffic for photography or tape-recording. The South Shore Line from Chicago enters the west side of town on 10th Street then swings diagonally one block to cross town, east-west, mainly on 11th Street. There was a handsome station with a booking office and waiting room on 11th Street East, just east of Franklin Street, and the company headquarters and workshops are at the east end of town, where most journeys terminate. At dusk an eight-car passenger train from Chicago trundled through 11th Street. When it stopped at the station the front end of the train was a long walk up the street from the station.

The South Shore Line has survived trade recessions and highway competition thanks largely to the development of heavy freight traffic. The company's 13 electric locomotives moved tremendous coal tonnage and general railway freight, and long freight trains worked through 11th Street. Occasionally other motive power is seen on the line as the South Shore Line has junctions with eight other railways for interchange freight. This was Friday evening and there were usually no freight operations at weekends so I was lucky to record two coupled, black, diesel locomotives looming out of the night on 11th Street East, drifting to a stop at the highway signals at Franklin Street and, on the green light, with engines churning and bell tolling, moving on west towards Chicago.

On expeditions like this I believe that the 'early bird catches the worm', so next morning I was up at six and walked into town and was rewarded by meeting one of my favourite interurban cars from the past, which I had no idea was still in existence. About 8am the line train appeared on 11th Street East from the workshops, heading west to work on the overhead line. Line car 1100, fitted with a wooden, elevating, overhead tower, pulled a cable-drum flatcar and a diesel switcher (shunter), ex-Buffalo Creek Railway, which moved this lash-up when a section of the overhead was isolated. This was the third incarnation for line car 1100. It was built in 1926 as a steel passenger and baggage car for the Indiana Service Corporation, which in 1930 was amalgamated into Sam Insull's 600-mile Indiana Railroad system centred on Indianapolis; the car was rebuilt in 1935 as one of that company's three railway post office cars with shorter passenger saloons and enlarged former baggage compartments for mailbags and sorting offices with postal clerks. I have a framed photograph at home of this car, then 376, scything the vegetation on the line to Muncie. As a result of the depression and highway competition, the Indiana Railroad system closed down piecemeal between 1937 and 1941, when car 376 was sold to the IR's northern neighbour, the South Shore Line, another Insull property, and here it was … still at work! It greeted me with a deep bass blast on its air horn as it squealed to a stop at the highway signals then moved its short train on along 11th Street West.

The passenger cars used traditional streetcar gongs repeatedly as they moved potently and ponderously through 11th Street with a rustling sound, heavy wheelbeats and a subdued, deep-bass drone of heavy electric traction motors. I recorded the 8.15 two-car train from Michigan City to Chicago stopping to pick up passengers at Michigan City station and moving on its way. I walked the line east to record the 9.05 two-car westbound shaking the residential neighbourhood as it drifted through the tunnel of trees on 11th Street East and applied slight power for a reverse curve over a brow shortly before arriving at the station. I got the next train to sound its horn – briefly, three times – by standing close to the rails in the middle of 11th Street West as the 8am two-car set from Chicago arrived in Michigan City at 9.25.

When I photographed this train unloading passengers and the morning newspapers at Michigan City station, the motorman, recognising a traction buff, leaned out of the window and handed me his three pages of hand-written train orders, issued by telephone at Chicago, Hammond and Gary, as a souvenir, still in my archives. The trains rolled through town at 2-hourly intervals eastbound and westbound and in the intervals I strolled around town photographing the architecture. I found a good bookshop on Washington Street and bought the definitive book on the South Shore: *The Last Interurban* by William D. Middleton, doyen of interurban writers, published only two years before my visit, a large, hardback book for $10, which crowned my pilgrimage to this last outpost of the interurban empire.

I also recall being able to buy postage stamps from a closed post office (it was Saturday afternoon) by talking to a postal clerk through the slot in the letter box he was clearing from inside the office, exchanging money and stamps through the slot. This was characteristic of the relaxed and informal attitude of people I met in rural North America. Later on the same tour I was photographing Trout Lake station in Michigan's upper peninsula with a diesel-headed freight train on the Soo Line (formerly the Minneapolis, St Paul & Sault Ste Marie Railroad) when the train crew invited me to ride in the cab on the rest of their long pick-up freight journey from Saulte Ste Marie to Marquette. I had to decline the offer because my hosts I was travelling with by car from Detroit were due further west long before the train reached Marquette at the end of the day.

Back in Michigan City, as it was Saturday there were four trains to South Bend that day, so finally I waited for the 1.25 two-car train from Michigan City for South Bend to connect with my return by coach to Detroit. This was supposed to be the 11.59 from Chicago and was running over an hour late when it arrived. It was good to be able to record a ride on an interurban, which made all the traditional electric traction sounds as we crossed the flat northern Indiana countryside of cornfields, woods and lakes. It covered the 32 miles from Michigan City to South Bend in 35 minutes with four intermediate stops and it cost me $1 and 7 dimes.

I recorded continuously from the stop at Rolling Prairie over the 17 miles to the arrival at South Bend. We stopped at Lake Park, Hudson Lake and New Carlisle, all 'flag stops' (request stops) with traditional 'wig-wag' crossing bells. Then we sped non-stop for 12 miles along the arrow-straight line on a ruling gradient of 1 in 500 to South Bend terminus in 12 minutes at

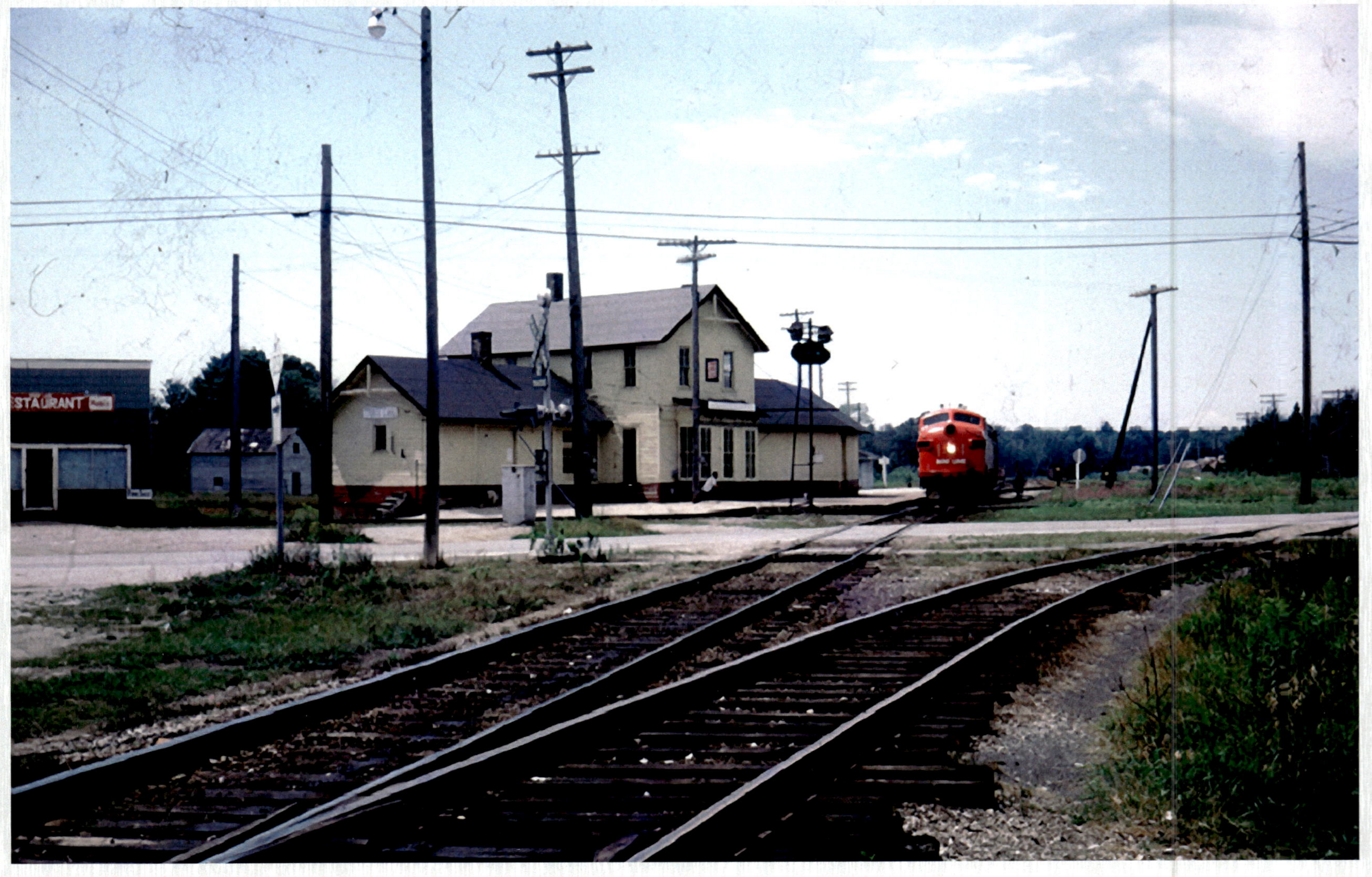

an average speed, start to stop, of 60mph, although the constant sound along this stretch made rather boring listening.

I had come to the South Shore Line 10 years before the traditional interurban scene changed, although street running had already ended in East Chicago and South Bend and the Chesapeake & Ohio Railway, one of the connecting lines, had taken control of the financially ailing South Shore company in 1967. In 1976 it filed to end the loss-making passenger service, only to be refused by the Interstate Commerce Commission. Freight operations turned over to diesel traction in 1981 and the passenger cars were around 55 years old when they were replaced in 1982-83 by new stock built in Japan to similar dimensions and outline but painted silver-grey with only a dash of orange in a stripe along the windows. The South Shore Line went bankrupt in 1989 and the Northern Indiana Commuter Transportation District was formed to run the passenger services with public funds

Trout Lake junction is a level crossing of two lines and the cornerwise station has platforms facing both tracks on the Soo Line (formerly the Minneapolis, St Paul & Sault Ste Marie Railroad) in Chippewa County on Michigan's upper peninsula. An obsolete style of post-war diesel-electric locomotive heads the pick-up freight from Sault Ste Marie to Marquette on 12 August 1972.

while a new Chicago, South Shore & South Bend Railroad company was formed to continue the diesel freight service as a subsidiary of the Anacosta & Pacific Railway. The line's fortunes then began to look up and further new passenger stock was delivered in 2001 and 2009 bringing the total to 68 single-deckers and 14 bi-level cars. The line has been extended at both ends from Randolph Street to Millennium

station in Chicago and from Bendix to South Bend airport, taking in a segment of the town. There are long-term plans to divert the line off the streets of Michigan City on to a private right of way but the cost and demolition involved is a deterrent. Finally, the venerated line car 1100 was retired in 2003 to the Illinois Railway Museum at Union after 77 years' service.

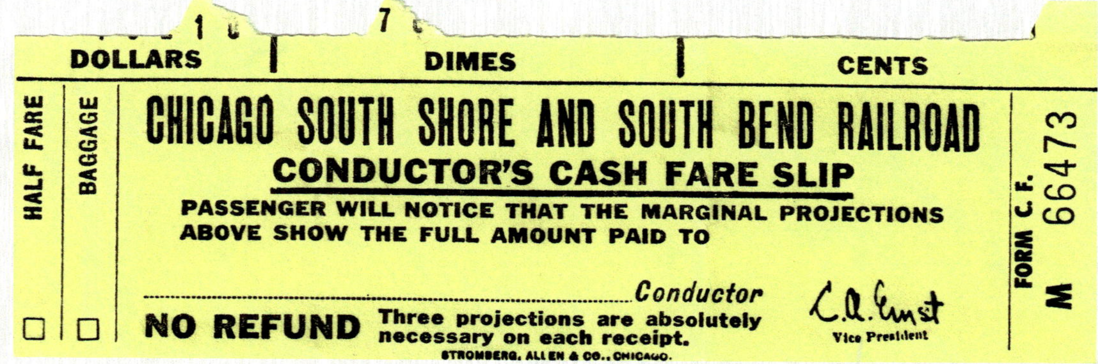

A ticket to ride America's last interurban, the South Shore Line, from Michigan City to South Bend, on 5 August 1972 – 32 miles for 1 dollar, 7 dimes.

Index